First published 2019

(c) 2019 Dominic Salles

About the Author

Dominic Salles still lives in Swindon, with his workaholic wife Deirdre, his jiu-jitsu-loving-engineer son, Harry, Harry's girlfriend Becky and Bob, the 15 year old rescue dog who refuses to die. His sister Jacey is world famous for her Spanish accent. She would be hilarious in her own YouTube channel. His daughter Jess has just become a teacher and coach to the Welsh women's Aussie Rules Football team. He drives a 2006 Prius.

His YouTube channel, Mr Salles Teaches English, will one day earn him a living. When that happens, he is going to train as a snowboard instructor.

He has just bought a longboard and is building thighs like The Rock because, you know, it will happen!

Introduction

700,000 students are going to take GCSE English Literature this year. Unless 350,000 of them buy this guide, so the grade boundaries explode, you are going to get grade 7, 8 or 9.

Unless, of course, you are just too busy to read it. Fine, just read the grade 9 essays which come with the guide, for free. You'll still get at least grade 7. Or cheat a bit, and memorise them, and get grade 8 or 9!

However you do it, Buy This Guide! Mr Salles wants you to smash the exam, love the novel, and then he wants to go snowboarding for 3 months. Only you can make this happen.

Another bonus. You get the novella for free, too. Listen, I know copies of this novella are cheap as chips and, if you just printed it off from the Internet, almost as cheap as the newspaper those chips are wrapped in.

So why did I include the novel with the chapter summaries? Because of the paragraphs. Bear with me. I have an English degree and I have read this novella a dozen times. It's flipping hard, because of the paragraphs. Great big, fat chunks of text, which go on for ever and are packed with too many ideas.

So to make it easier for a modern reader, I have added paragraph breaks for changes of **topic**, **time** and **talk**. It sounds simple. But the effect will transform your ability to understand just what on earth is going on! You might even enjoy it as a cracking good yarn.

None **of the wording has been changed.** It is the whole text of the novel.

It is a rare reader who doesn't know the central mystery already, but if you are lucky enough not to know about the relationship between Doctor Henry Jekyll and Mr Edward Hyde, you are in for a treat. Read the novel first, and experience the same mystery as a Victorian reader.

Next, you might choose to read the Chapter Summaries. These include all the main events of the chapter, with much analysis. I feel it is more natural to learn this way, rather than compartmentalising facts and analysis in different sections.

You will probably know by now that I believe every student can understand ideas at grade 7, 8 and 9. They are just ideas. It is just knowing stuff.

I don't expect every student who reads this guide to get those grades, because linking ideas together, with the right language and the right quotations is more of a skill. But an essay that would score a grade 4, can easily move to grade 5 or 6 with the introduction of grade 7 ideas. Everyone can do that!

Having said that, 53% of my YouTube viewers improve by at least 2 grades, 14% by 3 grades and another 14% improve by 4 grades or more!

28% go up by at least 3 grades...imagine how many more would do so if they read this guide.

So, you really can improve from grade 4 or 5 to grades 8 and 9. Indeed, if you use this guide, it will be almost impossible for you not to get at least a grade 7.

I have highlighted all the grade 7, 8 and 9 ideas in the summaries in bold, so you can make notes on the extra ideas that will improve your grade.

To be honest, you can get grade 7 and above just with that.

But you know there is much more to help you nail those grades. There really isn't a guide as good as this on the market – that's why I wrote it.

Contents Page

THE STRANGE CASE OF DR. JEKYLL AND MR. HYDE

by Robert Louis Stevenson

Chapter 1

STORY OF THE DOOR

MR. UTTERSON the lawyer was a man of a rugged countenance, that was never lighted by a smile; cold, scanty and embarrassed in discourse; backward in sentiment; lean, long, dusty, dreary, and yet somehow lovable. At friendly meetings, and when the wine was to his taste, something eminently human beaconed from his eye; something indeed which never found its way into his talk, but which spoke not only in these silent symbols of the after-dinner face, but more often and loudly in the acts of his life.

He was austere with himself; drank gin when he was alone, to mortify a taste for vintages; and though he enjoyed the theatre, had not crossed the doors of one for twenty years. But he had an approved tolerance for others; sometimes wondering, almost with envy, at the high pressure of spirits involved in their misdeeds; and in any extremity inclined to help rather than to reprove.

"I incline to Cain's heresy," he used to say quaintly: "I let my brother go to the devil in his own way." In this character, it was frequently his fortune to be the last reputable acquaintance and the last good influence in the lives of down-going men. And to such as these, so long as they came about his chambers, he never marked a shade of change in his demeanour.

No doubt the feat was easy to Mr. Utterson; for he was undemonstrative at the best, and even his friendship seemed to be founded in a similar catholicity of good-nature. It is the mark of a modest man to accept his friendly circle ready-made from the hands of opportunity; and that was the lawyer's way. His friends were those of his own blood or those whom he had known the longest; his affections, like ivy, were the growth of time, they implied no aptness in the object.

Hence, no doubt, the bond that united him to Mr. Richard Enfield, his distant kinsman, the well-known man about town. It was a nut to crack for many, what these two could see in each other, or what subject they could find in common. It was reported by those who encountered them in their Sunday walks, that they said nothing, looked singularly dull, and would hail with obvious relief the appearance of a friend. For all that, the two men put the greatest store by these excursions, counted them the chief jewel of each week, and not only set aside occasions of pleasure, but even resisted the calls of business, that they might enjoy them uninterrupted.

It chanced on one of these rambles that their way led them down a by-street in a busy quarter of London. The street was small and what is called quiet, but it drove a thriving trade on the week-days. The inhabitants were all doing well, it seemed, and all emulously hoping to do better still, and laying out the surplus of their gains in coquetry; so that the shop fronts stood along that thoroughfare with an air of invitation, like rows of smiling saleswomen.

Even on Sunday, when it veiled its more florid charms and lay comparatively empty of passage, the street shone out in contrast to its dingy neighbourhood, like a fire in a forest; and with its freshly painted shutters, well-polished brasses, and general cleanliness and gaiety of note, instantly caught and pleased the eye of the passenger.

Two doors from one corner, on the left hand going east, the line was broken by the entry of a court; and just at that point, a certain sinister block of building thrust forward its gable on the street. It was two stories high; showed no window, nothing but a door on the lower story and a blind forehead of discoloured wall on the upper; and bore in every feature, the marks of prolonged and sordid negligence.

The door, which was equipped with neither bell nor knocker, was blistered and distained. Tramps slouched into the recess and struck matches on the panels; children kept shop upon the steps; the schoolboy had tried his knife on the mouldings; and for close on a generation, no one had appeared to drive away these random visitors or to repair their ravages.

Mr. Enfield and the lawyer were on the other side of the by-street; but when they came abreast of the entry, the former lifted up his cane and pointed.

"Did you ever remark that door?" he asked; and when his companion had replied in the affirmative, "It is connected in my mind," added he, "with a very odd story."

"Indeed?" said Mr. Utterson, with a slight change of voice, "and what was that?"

"Well, it was this way," returned Mr. Enfield: "I was coming home from some place at the end of the world, about three o'clock of a black winter morning, and my way lay through a part of town where there was literally nothing to be seen but lamps. Street after street, and all the folks asleep—street after street, all lighted up as if for a procession and all as empty as a church—till at last I got into that state of mind when a man listens and listens and begins to long for the sight of a policeman.

All at once, I saw two figures: one a little man who was stumping along eastward at a good walk, and the other a girl of maybe eight or ten who was running as hard as she was able down a cross street. Well, sir, the two ran into one another naturally enough at the corner; and then came the horrible part of the thing; for the man trampled calmly over the child's body and left her screaming on the ground.

It sounds nothing to hear, but it was hellish to see. It wasn't like a man; it was like some damned Juggernaut. I gave a view-halloa, took to my heels, collared my gentleman, and brought him back to where there was already quite a group about the screaming child.

He was perfectly cool and made no resistance, but gave me one look, so ugly that it brought out the sweat on me like running. The people who had turned out were the girl's own family; and pretty soon, the doctor, for whom she had been sent, put in his appearance.

Well, the child was not much the worse, more frightened, according to the Sawbones; and there you might have supposed would be an end to it. But there was one curious circumstance. I had taken a loathing to my gentleman at first sight. So had the child's family, which was only natural.

But the doctor's case was what struck me. He was the usual cut-and-dry apothecary, of no particular age and colour, with a strong Edinburgh accent, and about as emotional as a bagpipe. Well, sir, he was like the rest of us; every time he looked at my prisoner, I saw that Sawbones turn sick and white with the desire to kill him. I knew what was in his mind, just as he knew what was in mine; and killing being out of the question, we did the next best.

We told the man we could and would make such a scandal out of this, as should make his name stink from one end of London to the other. If he had any friends or any credit, we undertook that he should lose them.

And all the time, as we were pitching it in red hot, we were keeping the women off him as best we could, for they were as wild as harpies. I never saw a circle of such hateful faces; and there was the man in the middle, with a kind of black, sneering coolness—frightened too, I could see that—but carrying it off, sir, really like Satan.

'If you choose to make capital out of this accident,' said he, 'I am naturally helpless. No gentleman but wishes to avoid a scene,' says he. 'Name your figure.'

Well, we screwed him up to a hundred pounds for the child's family; he would have clearly liked to stick out; but there was something about the lot of us that meant mischief, and at last he struck.

The next thing was to get the money; and where do you think he carried us but to that place with the door?— whipped out a key, went in, and presently came back with the matter of ten pounds in gold and a cheque for the balance on Coutts's, drawn payable to bearer and signed with a name that I can't mention, though it's one of the points of my story, but it was a name at least very well known and often printed. The figure was stiff; but the signature was good for more than that, if it was only genuine.

I took the liberty of pointing out to my gentleman that the whole business looked apocryphal, and that a man does not, in real life, walk into a cellar door at four in the morning and come out of it with another man's cheque for close upon a hundred pounds. But he was quite easy and sneering.

'Set your mind at rest,' says he, 'I will stay with you till the banks open and cash the cheque myself.'

So we all set off, the doctor, and the child's father, and our friend and myself, and passed the rest of the night in my chambers; and next day, when we had breakfasted, went in a body to the bank. I gave in the check myself, and said I had every reason to believe it was a forgery. Not a bit of it. The cheque was genuine."

"Tut-tut," said Mr. Utterson.

"I see you feel as I do," said Mr. Enfield. "Yes, it's a bad story. For my man was a fellow that nobody could have to do with, a really damnable man; and the person that drew the cheque is the very pink of the proprieties, celebrated too, and (what makes it worse) one of your fellows who do what they call good. Black-mail, I suppose; an honest man paying through the nose for some of the capers of his youth. Black-Mail House is what I call that place with the door, in consequence. Though even that, you know, is far from explaining all," he added, and with the words fell into a vein of musing.

From this he was recalled by Mr. Utterson asking rather suddenly: "And you don't know if the drawer of the cheque lives there?"

"A likely place, isn't it?" returned Mr. Enfield. "But I happen to have noticed his address; he lives in some square or other."

"And you never asked about the—place with the door?" said Mr. Utterson.

"No, sir: I had a delicacy," was the reply. "I feel very strongly about putting questions; it partakes too much of the style of the day of judgment. You start a question, and it's like starting a stone. You sit quietly on the top of a hill; and away the stone goes, starting others; and presently some bland old bird (the last you would have thought of) is knocked on the head in his own back-garden and the family have to change their name. No, sir, I make it a rule of mine: the more it looks like Queer Street, the less I ask."

"A very good rule, too," said the lawyer.

"But I have studied the place for myself," continued Mr. Enfield. "It seems scarcely a house. There is no other door, and nobody goes in or out of that one but, once in a great while, the gentleman of my adventure. There are three windows looking on the court on the first floor; none below; the windows are always shut but they're clean. And then there is a chimney which is generally smoking; so somebody must live there. And yet it's not so sure; for the buildings are so packed together about that court, that it's hard to say where one ends and another begins."

The pair walked on again for a while in silence; and then, "Enfield," said Mr. Utterson, "that's a good rule of yours."

"Yes, I think it is," returned Enfield.

"But for all that," continued the lawyer, "there's one point I want to ask: I want to ask the name of that man who walked over the child."

"Well," said Mr. Enfield, "I can't see what harm it would do. It was a man of the name of Hyde."

"H'm," said Mr. Utterson. "What sort of a man is he to see?"

"He is not easy to describe. There is something wrong with his appearance; something displeasing, something downright detestable. I never saw a man I so disliked, and yet I scarce know why. He must be deformed somewhere; he gives a strong feeling of deformity, although I couldn't specify the point. He's an extraordinary-looking man, and yet I really can name nothing out of the way. No, sir; I can make no hand of it; I can't describe him. And it's not want of memory; for I declare I can see him this moment."

Mr. Utterson again walked some way in silence and obviously under a weight of consideration.

"You are sure he used a key?" he inquired at last.

"My dear sir..." began Enfield, surprised out of himself.

"Yes, I know," said Utterson; "I know it must seem strange. The fact is, if I do not ask you the name of the other party, it is because I know it already. You see, Richard, your tale has gone home. If you have been inexact in any point, you had better correct it."

"I think you might have warned me," returned the other, with a touch of sullenness. "But I have been pedantically exact, as you call it. The fellow had a key; and what's more, he has it still. I saw him use it, not a week ago."

Mr. Utterson sighed deeply but said never a word; and the young man presently resumed. "Here is another lesson to say nothing," said he. "I am ashamed of my long tongue. Let us make a bargain never to refer to this again."

"With all my heart," said the lawyer. "I shake hands on that, Richard."

Chapter 2

SEARCH FOR MR. HYDE

THAT evening Mr. Utterson came home to his bachelor house in sombre spirits and sat down to dinner without relish. It was his custom of a Sunday, when this meal was over, to sit close by the fire, a volume of some dry divinity on his reading-desk, until the clock of the neighbouring church rang out the hour of twelve, when he would go soberly and gratefully to bed.

On this night, however, as soon as the cloth was taken away, he took up a candle and went into his business-room. There he opened his safe, took from the most private part of it a document endorsed on the envelope as Dr. Jekyll's Will, and sat down with a clouded brow to study its contents.

The will was holograph, for Mr. Utterson, though he took charge of it now that it was made, had refused to lend the least assistance in the making of it; it provided not only that, in case of the decease of Henry Jekyll, M.D., D.C.L., L.L.D., F.R.S., etc., all his possessions were to pass into the hands of his "friend and benefactor Edward Hyde," but that in case of Dr. Jekyll's "disappearance or unexplained absence for any period exceeding three calendar months," the said Edward Hyde should step into the said Henry Jekyll's shoes without further delay and free from any burthen or obligation, beyond the payment of a few small sums to the members of the doctor's household.

This document had long been the lawyer's eyesore. It offended him both as a lawyer and as a lover of the sane and customary sides of life, to whom the fanciful was the immodest. And hitherto it was his ignorance of Mr. Hyde that had swelled his indignation; now, by a sudden turn, it was his knowledge.

It was already bad enough when the name was but a name of which he could learn no more. It was worse when it began to be clothed upon with detestable attributes; and out of the shifting, insubstantial mists that had so long baffled his eye, there leaped up the sudden, definite presentment of a fiend.

"I thought it was madness," he said, as he replaced the obnoxious paper in the safe, "and now I begin to fear it is disgrace."

With that he blew out his candle, put on a great-coat, and set forth in the direction of Cavendish Square, that citadel of medicine, where his friend, the great Dr. Lanyon, had his house and received his crowding patients. "If any one knows, it will be Lanyon," he had thought.

The solemn butler knew and welcomed him; he was subjected to no stage of delay, but ushered direct from the door to the dining-room where Dr. Lanyon sat alone over his wine.

This was a hearty, healthy, dapper, red-faced gentleman, with a shock of hair prematurely white, and a boisterous and decided manner. At sight of Mr. Utterson, he sprang up from his chair and welcomed him with both hands. The geniality, as was the way of the man, was somewhat theatrical to the eye; but it reposed on genuine feeling.

For these two were old friends, old mates both at school and college, both thorough respecters of themselves and of each other, and, what does not always follow, men who thoroughly enjoyed each other's company.

After a little rambling talk, the lawyer led up to the subject which so disagreeably pre-occupied his mind.

"I suppose, Lanyon," said he "you and I must be the two oldest friends that Henry Jekyll has?"

"I wish the friends were younger," chuckled Dr. Lanyon. "But I suppose we are. And what of that? I see little of him now."

"Indeed?" said Utterson. "I thought you had a bond of common interest."

"We had," was the reply. "But it is more than ten years since Henry Jekyll became too fanciful for me. He began to go wrong, wrong in mind; and though of course I continue to take an interest in him for old sake's sake, as they say, I see and I have seen devilish little of the man. Such unscientific balderdash," added the doctor, flushing suddenly purple, "would have estranged Damon and Pythias."

This little spirit of temper was somewhat of a relief to Mr. Utterson. "They have only differed on some point of science," he thought; and being a man of no scientific passions (except in the matter of conveyancing), he even added: "It is nothing worse than that!" He gave his friend a few seconds to recover his composure, and then approached the question he had come to put. "Did you ever come across a protege of his—one Hyde?" he asked.

"Hyde?" repeated Lanyon. "No. Never heard of him. Since my time."

That was the amount of information that the lawyer carried back with him to the great, dark bed on which he tossed to and fro, until the small hours of the morning began to grow large. It was a night of little ease to his toiling mind, toiling in mere darkness and besieged by questions.

Six o'clock struck on the bells of the church that was so conveniently near to Mr. Utterson's dwelling, and still he was digging at the problem. Hitherto it had touched him on the intellectual side alone; but now his imagination also was engaged, or rather enslaved; and as he lay and tossed in the gross darkness of the night and the curtained room, Mr. Enfield's tale went by before his mind in a scroll of lighted pictures.

He would be aware of the great field of lamps of a nocturnal city; then of the figure of a man walking swiftly; then of a child running from the doctor's; and then these met, and that human Juggernaut trod the child down and passed on regardless of her screams.

Or else he would see a room in a rich house, where his friend lay asleep, dreaming and smiling at his dreams; and then the door of that room would be opened, the curtains of the bed plucked apart, the sleeper recalled, and lo! there would stand by his side a figure to whom power was given, and even at that dead hour, he must rise and do its bidding.

The figure in these two phases haunted the lawyer all night; and if at any time he dozed over, it was but to see it glide more stealthily through sleeping houses, or move the more swiftly and still the more swiftly, even to dizziness, through wider labyrinths of lamplighted city, and at every street-corner crush a child and leave her screaming.

And still the figure had no face by which he might know it; even in his dreams, it had no face, or one that baffled him and melted before his eyes; and thus it was that there sprang up and grew apace in the lawyer's mind a singularly strong, almost an inordinate, curiosity to behold the features of the real Mr. Hyde.

If he could but once set eyes on him, he thought the mystery would lighten and perhaps roll altogether away, as was the habit of mysterious things when well examined. He might see a reason for his friend's strange preference or bondage (call it which you please) and even for the startling clause of the will. At least it would be a face worth seeing: the face of a man who was without bowels of mercy: a face which had but to show itself to raise up, in the mind of the unimpressionable Enfield, a spirit of enduring hatred.

From that time forward, Mr. Utterson began to haunt the door in the by-street of shops. In the morning before office hours, at noon when business was plenty, and time scarce, at night under the face of the fogged city moon, by all lights and at all hours of solitude or concourse, the lawyer was to be found on his chosen post.

"If he be Mr. Hyde," he had thought, "I shall be Mr. Seek."

And at last his patience was rewarded. It was a fine dry night; frost in the air; the streets as clean as a ballroom floor; the lamps, unshaken, by any wind, drawing a regular pattern of light and shadow. By ten o'clock, when the shops were closed, the by-street was very solitary and, in spite of the low growl of London from all round, very silent.

Small sounds carried far; domestic sounds out of the houses were clearly audible on either side of the roadway; and the rumour of the approach of any passenger preceded him by a long time. Mr. Utterson had been some minutes at his post, when he was aware of an odd, light footstep drawing near.

In the course of his nightly patrols, he had long grown accustomed to the quaint effect with which the footfalls of a single person, while he is still a great way off, suddenly spring out distinct from the vast hum and clatter of the city. Yet his attention had never before been so sharply and decisively arrested; and it was with a strong, superstitious prevision of success that he withdrew into the entry of the court.

The steps drew swiftly nearer, and swelled out suddenly louder as they turned the end of the street. The lawyer, looking forth from the entry, could soon see what manner of man he had to deal with. He was small and very plainly dressed, and the look of him, even at that distance, went somehow strongly against the watcher's inclination.

But he made straight for the door, crossing the roadway to save time; and as he came, he drew a key from his pocket like one approaching home.

Mr. Utterson stepped out and touched him on the shoulder as he passed. "Mr. Hyde, I think?"

Mr. Hyde shrank back with a hissing intake of the breath. But his fear was only momentary; and though he did not look the lawyer in the face, he answered coolly enough: "That is my name. What do you want?"

"I see you are going in," returned the lawyer. "I am an old friend of Dr. Jekyll's—Mr. Utterson of Gaunt Street—you must have heard my name; and meeting you so conveniently, I thought you might admit me."

"You will not find Dr. Jekyll; he is from home," replied Mr. Hyde, blowing in the key. And then suddenly, but still without looking up, "How did you know me?" he asked.

"On your side," said Mr. Utterson, "will you do me a favour?"

"With pleasure," replied the other. "What shall it be?"

"Will you let me see your face?" asked the lawyer.

Mr. Hyde appeared to hesitate, and then, as if upon some sudden reflection, fronted about with an air of defiance; and the pair stared at each other pretty fixedly for a few seconds.

"Now I shall know you again," said Mr. Utterson. "It may be useful."

"Yes," returned Mr. Hyde, "it is as well we have, met; and a propos, you should have my address." And he gave a number of a street in Soho.

"Good God!" thought Mr. Utterson, "can he, too, have been thinking of the will?" But he kept his feelings to himself and only grunted in acknowledgment of the address.

"And now," said the other, "how did you know me?"

"By description," was the reply.

"Whose description?"

"We have common friends," said Mr. Utterson.

"Common friends?" echoed Mr. Hyde, a little hoarsely. "Who are they?"

"Jekyll, for instance," said the lawyer.

"He never told you," cried Mr. Hyde, with a flush of anger. "I did not think you would have lied."

"Come," said Mr. Utterson, "that is not fitting language."

The other snarled aloud into a savage laugh; and the next moment, with extraordinary quickness, he had unlocked the door and disappeared into the house.

The lawyer stood awhile when Mr. Hyde had left him, the picture of disquietude. Then he began slowly to mount the street, pausing every step or two and putting his hand to his brow like a man in mental perplexity. The problem he was thus debating as he walked, was one of a class that is rarely solved.

Mr. Hyde was pale and dwarfish, he gave an impression of deformity without any nameable malformation, he had a displeasing smile, he had borne himself to the lawyer with a sort of murderous mixture of timidity and boldness, and he spoke with a husky, whispering and somewhat broken voice; all these were points against him, but not all of these together could explain the hitherto unknown disgust, loathing, and fear with which Mr. Utterson regarded him.

"There must be something else," said the perplexed gentleman. "There is something more, if I could find a name for it. God bless me, the man seems hardly human! Something troglodytic, shall we say? or can it be the old story of Dr. Fell? or is it the mere radiance of a foul soul that thus transpires through, and transfigures, its clay continent? The last, I think; for, O my poor old Harry Jekyll, if ever I read Satan's signature upon a face, it is on that of your new friend."

Round the corner from the by-street, there was a square of ancient, handsome houses, now for the most part decayed from their high estate and let in flats and chambers to all sorts and conditions of men: map-engravers, architects, shady lawyers, and the agents of obscure enterprises.

One house, however, second from the corner, was still occupied entire; and at the door of this, which wore a great air of wealth and comfort, though it was now plunged in darkness except for the fan-light, Mr. Utterson stopped and knocked. A well-dressed, elderly servant opened the door.

"Is Dr. Jekyll at home, Poole?" asked the lawyer.

"I will see, Mr. Utterson," said Poole, admitting the visitor, as he spoke, into a large, low-roofed, comfortable hall, paved with flags, warmed (after the fashion of a country house) by a bright, open fire, and furnished with costly cabinets of oak. "Will you wait here by the fire, sir? or shall I give you a light in the dining room?"

"Here, thank you," said the lawyer, and he drew near and leaned on the tall fender. This hall, in which he was now left alone, was a pet fancy of his friend the doctor's; and Utterson himself was wont to speak of it as the pleasantest room in London.

But to-night there was a shudder in his blood; the face of Hyde sat heavy on his memory; he felt (what was rare with him) a nausea and distaste of life; and in the gloom of his spirits, he seemed to read a menace in the flickering of the firelight on the polished cabinets and the uneasy starting of the shadow on the roof.

He was ashamed of his relief, when Poole presently returned to announce that Dr. Jekyll was gone out.

"I saw Mr. Hyde go in by the old dissecting-room door, Poole," he said. "Is that right, when Dr. Jekyll is from home?"

"Quite right, Mr. Utterson, sir," replied the servant. "Mr. Hyde has a key."

"Your master seems to repose a great deal of trust in that young man, Poole," resumed the other musingly.

"Yes, sir, he do indeed," said Poole. "We have all orders to obey him."

"I do not think I ever met Mr. Hyde?" asked Utterson.

"O, dear no, sir. He never dines here," replied the butler. "Indeed we see very little of him on this side of the house; he mostly comes and goes by the laboratory."

"Well, good-night, Poole."

"Good-night, Mr. Utterson." And the lawyer set out homeward with a very heavy heart.

"Poor Harry Jekyll," he thought, "my mind misgives me he is in deep waters! He was wild when he was young; a long while ago to be sure; but in the law of God, there is no statute of limitations. Ay, it must be that; the ghost of some old sin, the cancer of some concealed disgrace: punishment coming, PEDE CLAUDO, years after memory has forgotten and self-love condoned the fault."

And the lawyer, scared by the thought, brooded a while on his own past, groping in all the corners of memory, lest by chance some Jack-in-the-Box of an old iniquity should leap to light there.

His past was fairly blameless; few men could read the rolls of their life with less apprehension; yet he was humbled to the dust by the many ill things he had done, and raised up again into a sober and fearful gratitude by the many that he had come so near to doing, yet avoided.

And then by a return on his former subject, he conceived a spark of hope. "This Master Hyde, if he were studied," thought he, "must have secrets of his own; black secrets, by the look of him; secrets compared to which poor Jekyll's worst would be like sunshine. Things cannot continue as they are. It turns me cold to think of this creature stealing like a thief to Harry's bedside; poor Harry, what a wakening! And the danger of it; for if this Hyde suspects the existence of the will, he may grow impatient to inherit. Ay, I must put my shoulder to the wheel if Jekyll will but let me," he added, "if Jekyll will only let me."

For once more he saw before his mind's eye, as clear as a transparency, the strange clauses of the will.

Chapter 3

DR. JEKYLL WAS QUITE AT EASE

A FORTNIGHT later, by excellent good fortune, the doctor gave one of his pleasant dinners to some five or six old cronies, all intelligent, reputable men and all judges of good wine; and Mr. Utterson so contrived that he remained behind after the others had departed. This was no new arrangement, but a thing that had befallen many scores of times.

Where Utterson was liked, he was liked well. Hosts loved to detain the dry lawyer, when the light-hearted and the loose-tongued had already their foot on the threshold; they liked to sit a while in his unobtrusive company, practising for solitude, sobering their minds in the man's rich silence after the expense and strain of gaiety.

To this rule, Dr. Jekyll was no exception; and as he now sat on the opposite side of the fire—a large, well-made, smooth-faced man of fifty, with something of a slyish cast perhaps, but every mark of capacity and kindness—you could see by his looks that he cherished for Mr. Utterson a sincere and warm affection.

"I have been wanting to speak to you, Jekyll," began the latter. "You know that will of yours?"

A close observer might have gathered that the topic was distasteful; but the doctor carried it off gaily.

"My poor Utterson," said he, "you are unfortunate in such a client. I never saw a man so distressed as you were by my will; unless it were that hide-bound pedant, Lanyon, at what he called my scientific heresies. Oh, I know he's a good fellow—you needn't frown—an excellent fellow, and I always mean to see more of him; but a hide-bound pedant for all that; an ignorant, blatant pedant. I was never more disappointed in any man than Lanyon."

"You know I never approved of it," pursued Utterson, ruthlessly disregarding the fresh topic.

"My will? Yes, certainly, I know that," said the doctor, a trifle sharply. "You have told me so."

"Well, I tell you so again," continued the lawyer. "I have been learning something of young Hyde."

The large handsome face of Dr. Jekyll grew pale to the very lips, and there came a blackness about his eyes. "I do not care to hear more," said he. "This is a matter I thought we had agreed to drop."

"What I heard was abominable," said Utterson.

"It can make no change. You do not understand my position," returned the doctor, with a certain incoherency of manner. "I am painfully situated, Utterson; my position is a very strange—a very strange one. It is one of those affairs that cannot be mended by talking."

"Jekyll," said Utterson, "you know me: I am a man to be trusted. Make a clean breast of this in confidence; and I make no doubt I can get you out of it."

"My good Utterson," said the doctor, "this is very good of you, this is downright good of you, and I cannot find words to thank you in. I believe you fully; I would trust you before any man alive, ay, before myself, if I could make the choice; but indeed it isn't what you fancy; it is not so bad as that; and just to put your good heart at rest, I will tell you one thing: the moment I choose, I can be rid of Mr. Hyde. I give you my hand upon that; and I thank you again and again; and I will just add one little word, Utterson, that I'm sure you'll take in good part: this is a private matter, and I beg of you to let it sleep."

Utterson reflected a little, looking in the fire.

"I have no doubt you are perfectly right," he said at last, getting to his feet.

"Well, but since we have touched upon this business, and for the last time I hope," continued the doctor, "there is one point I should like you to understand. I have really a very great interest in poor Hyde. I know you have seen him; he told me so; and I fear he was rude. But, I do sincerely take a great, a very great interest in that young man; and if I am taken away, Utterson, I wish you to promise me that you will bear with him and get his rights for him. I think you would, if you knew all; and it would be a weight off my mind if you would promise."

"I can't pretend that I shall ever like him," said the lawyer.

"I don't ask that," pleaded Jekyll, laying his hand upon the other's arm; "I only ask for justice; I only ask you to help him for my sake, when I am no longer here."

Utterson heaved an irrepressible sigh. "Well," said he, "I promise."

Chapter 4

THE CAREW MURDER CASE

NEARLY a year later, in the month of October, 18—-, London was startled by a crime of singular ferocity and rendered all the more notable by the high position of the victim. The details were few and startling. A maid servant living alone in a house not far from the river, had gone up-stairs to bed about eleven.

Although a fog rolled over the city in the small hours, the early part of the night was cloudless, and the lane, which the maid's window overlooked, was brilliantly lit by the full moon. It seems she was romantically given, for she sat down upon her box, which stood immediately under the window, and fell into a dream of musing.

Never (she used to say, with streaming tears, when she narrated that experience), never had she felt more at peace with all men or thought more kindly of the world. And as she so sat she became aware of an aged and beautiful gentleman with white hair, drawing near along the lane; and advancing to meet him, another and very small gentleman, to whom at first she paid less attention.

When they had come within speech (which was just under the maid's eyes) the older man bowed and accosted the other with a very pretty manner of politeness. It did not seem as if the subject of his address were of great importance; indeed, from his pointing, it sometimes appeared as if he were only inquiring his way; but the moon shone on his face as he spoke, and the girl was pleased to watch it, it seemed to breathe such an innocent and old-world kindness of disposition, yet with something high too, as of a well-founded self-content.

Presently her eye wandered to the other, and she was surprised to recognise in him a certain Mr. Hyde, who had once visited her master and for whom she had conceived a dislike. He had in his hand a heavy cane, with which he was trifling; but he answered never a word, and seemed to listen with an ill-contained impatience.

And then all of a sudden he broke out in a great flame of anger, stamping with his foot, brandishing the cane, and carrying on (as the maid described it) like a madman. The old gentleman took a step back, with the air of one very much surprised and a trifle hurt; and at that Mr. Hyde broke out of all bounds and clubbed him to the earth.

And next moment, with ape-like fury, he was trampling his victim under foot and hailing down a storm of blows, under which the bones were audibly shattered and the body jumped upon the roadway. At the horror of these sights and sounds, the maid fainted.

It was two o'clock when she came to herself and called for the police. The murderer was gone long ago; but there lay his victim in the middle of the lane, incredibly mangled. The stick with which the deed had been done, although it was of some rare and very tough and heavy wood, had broken in the middle under the stress of this insensate cruelty; and one splintered half had rolled in the neighbouring gutter—the other, without doubt, had been carried away by the murderer.

A purse and a gold watch were found upon the victim: but no cards or papers, except a sealed and stamped envelope, which he had been probably carrying to the post, and which bore the name and address of Mr. Utterson.

This was brought to the lawyer the next morning, before he was out of bed; and he had no sooner seen it, and been told the circumstances, than he shot out a solemn lip.

"I shall say nothing till I have seen the body," said he; "this may be very serious. Have the kindness to wait while I dress."

And with the same grave countenance he hurried through his breakfast and drove to the police station, whither the body had been carried. As soon as he came into the cell, he nodded.

"Yes," said he, "I recognise him. I am sorry to say that this is Sir Danvers Carew."

"Good God, sir," exclaimed the officer, "is it possible?" And the next moment his eye lighted up with professional ambition.

"This will make a deal of noise," he said. "And perhaps you can help us to the man." And he briefly narrated what the maid had seen, and showed the broken stick.

Mr. Utterson had already quailed at the name of Hyde; but when the stick was laid before him, he could doubt no longer; broken and battered as it was, he recognised it for one that he had himself presented many years before to Henry Jekyll.

"Is this Mr. Hyde a person of small stature?" he inquired.

"Particularly small and particularly wicked-looking, is what the maid calls him," said the officer.

Mr. Utterson reflected; and then, raising his head, "If you will come with me in my cab," he said, "I think I can take you to his house."

It was by this time about nine in the morning, and the first fog of the season. A great chocolate-coloured pall lowered over heaven, but the wind was continually charging and routing these embattled vapours; so that as the cab crawled from street to street, Mr. Utterson beheld a marvellous number of degrees and hues of twilight; for here it would be dark like the back-end of evening; and there would be a glow of a rich, lurid brown, like the light of some strange conflagration; and here, for a moment, the fog would be quite broken up, and a haggard shaft of daylight would glance in between the swirling wreaths.

The dismal quarter of Soho seen under these changing glimpses, with its muddy ways, and slatternly passengers, and its lamps, which had never been extinguished or had been kindled afresh to combat this mournful re-invasion of darkness, seemed, in the lawyer's eyes, like a district of some city in a nightmare.

The thoughts of his mind, besides, were of the gloomiest dye; and when he glanced at the companion of his drive, he was conscious of some touch of that terror of the law and the law's officers, which may at times assail the most honest.

As the cab drew up before the address indicated, the fog lifted a little and showed him a dingy street, a gin palace, a low French eating-house, a shop for the retail of penny numbers and twopenny salads, many ragged children huddled in the doorways, and many women of different nationalities passing out, key in hand, to have a morning glass; and the next moment the fog settled down again upon that part, as brown as umber, and cut him off from his blackguardly surroundings. This was the home of Henry Jekyll's favourite; of a man who was heir to a quarter of a million sterling.

An ivory-faced and silvery-haired old woman opened the door. She had an evil face, smoothed by hypocrisy; but her manners were excellent. Yes, she said, this was Mr. Hyde's, but he was not at home; he had been in that night very late, but had gone away again in less than an hour; there was nothing strange in that; his habits were very irregular, and he was often absent; for instance, it was nearly two months since she had seen him till yesterday.

"Very well, then, we wish to see his rooms," said the lawyer; and when the woman began to declare it was impossible, "I had better tell you who this person is," he added. "This is Inspector Newcomen of Scotland Yard."

A flash of odious joy appeared upon the woman's face. "Ah!" said she, "he is in trouble! What has he done?"

Mr. Utterson and the inspector exchanged glances. "He don't seem a very popular character," observed the latter. "And now, my good woman, just let me and this gentleman have a look about us."

In the whole extent of the house, which but for the old woman remained otherwise empty, Mr. Hyde had only used a couple of rooms; but these were furnished with luxury and good taste. A closet was filled with wine; the plate was of silver, the napery elegant; a good picture hung upon the walls, a gift (as Utterson supposed) from Henry Jekyll, who was much of a connoisseur; and the carpets were of many plies and agreeable in colour.

At this moment, however, the rooms bore every mark of having been recently and hurriedly ransacked; clothes lay about the floor, with their pockets inside out; lock-fast drawers stood open; and on the hearth there lay a pile of grey ashes, as though many papers had been burned.

From these embers the inspector disinterred the butt-end of a green cheque-book, which had resisted the action of the fire; the other half of the stick was found behind the door; and as this clinched his suspicions, the officer declared himself delighted.

A visit to the bank, where several thousand pounds were found to be lying to the murderer's credit, completed his gratification.

"You may depend upon it, sir," he told Mr. Utterson: "I have him in my hand. He must have lost his head, or he never would have left the stick or, above all, burned the cheque-book. Why, money's life to the man. We have nothing to do but wait for him at the bank, and get out the handbills."

This last, however, was not so easy of accomplishment; for Mr. Hyde had numbered few familiars—even the master of the servant-maid had only seen him twice; his family could nowhere be traced; he had never been photographed; and the few who could describe him differed widely, as common observers will.

Only on one point, were they agreed; and that was the haunting sense of unexpressed deformity with which the fugitive impressed his beholders.

Chapter 5

INCIDENT OF THE LETTER

IT was late in the afternoon, when Mr. Utterson found his way to Dr. Jekyll's door, where he was at once admitted by Poole, and carried down by the kitchen offices and across a yard which had once been a garden, to the building which was indifferently known as the laboratory or the dissecting-rooms.

The doctor had bought the house from the heirs of a celebrated surgeon; and his own tastes being rather chemical than anatomical, had changed the destination of the block at the bottom of the garden.

It was the first time that the lawyer had been received in that part of his friend's quarters; and he eyed the dingy, windowless structure with curiosity, and gazed round with a distasteful sense of strangeness as he crossed the theatre, once crowded with eager students and now lying gaunt and silent, the tables laden with chemical apparatus, the floor strewn with crates and littered with packing straw, and the light falling dimly through the foggy cupola.

At the further end, a flight of stairs mounted to a door covered with red baize; and through this, Mr. Utterson was at last received into the doctor's cabinet. It was a large room, fitted round with glass presses, furnished, among other things, with a cheval-glass and a business table, and looking out upon the court by three dusty windows barred with iron.

A fire burned in the grate; a lamp was set lighted on the chimney shelf, for even in the houses the fog began to lie thickly; and there, close up to the warmth, sat Dr. Jekyll, looking deadly sick. He did not rise to meet his visitor, but held out a cold hand and bade him welcome in a changed voice.

"And now," said Mr. Utterson, as soon as Poole had left them, "you have heard the news?"

The doctor shuddered. "They were crying it in the square," he said. "I heard them in my dining-room."

"One word," said the lawyer. "Carew was my client, but so are you, and I want to know what I am doing. You have not been mad enough to hide this fellow?"

"Utterson, I swear to God," cried the doctor, "I swear to God I will never set eyes on him again. I bind my honour to you that I am done with him in this world. It is all at an end. And indeed he does not want my help; you do not know him as I do; he is safe, he is quite safe; mark my words, he will never more be heard of."

The lawyer listened gloomily; he did not like his friend's feverish manner. "You seem pretty sure of him," said he; "and for your sake, I hope you may be right. If it came to a trial, your name might appear."

"I am quite sure of him," replied Jekyll; "I have grounds for certainty that I cannot share with any one. But there is one thing on which you may advise me. I have—I have received a letter; and I am at a loss whether I should show it to the police. I should like to leave it in your hands, Utterson; you would judge wisely, I am sure; I have so great a trust in you."

"You fear, I suppose, that it might lead to his detection?" asked the lawyer.

"No," said the other. "I cannot say that I care what becomes of Hyde; I am quite done with him. I was thinking of my own character, which this hateful business has rather exposed."

Utterson ruminated a while; he was surprised at his friend's selfishness, and yet relieved by it. "Well," said he, at last, "let me see the letter."

The letter was written in an odd, upright hand and signed "Edward Hyde": and it signified, briefly enough, that the writer's benefactor, Dr. Jekyll, whom he had long so unworthily repaid for a thousand generosities, need labour under no alarm for his safety, as he had means of escape on which he placed a sure dependence.

The lawyer liked this letter well enough; it put a better colour on the intimacy than he had looked for; and he blamed himself for some of his past suspicions.

"Have you the envelope?" he asked.

"I burned it," replied Jekyll, "before I thought what I was about. But it bore no postmark. The note was handed in."

"Shall I keep this and sleep upon it?" asked Utterson.

"I wish you to judge for me entirely," was the reply. "I have lost confidence in myself."

"Well, I shall consider," returned the lawyer. "And now one word more: it was Hyde who dictated the terms in your will about that disappearance?"

The doctor seemed seized with a qualm of faintness: he shut his mouth tight and nodded.

"I knew it," said Utterson. "He meant to murder you. You have had a fine escape."

"I have had what is far more to the purpose," returned the doctor solemnly: "I have had a lesson—O God, Utterson, what a lesson I have had!" And he covered his face for a moment with his hands.

On his way out, the lawyer stopped and had a word or two with Poole. "By the by," said he, "there was a letter handed in to-day: what was the messenger like?"

But Poole was positive nothing had come except by post; "and only circulars by that," he added.

This news sent off the visitor with his fears renewed. Plainly the letter had come by the laboratory door; possibly, indeed, it had been written in the cabinet; and if that were so, it must be differently judged, and handled with the more caution.

The newsboys, as he went, were crying themselves hoarse along the footways: "Special edition. Shocking murder of an M. P."

That was the funeral oration of one friend and client; and he could not help a certain apprehension lest the good name of another should be sucked down in the eddy of the scandal. It was, at least, a ticklish decision that he had to make; and self-reliant as he was by habit, he began to cherish a longing for advice. It was not to be had directly; but perhaps, he thought, it might be fished for.

Presently after, he sat on one side of his own hearth, with Mr. Guest, his head clerk, upon the other, and midway between, at a nicely calculated distance from the fire, a bottle of a particular old wine that had long dwelt unsunned in the foundations of his house.

The fog still slept on the wing above the drowned city, where the lamps glimmered like carbuncles; and through the muffle and smother of these fallen clouds, the procession of the town's life was still rolling in through the great arteries with a sound as of a mighty wind.

But the room was gay with firelight. In the bottle the acids were long ago resolved; the imperial dye had softened with time, as the colour grows richer in stained windows; and the glow of hot autumn afternoons on hillside vineyards was ready to be set free and to disperse the fogs of London.

Insensibly the lawyer melted. There was no man from whom he kept fewer secrets than Mr. Guest; and he was not always sure that he kept as many as he meant. Guest had often been on business to the doctor's; he knew Poole; he could scarce have failed to hear of Mr. Hyde's familiarity about the house; he might draw conclusions: was it not as well, then, that he should see a letter which put that mystery to rights? and above all since Guest, being a great student and critic of handwriting, would consider the step natural and obliging? The clerk, besides, was a man of counsel; he would scarce read so strange a document without dropping a remark; and by that remark Mr. Utterson might shape his future course.

"This is a sad business about Sir Danvers," he said.

"Yes, sir, indeed. It has elicited a great deal of public feeling," returned Guest. "The man, of course, was mad."

"I should like to hear your views on that," replied Utterson. "I have a document here in his handwriting; it is between ourselves, for I scarce know what to do about it; it is an ugly business at the best. But there it is; quite in your way a murderer's autograph."

Guest's eyes brightened, and he sat down at once and studied it with passion. "No, sir," he said: "not mad; but it is an odd hand."

"And by all accounts a very odd writer," added the lawyer.

Just then the servant entered with a note.

"Is that from Dr. Jekyll, sir?" inquired the clerk. "I thought I knew the writing. Anything private, Mr. Utterson?"

"Only an invitation to dinner. Why? Do you want to see it?"

"One moment. I thank you, sir"; and the clerk laid the two sheets of paper alongside and sedulously compared their contents. "Thank you, sir," he said at last, returning both; "it's a very interesting autograph."

There was a pause, during which Mr. Utterson struggled with himself. "Why did you compare them, Guest?" he inquired suddenly.

"Well, sir," returned the clerk, "there's a rather singular resemblance; the two hands are in many points identical: only differently sloped."

"Rather quaint," said Utterson.

"It is, as you say, rather quaint," returned Guest.

"I wouldn't speak of this note, you know," said the master.

"No, sir," said the clerk. "I understand."

But no sooner was Mr. Utterson alone that night than he locked the note into his safe, where it reposed from that time forward.

"What!" he thought. "Henry Jekyll forge for a murderer!"

And his blood ran cold in his veins.

Chapter 6

REMARKABLE INCIDENT OF DR. LANYON

TIME ran on; thousands of pounds were offered in reward, for the death of Sir Danvers was resented as a public injury; but Mr. Hyde had disappeared out of the ken of the police as though he had never existed. Much of his past was unearthed, indeed, and all disreputable: tales came out of the man's cruelty, at once so callous and violent; of his vile life, of his strange associates, of the hatred that seemed to have surrounded his career; but of his present whereabouts, not a whisper.

From the time he had left the house in Soho on the morning of the murder, he was simply blotted out; and gradually, as time drew on, Mr. Utterson began to recover from the hotness of his alarm, and to grow more at quiet with himself. The death of Sir Danvers was, to his way of thinking, more than paid for by the disappearance of Mr. Hyde.

Now that that evil influence had been withdrawn, a new life began for Dr. Jekyll. He came out of his seclusion, renewed relations with his friends, became once more their familiar guest and entertainer; and whilst he had always been known for charities, he was now no less distinguished for religion.

He was busy, he was much in the open air, he did good; his face seemed to open and brighten, as if with an inward consciousness of service; and for more than two months, the doctor was at peace.

On the 8th of January Utterson had dined at the doctor's with a small party; Lanyon had been there; and the face of the host had looked from one to the other as in the old days when the trio were inseparable friends.

On the 12th, and again on the 14th, the door was shut against the lawyer. "The doctor was confined to the house," Poole said, "and saw no one."

On the 15th, he tried again, and was again refused; and having now been used for the last two months to see his friend almost daily, he found this return of solitude to weigh upon his spirits. The fifth night he had in Guest to dine with him; and the sixth he betook himself to Dr. Lanyon's.

There at least he was not denied admittance; but when he came in, he was shocked at the change which had taken place in the doctor's appearance. He had his death-warrant written legibly upon his face.

The rosy man had grown pale; his flesh had fallen away; he was visibly balder and older; and yet it was not so much, these tokens of a swift physical decay that arrested the lawyer's notice, as a look in the eye and quality of manner that seemed to testify to some deep-seated terror of the mind.

It was unlikely that the doctor should fear death; and yet that was what Utterson was tempted to suspect. "Yes," he thought; "he is a doctor, he must know his own state and that his days are counted; and the knowledge is more than he can bear."

And yet when Utterson remarked on his ill-looks, it was with an air of greatness that Lanyon declared himself a doomed man.

"I have had a shock," he said, "and I shall never recover. It is a question of weeks. Well, life has been pleasant; I liked it; yes, sir, I used to like it. I sometimes think if we knew all, we should be more glad to get away."

"Jekyll is ill, too," observed Utterson. "Have you seen him?"

But Lanyon's face changed, and he held up a trembling hand. "I wish to see or hear no more of Dr. Jekyll," he said in a loud, unsteady voice. "I am quite done with that person; and I beg that you will spare me any allusion to one whom I regard as dead."

"Tut-tut," said Mr. Utterson; and then after a considerable pause, "Can't I do anything?" he inquired. "We are three very old friends, Lanyon; we shall not live to make others."

"Nothing can be done," returned Lanyon; "ask himself."

"He will not see me," said the lawyer.

"I am not surprised at that," was the reply. "Some day, Utterson, after I am dead, you may perhaps come to learn the right and wrong of this. I cannot tell you. And in the meantime, if you can sit and talk with me of other things, for God's sake, stay and do so; but if you cannot keep clear of this accursed topic, then, in God's name, go, for I cannot bear it."

As soon as he got home, Utterson sat down and wrote to Jekyll, complaining of his exclusion from the house, and asking the cause of this unhappy break with Lanyon; and the next day brought him a long answer, often very pathetically worded, and sometimes darkly mysterious in drift. The quarrel with Lanyon was incurable.

"I do not blame our old friend," Jekyll wrote, "but I share his view that we must never meet. I mean from henceforth to lead a life of extreme seclusion; you must not be surprised, nor must you doubt my friendship, if my door is often shut even to you. You must suffer me to go my own dark way. I have brought on myself a punishment and a danger that I cannot name. If I am the chief of sinners, I am the chief of sufferers also.

I could not think that this earth contained a place for sufferings and terrors so unmanning; and you can do but one thing, Utterson, to lighten this destiny, and that is to respect my silence."

Utterson was amazed; the dark influence of Hyde had been withdrawn, the doctor had returned to his old tasks and amities; a week ago, the prospect had smiled with every promise of a cheerful and an honoured age; and now in a moment, friendship, and peace of mind, and the whole tenor of his life were wrecked. So great and unprepared a change pointed to madness; but in view of Lanyon's manner and words, there must lie for it some deeper ground.

A week afterwards Dr. Lanyon took to his bed, and in something less than a fortnight he was dead. The night after the funeral, at which he had been sadly affected, Utterson locked the door of his business room, and sitting there by the light of a melancholy candle, drew out and set before him an envelope addressed by the hand and sealed with the seal of his dead friend.

"PRIVATE: for the hands of G. J. Utterson ALONE and in case of his predecease to be destroyed unread," so it was emphatically superscribed; and the lawyer dreaded to behold the contents.

"I have buried one friend to-day," he thought: "what if this should cost me another?"

And then he condemned the fear as a disloyalty, and broke the seal.

Within there was another enclosure, likewise sealed, and marked upon the cover as "not to be opened till the death or disappearance of Dr. Henry Jekyll."

Utterson could not trust his eyes. Yes, it was disappearance; here again, as in the mad will which he had long ago restored to its author, here again were the idea of a disappearance and the name of Henry Jekyll bracketed. But in the will, that idea had sprung from the sinister suggestion of the man Hyde; it was set there with a purpose all too plain and horrible. Written by the hand of Lanyon, what should it mean?

A great curiosity came on the trustee, to disregard the prohibition and dive at once to the bottom of these mysteries; but professional honour and faith to his dead friend were stringent obligations; and the packet slept in the inmost corner of his private safe.

It is one thing to mortify curiosity, another to conquer it; and it may be doubted if, from that day forth, Utterson desired the society of his surviving friend with the same eagerness. He thought of him kindly; but his thoughts were disquieted and fearful.

He went to call indeed; but he was perhaps relieved to be denied admittance; perhaps, in his heart, he preferred to speak with Poole upon the doorstep and surrounded by the air and sounds of the open city, rather than to be admitted into that house of voluntary bondage, and to sit and speak with its inscrutable recluse. Poole had, indeed, no very pleasant news to communicate.

The doctor, it appeared, now more than ever confined himself to the cabinet over the laboratory, where he would sometimes even sleep; he was out of spirits, he had grown very silent, he did not read; it seemed as if he had something on his mind. Utterson became so used to the unvarying character of these reports, that he fell off little by little in the frequency of his visits.

Chapter 7

INCIDENT AT THE WINDOW

IT chanced on Sunday, when Mr. Utterson was on his usual walk with Mr. Enfield, that their way lay once again through the by-street; and that when they came in front of the door, both stopped to gaze on it.

"Well," said Enfield, "that story's at an end at least. We shall never see more of Mr. Hyde."

"I hope not," said Utterson. "Did I ever tell you that I once saw him, and shared your feeling of repulsion?"

"It was impossible to do the one without the other," returned Enfield. "And by the way, what an ass you must have thought me, not to know that this was a back way to Dr. Jekyll's! It was partly your own fault that I found it out, even when I did."

"So you found it out, did you?" said Utterson. "But if that be so, we may step into the court and take a look at the windows. To tell you the truth, I am uneasy about poor Jekyll; and even outside, I feel as if the presence of a friend might do him good."

The court was very cool and a little damp, and full of premature twilight, although the sky, high up overhead, was still bright with sunset. The middle one of the three windows was half-way open; and sitting close beside it, taking the air with an infinite sadness of mien, like some disconsolate prisoner, Utterson saw Dr. Jekyll.

"What! Jekyll!" he cried. "I trust you are better."

"I am very low, Utterson," replied the doctor, drearily, "very low. It will not last long, thank God."

"You stay too much indoors," said the lawyer. "You should be out, whipping up the circulation like Mr. Enfield and me. (This is my cousin—Mr. Enfield—Dr. Jekyll.) Come, now; get your hat and take a quick turn with us."

"You are very good," sighed the other. "I should like to very much; but no, no, no, it is quite impossible; I dare not. But indeed, Utterson, I am very glad to see you; this is really a great pleasure; I would ask you and Mr. Enfield up, but the place is really not fit."

"Why then," said the lawyer, good-naturedly, "the best thing we can do is to stay down here and speak with you from where we are."

"That is just what I was about to venture to propose," returned the doctor with a smile. But the words were hardly uttered, before the smile was struck out of his face and succeeded by an expression of such abject terror and despair, as froze the very blood of the two gentlemen below.

They saw it but for a glimpse, for the window was instantly thrust down; but that glimpse had been sufficient, and they turned and left the court without a word. In silence, too, they traversed the by-street; and it was not until they had come into a neighbouring thoroughfare, where even upon a Sunday there were still some stirrings of life, that Mr. Utterson at last turned and looked at his companion. They were both pale; and there was an answering horror in their eyes.

"God forgive us, God forgive us," said Mr. Utterson.

But Mr. Enfield only nodded his head very seriously and walked on once more in silence.

Chapter 8

THE LAST NIGHT

MR. UTTERSON was sitting by his fireside one evening after dinner, when he was surprised to receive a visit from Poole.

"Bless me, Poole, what brings you here?" he cried; and then taking a second look at him, "What ails you?" he added; "is the doctor ill?"

"Mr. Utterson," said the man, "there is something wrong."

"Take a seat, and here is a glass of wine for you," said the lawyer. "Now, take your time, and tell me plainly what you want."

"You know the doctor's ways, sir," replied Poole, "and how he shuts himself up. Well, he's shut up again in the cabinet; and I don't like it, sir—I wish I may die if I like it. Mr. Utterson, sir, I'm afraid."

"Now, my good man," said the lawyer, "be explicit. What are you afraid of?"

"I've been afraid for about a week," returned Poole, doggedly disregarding the question, "and I can bear it no more."

The man's appearance amply bore out his words; his manner was altered for the worse; and except for the moment when he had first announced his terror, he had not once looked the lawyer in the face. Even now, he sat with the glass of wine untasted on his knee, and his eyes directed to a corner of the floor.

"I can bear it no more," he repeated.

"Come," said the lawyer, "I see you have some good reason, Poole; I see there is something seriously amiss. Try to tell me what it is."

"I think there's been foul play," said Poole, hoarsely.

"Foul play!" cried the lawyer, a good deal frightened and rather inclined to be irritated in consequence. "What foul play? What does the man mean?"

"I daren't say, sir," was the answer; "but will you come along with me and see for yourself?"

Mr. Utterson's only answer was to rise and get his hat and great-coat; but he observed with wonder the greatness of the relief that appeared upon the butler's face, and perhaps with no less, that the wine was still untasted when he set it down to follow.

It was a wild, cold, seasonable night of March, with a pale moon, lying on her back as though the wind had tilted her, and a flying wrack of the most diaphanous and lawny texture.

The wind made talking difficult, and flecked the blood into the face. It seemed to have swept the streets unusually bare of passengers, besides; for Mr. Utterson thought he had never seen that part of London so deserted.

He could have wished it otherwise; never in his life had he been conscious of so sharp a wish to see and touch his fellow-creatures; for struggle as he might, there was borne in upon his mind a crushing anticipation of calamity.

The square, when they got there, was all full of wind and dust, and the thin trees in the garden were lashing themselves along the railing. Poole, who had kept all the way a pace or two ahead, now pulled up in the middle of the pavement, and in spite of the biting weather, took off his hat and mopped his brow with a red pocket-handkerchief.

But for all the hurry of his coming, these were not the dews of exertion that he wiped away, but the moisture of some strangling anguish; for his face was white and his voice, when he spoke, harsh and broken.

"Well, sir," he said, "here we are, and God grant there be nothing wrong."

"Amen, Poole," said the lawyer.

Thereupon the servant knocked in a very guarded manner; the door was opened on the chain; and a voice asked from within, "Is that you, Poole?"

"It's all right," said Poole. "Open the door." The hall, when they entered it, was brightly lighted up; the fire was built high; and about the hearth the whole of the servants, men and women, stood huddled together like a flock of sheep.

At the sight of Mr. Utterson, the housemaid broke into hysterical whimpering; and the cook, crying out, "Bless God! it's Mr. Utterson," ran forward as if to take him in her arms.

"What, what? Are you all here?" said the lawyer peevishly. "Very irregular, very unseemly; your master would be far from pleased."

"They're all afraid," said Poole.

Blank silence followed, no one protesting; only the maid lifted up her voice and now wept loudly.

"Hold your tongue!" Poole said to her, with a ferocity of accent that testified to his own jangled nerves; and indeed, when the girl had so suddenly raised the note of her lamentation, they had all started and turned toward the inner door with faces of dreadful expectation.

"And now," continued the butler, addressing the knife-boy, "reach me a candle, and we'll get this through hands at once." And then he begged Mr. Utterson to follow him, and led the way to the back-garden.

"Now, sir," said he, "you come as gently as you can. I want you to hear, and I don't want you to be heard. And see here, sir, if by any chance he was to ask you in, don't go."

Mr. Utterson's nerves, at this unlooked-for termination, gave a jerk that nearly threw him from his balance; but he re-collected his courage and followed the butler into the laboratory building and through the surgical theatre, with its lumber of crates and bottles, to the foot of the stair.

Here Poole motioned him to stand on one side and listen; while he himself, setting down the candle and making a great and obvious call on his resolution, mounted the steps and knocked with a somewhat uncertain hand on the red baize of the cabinet door.

"Mr. Utterson, sir, asking to see you," he called; and even as he did so, once more violently signed to the lawyer to give ear.

A voice answered from within: "Tell him I cannot see any one," it said complainingly.

"Thank you, sir," said Poole, with a note of something like triumph in his voice; and taking up his candle, he led Mr. Utterson back across the yard and into the great kitchen, where the fire was out and the beetles were leaping on the floor.

"Sir," he said, looking Mr. Utterson in the eyes, "was that my master's voice?"

"It seems much changed," replied the lawyer, very pale, but giving look for look.

"Changed? Well, yes, I think so," said the butler. "Have I been twenty years in this man's house, to be deceived about his voice? No, sir; master's made away with; he was made, away with eight days ago, when we heard him cry out upon the name of God; and who's in there instead of him, and why it stays there, is a thing that cries to Heaven, Mr. Utterson!"

"This is a very strange tale, Poole; this is rather a wild tale, my man," said Mr. Utterson, biting his finger. "Suppose it were as you suppose, supposing Dr. Jekyll to have been—well, murdered, what could induce the murderer to stay? That won't hold water; it doesn't commend itself to reason."

"Well, Mr. Utterson, you are a hard man to satisfy, but I'll do it yet," said Poole. "All this last week (you must know) him, or it, or whatever it is that lives in that cabinet, has been crying night and day for some sort of medicine and cannot get it to his mind. It was sometimes his way—the master's, that is—to write his orders on a sheet of paper and throw it on the stair. We've had nothing else this week back; nothing but papers, and a closed door, and the very meals left there to be smuggled in when nobody was looking. Well, sir, every day, ay, and twice and thrice in the same day, there have been orders and complaints, and I have been sent flying to all the wholesale chemists in town. Every time I brought the stuff back, there would be another paper telling me to return it, because it was not pure, and another order to a different firm. This drug is wanted bitter bad, sir, whatever for."

"Have you any of these papers?" asked Mr. Utterson.

Poole felt in his pocket and handed out a crumpled note, which the lawyer, bending nearer to the candle, carefully examined.

Its contents ran thus: "Dr. Jekyll presents his compliments to Messrs. Maw. He assures them that their last sample is impure and quite useless for his present purpose. In the year 18—-, Dr. J. purchased a somewhat large quantity from Messrs. M. He now begs them to search with the most sedulous care, and should any of the same quality be left, to forward it to him at once. Expense is no consideration. The importance of this to Dr. J. can hardly be exaggerated."

So far the letter had run composedly enough, but here with a sudden splutter of the pen, the writer's emotion had broken loose.

"For God's sake," he had added, "find me some of the old."

"This is a strange note," said Mr. Utterson; and then sharply, "How do you come to have it open?"

"The man at Maw's was main angry, sir, and he threw it back to me like so much dirt," returned Poole.

"This is unquestionably the doctor's hand, do you know?" resumed the lawyer.

"I thought it looked like it," said the servant rather sulkily; and then, with another voice, "But what matters hand-of-write?" he said. "I've seen him!"

"Seen him?" repeated Mr. Utterson. "Well?"

"That's it!" said Poole. "It was this way. I came suddenly into the theatre from the garden. It seems he had slipped out to look for this drug or whatever it is; for the cabinet door was open, and there he was at the far end of the room digging among the crates. He looked up when I came in, gave a kind of cry, and whipped up-stairs into the cabinet. It was but for one minute that I saw him, but the hair stood upon my head like quills. Sir, if that was my master, why had he a mask upon his face? If it was my master, why did he cry out like a rat, and run from me? I have served him long enough. And then..."

The man paused and passed his hand over his face.

"These are all very strange circumstances," said Mr. Utterson, "but I think I begin to see daylight. Your master, Poole, is plainly seized with one of those maladies that both torture and deform the sufferer; hence, for aught I know, the alteration of his voice; hence the mask and the avoidance of his friends; hence his eagerness to find this drug, by means of which the poor soul retains some hope of ultimate recovery—God grant that he be not deceived! There is my explanation; it is sad enough, Poole, ay, and appalling to consider; but it is plain and natural, hangs well together, and delivers us from all exorbitant alarms."

"Sir," said the butler, turning to a sort of mottled pallor, "that thing was not my master, and there's the truth. My master" here he looked round him and began to whisper—"is a tall, fine build of a man, and this was more of a dwarf."

Utterson attempted to protest.

"O, sir," cried Poole, "do you think I do not know my master after twenty years? Do you think I do not know where his head comes to in the cabinet door, where I saw him every morning of my life? No, Sir, that thing in the mask was never Dr. Jekyll—God knows what it was, but it was never Dr. Jekyll; and it is the belief of my heart that there was murder done."

"Poole," replied the lawyer, "if you say that, it will become my duty to make certain. Much as I desire to spare your master's feelings, much as I am puzzled by this note which seems to prove him to be still alive, I shall consider it my duty to break in that door."

"Ah Mr. Utterson, that's talking!" cried the butler.

"And now comes the second question," resumed Utterson: "Who is going to do it?"

"Why, you and me," was the undaunted reply.

"That's very well said," returned the lawyer; "and whatever comes of it, I shall make it my business to see you are no loser."

"There is an axe in the theatre," continued Poole; "and you might take the kitchen poker for yourself."

The lawyer took that rude but weighty instrument into his hand, and balanced it. "Do you know, Poole," he said, looking up, "that you and I are about to place ourselves in a position of some peril?"

"You may say so, sir, indeed," returned the butler.

"It is well, then, that we should be frank," said the other. "We both think more than we have said; let us make a clean breast. This masked figure that you saw, did you recognise it?"

"Well, sir, it went so quick, and the creature was so doubled up, that I could hardly swear to that," was the answer. "But if you mean, was it Mr. Hyde?—why, yes, I think it was! You see, it was much of the same bigness; and it had the same quick, light way with it; and then who else could have got in by the laboratory door? You have not forgot, sir that at the time of the murder he had still the key with him? But that's not all. I don't know, Mr. Utterson, if ever you met this Mr. Hyde?"

"Yes," said the lawyer, "I once spoke with him."

"Then you must know as well as the rest of us that there was something queer about that gentleman— something that gave a man a turn—I don't know rightly how to say it, sir, beyond this: that you felt it in your marrow kind of cold and thin."

"I own I felt something of what you describe," said Mr. Utterson.

"Quite so, sir," returned Poole. "Well, when that masked thing like a monkey jumped from among the chemicals and whipped into the cabinet, it went down my spine like ice. Oh, I know it's not evidence, Mr. Utterson. I'm book-learned enough for that; but a man has his feelings, and I give you my Bible-word it was Mr. Hyde!"

"Ay, ay," said the lawyer. "My fears incline to the same point. Evil, I fear, founded—evil was sure to come— of that connection. Ay, truly, I believe you; I believe poor Harry is killed; and I believe his murderer (for what purpose, God alone can tell) is still lurking in his victim's room. Well, let our name be vengeance. Call Bradshaw."

The footman came at the summons, very white and nervous.

"Pull yourself together, Bradshaw," said the lawyer. "This suspense, I know, is telling upon all of you; but it is now our intention to make an end of it. Poole, here, and I are going to force our way into the cabinet. If all is well, my shoulders are broad enough to bear the blame. Meanwhile, lest anything should really be amiss, or any malefactor seek to escape by the back, you and the boy must go round the corner with a pair of good sticks and take your post at the laboratory door. We give you ten minutes to get to your stations."

As Bradshaw left, the lawyer looked at his watch. "And now, Poole, let us get to ours," he said; and taking the poker under his arm, led the way into the yard.

The scud had banked over the moon, and it was now quite dark. The wind, which only broke in puffs and draughts into that deep well of building, tossed the light of the candle to and fro about their steps, until they came into the shelter of the theatre, where they sat down silently to wait. London hummed solemnly all around; but nearer at hand, the stillness was only broken by the sounds of a footfall moving to and fro along the cabinet floor.

"So it will walk all day, sir," whispered Poole; "ay, and the better part of the night. Only when a new sample comes from the chemist, there's a bit of a break. Ah, it's an ill conscience that's such an enemy to rest! Ah, sir, there's blood foully shed in every step of it! But hark again, a little closer—put your heart in your ears, Mr. Utterson, and tell me, is that the doctor's foot?"

The steps fell lightly and oddly, with a certain swing, for all they went so slowly; it was different indeed from the heavy creaking tread of Henry Jekyll. Utterson sighed. "Is there never anything else?" he asked.

Poole nodded. "Once," he said. "Once I heard it weeping!"

"Weeping? how that?" said the lawyer, conscious of a sudden chill of horror.

"Weeping like a woman or a lost soul," said the butler. "I came away with that upon my heart, that I could have wept too."

But now the ten minutes drew to an end. Poole disinterred the axe from under a stack of packing straw; the candle was set upon the nearest table to light them to the attack; and they drew near with bated breath to where that patient foot was still going up and down, up and down, in the quiet of the night.

"Jekyll," cried Utterson, with a loud voice, "I demand to see you." He paused a moment, but there came no reply.

"I give you fair warning, our suspicions are aroused, and I must and shall see you," he resumed; "if not by fair means, then by foul! if not of your consent, then by brute force!"

"Utterson," said the voice, "for God's sake, have mercy!"

"Ah, that's not Jekyll's voice—it's Hyde's!" cried Utterson. "Down with the door, Poole!"

Poole swung the axe over his shoulder; the blow shook the building, and the red baize door leaped against the lock and hinges. A dismal screech, as of mere animal terror, rang from the cabinet.

Up went the axe again, and again the panels crashed and the frame bounded; four times the blow fell; but the wood was tough and the fittings were of excellent workmanship; and it was not until the fifth, that the lock burst in sunder and the wreck of the door fell inwards on the carpet.

The besiegers, appalled by their own riot and the stillness that had succeeded, stood back a little and peered in. There lay the cabinet before their eyes in the quiet lamplight, a good fire glowing and chattering on the hearth, the kettle singing its thin strain, a drawer or two open, papers neatly set forth on the business-table, and nearer the fire, the things laid out for tea: the quietest room, you would have said, and, but for the glazed presses full of chemicals, the most commonplace that night in London.

Right in the midst there lay the body of a man sorely contorted and still twitching. They drew near on tiptoe, turned it on its back and beheld the face of Edward Hyde. He was dressed in clothes far too large for him, clothes of the doctor's bigness; the cords of his face still moved with a semblance of life, but life was quite gone; and by the crushed phial in the hand and the strong smell of kernels that hung upon the air, Utterson knew that he was looking on the body of a self-destroyer.

"We have come too late," he said sternly, "whether to save or punish. Hyde is gone to his account; and it only remains for us to find the body of your master."

The far greater proportion of the building was occupied by the theatre, which filled almost the whole ground story and was lighted from above, and by the cabinet, which formed an upper story at one end and looked upon the court.

A corridor joined the theatre to the door on the by-street; and with this the cabinet communicated separately by a second flight of stairs. There were besides a few dark closets and a spacious cellar. All these they now thoroughly examined. Each closet needed but a glance, for all were empty, and all, by the dust that fell from their doors, had stood long unopened.

The cellar, indeed, was filled with crazy lumber, mostly dating from the times of the surgeon who was Jekyll's predecessor; but even as they opened the door they were advertised of the uselessness of further search, by the fall of a perfect mat of cobweb which had for years sealed up the entrance. Nowhere was there any trace of Henry Jekyll, dead or alive.

Poole stamped on the flags of the corridor. "He must be buried here," he said, hearkening to the sound.

"Or he may have fled," said Utterson, and he turned to examine the door in the by-street. It was locked; and lying near by on the flags, they found the key, already stained with rust.

"This does not look like use," observed the lawyer.

"Use!" echoed Poole. "Do you not see, sir, it is broken? much as if a man had stamped on it."

"Ay," continued Utterson, "and the fractures, too, are rusty."

The two men looked at each other with a scare.

"This is beyond me, Poole," said the lawyer. "Let us go back to the cabinet."

They mounted the stair in silence, and still with an occasional awe-struck glance at the dead body, proceeded more thoroughly to examine the contents of the cabinet. At one table, there were traces of chemical work, various measured heaps of some white salt being laid on glass saucers, as though for an experiment in which the unhappy man had been prevented.

"That is the same drug that I was always bringing him," said Poole; and even as he spoke, the kettle with a startling noise boiled over.

This brought them to the fireside, where the easy-chair was drawn cosily up, and the tea-things stood ready to the sitter's elbow, the very sugar in the cup. There were several books on a shelf; one lay beside the tea-things open, and Utterson was amazed to find it a copy of a pious work, for which Jekyll had several times expressed a great esteem, annotated, in his own hand, with startling blasphemies.

Next, in the course of their review of the chamber, the searchers came to the cheval glass, into whose depths they looked with an involuntary horror. But it was so turned as to show them nothing but the rosy glow playing on the roof, the fire sparkling in a hundred repetitions along the glazed front of the presses, and their own pale and fearful countenances stooping to look in.

"This glass have seen some strange things, sir," whispered Poole.

"And surely none stranger than itself," echoed the lawyer in the same tones. "For what did Jekyll"—he caught himself up at the word with a start, and then conquering the weakness—"what could Jekyll want with it?" he said.

"You may say that!" said Poole.

Next they turned to the business-table. On the desk among the neat array of papers, a large envelope was uppermost, and bore, in the doctor's hand, the name of Mr. Utterson. The lawyer unsealed it, and several enclosures fell to the floor.

The first was a will, drawn in the same eccentric terms as the one which he had returned six months before, to serve as a testament in case of death and as a deed of gift in case of disappearance; but, in place of the name of Edward Hyde, the lawyer, with indescribable amazement, read the name of Gabriel John Utterson. He looked at Poole, and then back at the paper, and last of all at the dead malefactor stretched upon the carpet.

"My head goes round," he said. "He has been all these days in possession; he had no cause to like me; he must have raged to see himself displaced; and he has not destroyed this document."

He caught up the next paper; it was a brief note in the doctor's hand and dated at the top.

"O Poole!" the lawyer cried, "he was alive and here this day. He cannot have been disposed of in so short a space, he must be still alive, he must have fled! And then, why fled? and how? and in that case, can we venture to declare this suicide? Oh, we must be careful. I foresee that we may yet involve your master in some dire catastrophe."

"Why don't you read it, sir?" asked Poole.

"Because I fear," replied the lawyer solemnly. "God grant I have no cause for it!" And with that he brought the paper to his eyes and read as follows:

"MY DEAR UTTERSON,—When this shall fall into your hands, I shall have disappeared, under what circumstances I have not the penetration to foresee, but my instinct and all the circumstances of my nameless situation tell me that the end is sure and must be early. Go then, and first read the narrative which Lanyon warned me he was to place in your hands; and if you care to hear more, turn to the confession of

       "Your unworthy and unhappy friend,
          "HENRY JEKYLL."

"There was a third enclosure?" asked Utterson.

"Here, sir," said Poole, and gave into his hands a considerable packet sealed in several places.

The lawyer put it in his pocket.

"I would say nothing of this paper. If your master has fled or is dead, we may at least save his credit. It is now ten; I must go home and read these documents in quiet; but I shall be back before midnight, when we shall send for the police."

They went out, locking the door of the theatre behind them; and Utterson, once more leaving the servants gathered about the fire in the hall, trudged back to his office to read the two narratives in which this mystery was now to be explained.

Chapter 9

DR. LANYON'S NARRATIVE

ON the ninth of January, now four days ago, I received by the evening delivery a registered envelope, addressed in the hand of my colleague and old school-companion, Henry Jekyll. I was a good deal surprised by this; for we were by no means in the habit of correspondence; I had seen the man, dined with him, indeed, the night before; and I could imagine nothing in our intercourse that should justify formality of registration. The contents increased my wonder; for this is how the letter ran:

"10th December, 18—-

"DEAR LANYON,

You are one of my oldest friends; and although we may have differed at times on scientific questions, I cannot remember, at least on my side, any break in our affection. There was never a day when, if you had said to me, 'Jekyll, my life, my honour, my reason, depend upon you,' I would not have sacrificed my left hand to help you. Lanyon, my life, my honour my reason, are all at your mercy; if you fail me to-night I am lost. You might suppose, after this preface, that I am going to ask you for something dishonourable to grant. Judge for yourself.

"I want you to postpone all other engagements for to-night—ay, even if you were summoned to the bedside of an emperor; to take a cab, unless your carriage should be actually at the door; and with this letter in your hand for consultation, to drive straight to my house.

Poole, my butler, has his orders; you will find, him waiting your arrival with a locksmith. The door of my cabinet is then to be forced: and you are to go in alone; to open the glazed press (letter E) on the left hand, breaking the lock if it be shut; and to draw out, with all its contents as they stand, the fourth drawer from the top or (which is the same thing) the third from the bottom. In my extreme distress of wind, I have a morbid fear of misdirecting you; but even if I am in error, you may know the right drawer by its contents: some powders, a phial and a paper book. This drawer I beg of you to carry back with you to Cavendish Square exactly as it stands.

"That is the first part of the service: now for the second. You should be back, if you set out at once on the receipt of this, long before midnight; but I will leave you that amount of margin, not only in the fear of one of those obstacles that can neither be prevented nor fore-seen, but because an hour when your servants are in bed is to be preferred for what will then remain to do.

At midnight, then, I have to ask you to be alone in your consulting-room, to admit with your own hand into the house a man who will present himself in my name, and to place in his hands the drawer that you will have brought with you from my cabinet. Then you will have played your part and earned my gratitude completely.

Five minutes afterwards, if you insist upon an explanation, you will have understood that these arrangements are of capital importance; and that by the neglect of one of them, fantastic as they must appear, you might have charged your conscience with my death or the shipwreck of my reason.

"Confident as I am that you will not trifle with this appeal, my heart sinks and my hand trembles at the bare thought of such a possibility. Think of me at this hour, in a strange place, labouring under a blackness of distress that no fancy can exaggerate, and yet well aware that, if you will but punctually serve me, my troubles will roll away like a story that is told. Serve me, my dear Lanyon, and save Your friend,

"H. J.

"P. S. I had already sealed this up when a fresh terror struck upon my soul. It is possible that the post office may fail me, and this letter not come into your hands until to-morrow morning.

In that case, dear Lanyon, do my errand when it shall be most convenient for you in the course of the day; and once more expect my messenger at midnight. It may then already be too late; and if that night passes without event, you will know that you have seen the last of Henry Jekyll."

Upon the reading of this letter, I made sure my colleague was insane; but till that was proved beyond the possibility of doubt, I felt bound to do as he requested. The less I understood of this farrago, the less I was in a position to judge of its importance; and an appeal so worded could not be set aside without a grave responsibility.

I rose accordingly from table, got into a hansom, and drove straight to Jekyll's house. The butler was awaiting my arrival; he had received by the same post as mine a registered letter of instruction, and had sent at once for a locksmith and a carpenter.

The tradesmen came while we were yet speaking; and we moved in a body to old Dr. Denman's surgical theatre, from which (as you are doubtless aware) Jekyll's private cabinet is most conveniently entered. The door was very strong, the lock excellent; the carpenter avowed he would have great trouble and have to do much damage, if force were to be used; and the locksmith was near despair. But this last was a handy fellow, and after two hours' work, the door stood open. The press marked E was unlocked; and I took out the drawer, had it filled up with straw and tied in a sheet, and returned with it to Cavendish Square.

Here I proceeded to examine its contents. The powders were neatly enough made up, but not with the nicety of the dispensing chemist; so that it was plain they were of Jekyll's private manufacture; and when I opened one of the wrappers I found what seemed to me a simple crystalline salt of a white colour.

The phial, to which I next turned my attention, might have been about half-full of a blood-red liquor, which was highly pungent to the sense of smell and seemed to me to contain phosphorus and some volatile ether. At the other ingredients I could make no guess.

The book was an ordinary version-book and contained little but a series of dates. These covered a period of many years, but I observed that the entries ceased nearly a year ago and quite abruptly.

Here and there a brief remark was appended to a date, usually no more than a single word: "double" occurring perhaps six times in a total of several hundred entries; and once very early in the list and followed by several marks of exclamation, "total failure!!!"

All this, though it whetted my curiosity, told me little that was definite. Here were a phial of some tincture, a paper of some salt, and the record of a series of experiments that had led (like too many of Jekyll's investigations) to no end of practical usefulness.

How could the presence of these articles in my house affect either the honour, the sanity, or the life of my flighty colleague? If his messenger could go to one place, why could he not go to another? And even granting some impediment, why was this gentleman to be received by me in secret? The more I reflected the more convinced I grew that I was dealing with a case of cerebral disease: and though I dismissed my servants to bed, I loaded an old revolver, that I might be found in some posture of self-defence.

Twelve o'clock had scarce rung out over London, ere the knocker sounded very gently on the door. I went myself at the summons, and found a small man crouching against the pillars of the portico.

"Are you come from Dr. Jekyll?" I asked.

He told me "yes" by a constrained gesture; and when I had bidden him enter, he did not obey me without a searching backward glance into the darkness of the square. There was a policeman not far off, advancing with his bull's eye open; and at the sight, I thought my visitor started and made greater haste.

These particulars struck me, I confess, disagreeably; and as I followed him into the bright light of the consulting-room, I kept my hand ready on my weapon. Here, at last, I had a chance of clearly seeing him. I had never set eyes on him before, so much was certain.

He was small, as I have said; I was struck besides with the shocking expression of his face, with his remarkable combination of great muscular activity and great apparent debility of constitution, and—last but not least— with the odd, subjective disturbance caused by his neighbourhood.

This bore some resemblance to incipient rigour, and was accompanied by a marked sinking of the pulse. At the time, I set it down to some idiosyncratic, personal distaste, and merely wondered at the acuteness of the symptoms; but I have since had reason to believe the cause to lie much deeper in the nature of man, and to turn on some nobler hinge than the principle of hatred.

This person (who had thus, from the first moment of his entrance, struck in me what I can only describe as a disgustful curiosity) was dressed in a fashion that would have made an ordinary person laughable; his clothes, that is to say, although they were of rich and sober fabric, were enormously too large for him in every measurement—the trousers hanging on his legs and rolled up to keep them from the ground, the waist of the coat below his haunches, and the collar sprawling wide upon his shoulders.

Strange to relate, this ludicrous accoutrement was far from moving me to laughter. Rather, as there was something abnormal and misbegotten in the very essence of the creature that now faced me— something seizing, surprising, and revolting—this fresh disparity seemed but to fit in with and to reinforce it; so that to my interest in the man's nature and character, there was added a curiosity as to his origin, his life, his fortune and status in the world.

These observations, though they have taken so great a space to be set down in, were yet the work of a few seconds. My visitor was, indeed, on fire with sombre excitement.

"Have you got it?" he cried. "Have you got it?" And so lively was his impatience that he even laid his hand upon my arm and sought to shake me.

I put him back, conscious at his touch of a certain icy pang along my blood.

"Come, sir," said I. "You forget that I have not yet the pleasure of your acquaintance. Be seated, if you please."

And I showed him an example, and sat down myself in my customary seat and with as fair an imitation of my ordinary manner to a patient, as the lateness of the hour, the nature of my pre-occupations, and the horror I had of my visitor, would suffer me to muster.

"I beg your pardon, Dr. Lanyon," he replied civilly enough. "What you say is very well founded; and my impatience has shown its heels to my politeness. I come here at the instance of your colleague, Dr. Henry Jekyll, on a piece of business of some moment; and I understood..." He paused and put his hand to his throat, and I could see, in spite of his collected manner, that he was wrestling against the approaches of the hysteria—"I understood, a drawer..."

But here I took pity on my visitor's suspense, and some perhaps on my own growing curiosity.

"There it is, sir," said I, pointing to the drawer, where it lay on the floor behind a table and still covered with the sheet.

He sprang to it, and then paused, and laid his hand upon his heart: I could hear his teeth grate with the convulsive action of his jaws; and his face was so ghastly to see that I grew alarmed both for his life and reason.

"Compose yourself," said I.

He turned a dreadful smile to me, and as if with the decision of despair, plucked away the sheet. At sight of the contents, he uttered one loud sob of such immense relief that I sat petrified.

And the next moment, in a voice that was already fairly well under control, "Have you a graduated glass?" he asked.

I rose from my place with something of an effort and gave him what he asked.

He thanked me with a smiling nod, measured out a few minims of the red tincture and added one of the powders. The mixture, which was at first of a reddish hue, began, in proportion as the crystals melted, to brighten in colour, to effervesce audibly, and to throw off small fumes of vapour.

Suddenly and at the same moment, the ebullition ceased and the compound changed to a dark purple, which faded again more slowly to a watery green. My visitor, who had watched these metamorphoses with a keen eye, smiled, set down the glass upon the table, and then turned and looked upon me with an air of scrutiny.

"And now," said he, "to settle what remains. Will you be wise? Will you be guided? Will you suffer me to take this glass in my hand and to go forth from your house without further parley? Or has the greed of curiosity too much command of you?

Think before you answer, for it shall be done as you decide. As you decide, you shall be left as you were before, and neither richer nor wiser, unless the sense of service rendered to a man in mortal distress may be counted as a kind of riches of the soul.

Or, if you shall so prefer to choose, a new province of knowledge and new avenues to fame and power shall be laid open to you, here, in this room, upon the instant; and your sight shall be blasted by a prodigy to stagger the unbelief of Satan."

"Sir," said I, affecting a coolness that I was far from truly possessing, "you speak enigmas, and you will perhaps not wonder that I hear you with no very strong impression of belief. But I have gone too far in the way of inexplicable services to pause before I see the end."

"It is well," replied my visitor. "Lanyon, you remember your vows: what follows is under the seal of our profession. And now, you who have so long been bound to the most narrow and material views, you who have denied the virtue of transcendental medicine, you who have derided your superiors— behold!"

He put the glass to his lips and drank at one gulp. A cry followed; he reeled, staggered, clutched at the table and held on, staring with injected eyes, gasping with open mouth; and as I looked there came, I thought, a change—he seemed to swell— his face became suddenly black and the features seemed to melt and alter— and the next moment, I had sprung to my feet and leaped back against the wall, my arm raised to shield me from that prodigy, my mind submerged in terror.

"O God!" I screamed, and "O God!" again and again; for there before my eyes—pale and shaken, and half-fainting, and groping before him with his hands, like a man restored from death— there stood Henry Jekyll!

What he told me in the next hour, I cannot bring my mind to set on paper. I saw what I saw, I heard what I heard, and my soul sickened at it; and yet now when that sight has faded from my eyes, I ask myself if I believe it, and I cannot answer.

My life is shaken to its roots; sleep has left me; the deadliest terror sits by me at all hours of the day and night; I feel that my days are numbered, and that I must die; and yet I shall die incredulous.

As for the moral turpitude that man unveiled to me, even with tears of penitence, I cannot, even in memory, dwell on it without a start of horror. I will say but one thing, Utterson, and that (if you can bring your mind to credit it) will be more than enough.

The creature who crept into my house that night was, on Jekyll's own confession, known by the name of Hyde and hunted for in every corner of the land as the murderer of Carew.

HASTIE LANYON

Chapter 10

HENRY JEKYLL'S FULL STATEMENT OF THE CASE

I WAS born in the year 18—- to a large fortune, endowed besides with excellent parts, inclined by nature to industry, fond of the respect of the wise and good among my fellow-men, and thus, as might have been supposed, with every guarantee of an honourable and distinguished future.

And indeed the worst of my faults was a certain impatient gaiety of disposition, such as has made the happiness of many, but such as I found it hard to reconcile with my imperious desire to carry my head high, and wear a more than commonly grave countenance before the public.

Hence it came about that I concealed my pleasures; and that when I reached years of reflection, and began to look round me and take stock of my progress and position in the world, I stood already committed to a profound duplicity of life.

Many a man would have even blazoned such irregularities as I was guilty of; but from the high views that I had set before me, I regarded and hid them with an almost morbid sense of shame. It was thus rather the exacting nature of my aspirations than any particular degradation in my faults, that made me what I was and, with even a deeper trench than in the majority of men, severed in me those provinces of good and ill which divide and compound man's dual nature.

In this case, I was driven to reflect deeply and inveterately on that hard law of life, which lies at the root of religion and is one of the most plentiful springs of distress. Though so profound a double-dealer, I was in no sense a hypocrite; both sides of me were in dead earnest; I was no more myself when I laid aside restraint and plunged in shame, than when I laboured, in the eye of day, at the furtherance of knowledge or the relief of sorrow and suffering.

And it chanced that the direction of my scientific studies, which led wholly toward the mystic and the transcendental, re-acted and shed a strong light on this consciousness of the perennial war among my members. With every day, and from both sides of my intelligence, the moral and the intellectual, I thus drew steadily nearer to that truth, by whose partial discovery I have been doomed to such a dreadful shipwreck: that man is not truly one, but truly two. I say two, because the state of my own knowledge does not pass beyond that point.

Others will follow, others will outstrip me on the same lines; and I hazard the guess that man will be ultimately known for a mere polity of multifarious, incongruous, and independent denizens. I, for my part, from the nature of my life, advanced infallibly in one direction and in one direction only.

It was on the moral side, and in my own person, that I learned to recognise the thorough and primitive duality of man; I saw that, of the two natures that contended in the field of my consciousness, even if I could rightly be said to be either, it was only because I was radically both; and from an early date, even before the course of my scientific discoveries had begun to suggest the most naked possibility of such a miracle, I had learned to dwell with pleasure, as a beloved day-dream, on the thought of the separation of these elements.

If each, I told myself, could but be housed in separate identities, life would be relieved of all that was unbearable; the unjust delivered from the aspirations might go his way, and remorse of his more upright twin; and the just could walk steadfastly and securely on his upward path, doing the good things in which he found his pleasure, and no longer exposed to disgrace and penitence by the hands of this extraneous evil. It was the curse of mankind that these incongruous fagots were thus bound together that in the agonised womb of consciousness, these polar twins should be continuously struggling. How, then, were they dissociated?

I was so far in my reflections when, as I have said, a side-light began to shine upon the subject from the laboratory table. I began to perceive more deeply than it has ever yet been stated, the trembling immateriality, the mist-like transience of this seemingly so solid body in which we walk attired. Certain agents I found to have the power to shake and to pluck back that fleshly vestment, even as a wind might toss the curtains of a pavilion.

For two good reasons, I will not enter deeply into this scientific branch of my confession. First, because I have been made to learn that the doom and burthen of our life is bound for ever on man's shoulders, and when the attempt is made to cast it off, it but returns upon us with more unfamiliar and more awful pressure.

Second, because, as my narrative will make, alas! too evident, my discoveries were incomplete. Enough, then, that I not only recognised my natural body for the mere aura and effulgence of certain of the powers that made up my spirit, but managed to compound a drug by which these powers should be dethroned from their supremacy, and a second form and countenance substituted, none the less natural to me because they were the expression, and bore the stamp, of lower elements in my soul.

I hesitated long before I put this theory to the test of practice. I knew well that I risked death; for any drug that so potently controlled and shook the very fortress of identity, might by the least scruple of an overdose or at the least inopportunity in the moment of exhibition, utterly blot out that immaterial tabernacle which looked to it to change.

But the temptation of a discovery so singular and profound, at last overcame the suggestions of alarm. I had long since prepared my tincture; I purchased at once, from a firm of wholesale chemists, a large quantity of a particular salt which I knew, from my experiments, to be the last ingredient required; and late one accursed night, I compounded the elements, watched them boil and smoke together in the glass, and when the ebullition had subsided, with a strong glow of courage, drank off the potion.

The most racking pangs succeeded: a grinding in the bones, deadly nausea, and a horror of the spirit that cannot be exceeded at the hour of birth or death. Then these agonies began swiftly to subside, and I came to myself as if out of a great sickness.

There was something strange in my sensations, something indescribably new and, from its very novelty, incredibly sweet. I felt younger, lighter, happier in body; within I was conscious of a heady recklessness, a current of disordered sensual images running like a mill-race in my fancy, a solution of the bonds of obligation, an unknown but not an innocent freedom of the soul. I knew myself, at the first breath of this new life, to be more wicked, tenfold more wicked, sold a slave to my original evil; and the thought, in that moment, braced and delighted me like wine. I stretched out my hands, exulting in the freshness of these sensations; and in the act, I was suddenly aware that I had lost in stature.

There was no mirror, at that date, in my room; that which stands beside me as I write, was brought there later on and for the very purpose of these transformations. The night, however, was far gone into the morning—the morning, black as it was, was nearly ripe for the conception of the day—the inmates of my house were locked in the most rigorous hours of slumber; and I determined, flushed as I was with hope and triumph, to venture in my new shape as far as to my bedroom.

I crossed the yard, wherein the constellations looked down upon me, I could have thought, with wonder, the first creature of that sort that their unsleeping vigilance had yet disclosed to them; I stole through the corridors, a stranger in my own house; and coming to my room, I saw for the first time the appearance of Edward Hyde.

I must here speak by theory alone, saying not that which I know, but that which I suppose to be most probable. The evil side of my nature, to which I had now transferred the stamping efficacy, was less robust and less developed than the good which I had just deposed.

Again, in the course of my life, which had been, after all, nine-tenths a life of effort, virtue, and control, it had been much less exercised and much less exhausted. And hence, as I think, it came about that Edward Hyde was so much smaller, slighter, and younger than Henry Jekyll. Even as good shone upon the countenance of the one, evil was written broadly and plainly on the face of the other.

Evil besides (which I must still believe to be the lethal side of man) had left on that body an imprint of deformity and decay. And yet when I looked upon that ugly idol in the glass, I was conscious of no repugnance, rather of a leap of welcome. This, too, was myself. It seemed natural and human. In my eyes it bore a livelier image of the spirit, it seemed more express and single, than the imperfect and divided countenance I had been hitherto accustomed to call mine. And in so far I was doubtless right.

I have observed that when I wore the semblance of Edward Hyde, none could come near to me at first without a visible misgiving of the flesh. This, as I take it, was because all human beings, as we meet them, are commingled out of good and evil: and Edward Hyde, alone in the ranks of mankind, was pure evil.

I lingered but a moment at the mirror: the second and conclusive experiment had yet to be attempted; it yet remained to be seen if I had lost my identity beyond redemption and must flee before daylight from a house that was no longer mine; and hurrying back to my cabinet, I once more prepared and drank the cup, once more suffered the pangs of dissolution, and came to myself once more with the character, the stature, and the face of Henry Jekyll.

That night I had come to the fatal cross-roads. Had I approached my discovery in a more noble spirit, had I risked the experiment while under the empire of generous or pious aspirations, all must have been otherwise, and from these agonies of death and birth, I had come forth an angel instead of a fiend. The drug had no discriminating action; it was neither diabolical nor divine; it but shook the doors of the prison-house of my disposition; and like the captives of Philippi, that which stood within ran forth.

At that time my virtue slumbered; my evil, kept awake by ambition, was alert and swift to seize the occasion; and the thing that was projected was Edward Hyde. Hence, although I had now two characters as well as two appearances, one was wholly evil, and the other was still the old Henry Jekyll, that incongruous compound of whose reformation and improvement I had already learned to despair. The movement was thus wholly toward the worse.

Even at that time, I had not yet conquered my aversion to the dryness of a life of study. I would still be merrily disposed at times; and as my pleasures were (to say the least) undignified, and I was not only well known and highly considered, but growing toward the elderly man, this incoherency of my life was daily growing more unwelcome.

It was on this side that my new power tempted me until I fell in slavery. I had but to drink the cup, to doff at once the body of the noted professor, and to assume, like a thick cloak, that of Edward Hyde. I smiled at the notion; it seemed to me at the time to be humorous; and I made my preparations with the most studious care.

I took and furnished that house in Soho, to which Hyde was tracked by the police; and engaged as housekeeper a creature whom I well knew to be silent and unscrupulous. On the other side, I announced to my servants that a Mr. Hyde (whom I described) was to have full liberty and power about my house in the square; and to parry mishaps, I even called and made myself a familiar object, in my second character.

I next drew up that will to which you so much objected; so that if anything befell me in the person of Dr. Jekyll, I could enter on that of Edward Hyde without pecuniary loss. And thus fortified, as I supposed, on every side, I began to profit by the strange immunities of my position.

Men have before hired bravos to transact their crimes, while their own person and reputation sat under shelter. I was the first that ever did so for his pleasures. I was the first that could thus plod in the public eye with a load of genial respectability, and in a moment, like a schoolboy, strip off these lendings and spring headlong into the sea of liberty. But for me, in my impenetrable mantle, the safety was complete.

Think of it—I did not even exist! Let me but escape into my laboratory door, give me but a second or two to mix and swallow the draught that I had always standing ready; and whatever he had done, Edward Hyde would pass away like the stain of breath upon a mirror; and there in his stead, quietly at home, trimming the midnight lamp in his study, a man who could afford to laugh at suspicion, would be Henry Jekyll.

The pleasures which I made haste to seek in my disguise were, as I have said, undignified; I would scarce use a harder term. But in the hands of Edward Hyde, they soon began to turn toward the monstrous. When I would come back from these excursions, I was often plunged into a kind of wonder at my vicarious depravity. This familiar that I called out of my own soul, and sent forth alone to do his good pleasure, was a being inherently malign and villainous; his every act and thought centred on self; drinking pleasure with bestial avidity from any degree of torture to another; relentless like a man of stone.

Henry Jekyll stood at times aghast before the acts of Edward Hyde; but the situation was apart from ordinary laws, and insidiously relaxed the grasp of conscience. It was Hyde, after all, and Hyde alone, that was guilty. Jekyll was no worse; he woke again to his good qualities seemingly unimpaired; he would even make haste, where it was possible, to undo the evil done by Hyde. And thus his conscience slumbered.

Into the details of the infamy at which I thus connived (for even now I can scarce grant that I committed it) I have no design of entering; I mean but to point out the warnings and the successive steps with which my chastisement approached.

I met with one accident which, as it brought on no consequence, I shall no more than mention. An act of cruelty to a child aroused against me the anger of a passer-by, whom I recognised the other day in the person of your kinsman; the doctor and the child's family joined him; there were moments when I feared for my life; and at last, in order to pacify their too just resentment, Edward Hyde had to bring them to the door, and pay them in a cheque drawn in the name of Henry Jekyll.

But this danger was easily eliminated from the future, by opening an account at another bank in the name of Edward Hyde himself; and when, by sloping my own hand backward, I had supplied my double with a signature, I thought I sat beyond the reach of fate.

Some two months before the murder of Sir Danvers, I had been out for one of my adventures, had returned at a late hour, and woke the next day in bed with somewhat odd sensations. It was in vain I looked about me; in vain I saw the decent furniture and tall proportions of my room in the square; in vain that I recognised the pattern of the bed-curtains and the design of the mahogany frame; something still kept insisting that I was not where I was, that I had not wakened where I seemed to be, but in the little room in Soho where I was accustomed to sleep in the body of Edward Hyde.

I smiled to myself, and, in my psychological way began lazily to inquire into the elements of this illusion, occasionally, even as I did so, dropping back into a comfortable morning doze. I was still so engaged when, in one of my more wakeful moments, my eyes fell upon my hand. Now the hand of Henry Jekyll (as you have often remarked) was professional in shape and size: it was large, firm, white, and comely.

But the hand which I now saw, clearly enough, in the yellow light of a mid-London morning, lying half shut on the bed-clothes, was lean, corded, knuckly, of a dusky pallor and thickly shaded with a swart growth of hair. It was the hand of Edward Hyde.

I must have stared upon it for near half a minute, sunk as I was in the mere stupidity of wonder, before terror woke up in my breast as sudden and startling as the crash of cymbals; and bounding from my bed, I rushed to the mirror. At the sight that met my eyes, my blood was changed into something exquisitely thin and icy.

Yes, I had gone to bed Henry Jekyll, I had awakened Edward Hyde. How was this to be explained? I asked myself, and then, with another bound of terror—how was it to be remedied? It was well on in the morning; the servants were up; all my drugs were in the cabinet—a long journey down two pairs of stairs, through the back passage, across the open court and through the anatomical theatre, from where I was then standing horror-struck. It might indeed be possible to cover my face; but of what use was that, when I was unable to conceal the alteration in my stature?

And then with an overpowering sweetness of relief, it came back upon my mind that the servants were already used to the coming and going of my second self. I had soon dressed, as well as I was able, in clothes of my own size: had soon passed through the house, where Bradshaw stared and drew back at seeing Mr. Hyde at such an hour and in such a strange array; and ten minutes later, Dr. Jekyll had returned to his own shape and was sitting down, with a darkened brow, to make a feint of breakfasting.

Small indeed was my appetite. This inexplicable incident, this reversal of my previous experience, seemed, like the Babylonian finger on the wall, to be spelling out the letters of my judgment; and I began to reflect more seriously than ever before on the issues and possibilities of my double existence. That part of me which I had the power of projecting, had lately been much exercised and nourished; it had seemed to me of late as though the body of Edward Hyde had grown in stature, as though (when I wore that form) I were conscious of a more generous tide of blood; and I began to spy a danger that, if this were much prolonged, the balance of my nature might be permanently overthrown, the power of voluntary change be forfeited, and the character of Edward Hyde become irrevocably mine.

The power of the drug had not been always equally displayed. Once, very early in my career, it had totally failed me; since then I had been obliged on more than one occasion to double, and once, with infinite risk of death, to treble the amount; and these rare uncertainties had cast hitherto the sole shadow on my contentment.

Now, however, and in the light of that morning's accident, I was led to remark that whereas, in the beginning, the difficulty had been to throw off the body of Jekyll, it had of late gradually but decidedly transferred itself to the other side. All things therefore seemed to point to this: that I was slowly losing hold of my original and better self, and becoming slowly incorporated with my second and worse.

Between these two, I now felt I had to choose. My two natures had memory in common, but all other faculties were most unequally shared between them. Jekyll (who was composite) now with the most sensitive apprehensions, now with a greedy gusto, projected and shared in the pleasures and adventures of Hyde; but Hyde was indifferent to Jekyll, or but remembered him as the mountain bandit remembers the cavern in which he conceals himself from pursuit. Jekyll had more than a father's interest; Hyde had more than a son's indifference.

To cast in my lot with Jekyll, was to die to those appetites which I had long secretly indulged and had of late begun to pamper. To cast it in with Hyde, was to die to a thousand interests and aspirations, and to become, at a blow and for ever, despised and friendless.

The bargain might appear unequal; but there was still another consideration in the scales; for while Jekyll would suffer smartingly in the fires of abstinence, Hyde would be not even conscious of all that he had lost. Strange as my circumstances were, the terms of this debate are as old and commonplace as man; much the same inducements and alarms cast the die for any tempted and trembling sinner; and it fell out with me, as it falls with so vast a majority of my fellows, that I chose the better part and was found wanting in the strength to keep to it.

Yes, I preferred the elderly and discontented doctor, surrounded by friends and cherishing honest hopes; and bade a resolute farewell to the liberty, the comparative youth, the light step, leaping impulses and secret pleasures, that I had enjoyed in the disguise of Hyde.

I made this choice perhaps with some unconscious reservation, for I neither gave up the house in Soho, nor destroyed the clothes of Edward Hyde, which still lay ready in my cabinet. For two months, however, I was true to my determination; for two months I led a life of such severity as I had never before attained to, and enjoyed the compensations of an approving conscience. But time began at last to obliterate the freshness of my alarm; the praises of conscience began to grow into a thing of course; I began to be tortured with throes and longings, as of Hyde struggling after freedom; and at last, in an hour of moral weakness, I once again compounded and swallowed the transforming draught.

I do not suppose that, when a drunkard reasons with himself upon his vice, he is once out of five hundred times affected by the dangers that he runs through his brutish, physical insensibility; neither had I, long as I had considered my position, made enough allowance for the complete moral insensibility and insensate readiness to evil, which were the leading characters of Edward Hyde.

Yet it was by these that I was punished. My devil had been long caged, he came out roaring. I was conscious, even when I took the draught, of a more unbridled, a more furious propensity to ill. It must have been this, I suppose, that stirred in my soul that tempest of impatience with which I listened to the civilities of my unhappy victim; I declare, at least, before God, no man morally sane could have been guilty of that crime upon so pitiful a provocation; and that I struck in no more reasonable spirit than that in which a sick child may break a plaything.

But I had voluntarily stripped myself of all those balancing instincts by which even the worst of us continues to walk with some degree of steadiness among temptations; and in my case, to be tempted, however slightly, was to fall.

Instantly the spirit of hell awoke in me and raged. With a transport of glee, I mauled the unresisting body, tasting delight from every blow; and it was not till weariness had begun to succeed, that I was suddenly, in the top fit of my delirium, struck through the heart by a cold thrill of terror.

A mist dispersed; I saw my life to be forfeit; and fled from the scene of these excesses, at once glorying and trembling, my lust of evil gratified and stimulated, my love of life screwed to the topmost peg.

I ran to the house in Soho, and (to make assurance doubly sure) destroyed my papers; thence I set out through the lamplit streets, in the same divided ecstasy of mind, gloating on my crime, light-headedly devising others in the future, and yet still hastening and still hearkening in my wake for the steps of the avenger.

Hyde had a song upon his lips as he compounded the draught, and as he drank it, pledged the dead man. The pangs of transformation had not done tearing him, before Henry Jekyll, with streaming tears of gratitude and remorse, had fallen upon his knees and lifted his clasped hands to God.

The veil of self-indulgence was rent from head to foot, I saw my life as a whole: I followed it up from the days of childhood, when I had walked with my father's hand, and through the self-denying toils of my professional life, to arrive again and again, with the same sense of unreality, at the damned horrors of the evening.

I could have screamed aloud; I sought with tears and prayers to smother down the crowd of hideous images and sounds with which my memory swarmed against me; and still, between the petitions, the ugly face of my iniquity stared into my soul.

As the acuteness of this remorse began to die away, it was succeeded by a sense of joy. The problem of my conduct was solved. Hyde was thenceforth impossible; whether I would or not, I was now confined to the better part of my existence; and oh, how I rejoiced to think it! with what willing humility, I embraced anew the restrictions of natural life! with what sincere renunciation, I locked the door by which I had so often gone and come, and ground the key under my heel!

The next day, came the news that the murder had been overlooked, that the guilt of Hyde was patent to the world, and that the victim was a man high in public estimation. It was not only a crime, it had been a tragic folly. I think I was glad to know it; I think I was glad to have my better impulses thus buttressed and guarded by the terrors of the scaffold. Jekyll was now my city of refuge; let but Hyde peep out an instant, and the hands of all men would be raised to take and slay him.

I resolved in my future conduct to redeem the past; and I can say with honesty that my resolve was fruitful of some good. You know yourself how earnestly in the last months of last year, I laboured to relieve suffering; you know that much was done for others, and that the days passed quietly, almost happily for myself.

Nor can I truly say that I wearied of this beneficent and innocent life; I think instead that I daily enjoyed it more completely; but I was still cursed with my duality of purpose; and as the first edge of my penitence wore off, the lower side of me, so long indulged, so recently chained down, began to growl for licence.

Not that I dreamed of resuscitating Hyde; the bare idea of that would startle me to frenzy: no, it was in my own person, that I was once more tempted to trifle with my conscience; and it was as an ordinary secret sinner, that I at last fell before the assaults of temptation.

There comes an end to all things; the most capacious measure is filled at last; and this brief condescension to evil finally destroyed the balance of my soul. And yet I was not alarmed; the fall seemed natural, like a return to the old days before I had made discovery.

It was a fine, clear, January day, wet under foot where the frost had melted, but cloudless overhead; and the Regent's Park was full of winter chirrupings and sweet with spring odours. I sat in the sun on a bench; the animal within me licking the chops of memory; the spiritual side a little drowsed, promising subsequent penitence, but not yet moved to begin.

After all, I reflected, I was like my neighbours; and then I smiled, comparing myself with other men, comparing my active goodwill with the lazy cruelty of their neglect. And at the very moment of that vain-glorious thought, a qualm came over me, a horrid nausea and the most deadly shuddering.

These passed away, and left me faint; and then as in its turn the faintness subsided, I began to be aware of a change in the temper of my thoughts, a greater boldness, a contempt of danger, a solution of the bonds of obligation. I looked down; my clothes hung formlessly on my shrunken limbs; the hand that lay on my knee was corded and hairy.

I was once more Edward Hyde. A moment before I had been safe of all men's respect, wealthy, beloved—the cloth laying for me in the dining-room at home; and now I was the common quarry of mankind, hunted, houseless, a known murderer, thrall to the gallows.

My reason wavered, but it did not fail me utterly. I have more than once observed that, in my second character, my faculties seemed sharpened to a point and my spirits more tensely elastic; thus it came about that, where Jekyll perhaps might have succumbed, Hyde rose to the importance of the moment.

My drugs were in one of the presses of my cabinet; how was I to reach them? That was the problem that (crushing my temples in my hands) I set myself to solve. The laboratory door I had closed. If I sought to enter by the house, my own servants would consign me to the gallows.

I saw I must employ another hand, and thought of Lanyon. How was he to be reached? how persuaded? Supposing that I escaped capture in the streets, how was I to make my way into his presence? and how should I, an unknown and displeasing visitor, prevail on the famous physician to rifle the study of his colleague, Dr. Jekyll?

Then I remembered that of my original character, one part remained to me: I could write my own hand; and once I had conceived that kindling spark, the way that I must follow became lighted up from end to end.

Thereupon, I arranged my clothes as best I could, and summoning a passing hansom, drove to an hotel in Portland Street, the name of which I chanced to remember. At my appearance (which was indeed comical enough, however tragic a fate these garments covered) the driver could not conceal his mirth. I gnashed my teeth upon him with a gust of devilish fury; and the smile withered from his face—happily for him—yet more happily for myself, for in another instant I had certainly dragged him from his perch.

At the inn, as I entered, I looked about me with so black a countenance as made the attendants tremble; not a look did they exchange in my presence; but obsequiously took my orders, led me to a private room, and brought me wherewithal to write.

Hyde in danger of his life was a creature new to me; shaken with inordinate anger, strung to the pitch of murder, lusting to inflict pain. Yet the creature was astute; mastered his fury with a great effort of the will; composed his two important letters, one to Lanyon and one to Poole; and that he might receive actual evidence of their being posted, sent them out with directions that they should be registered.

Thenceforward, he sat all day over the fire in the private room, gnawing his nails; there he dined, sitting alone with his fears, the waiter visibly quailing before his eye; and thence, when the night was fully come, he set forth in the corner of a closed cab, and was driven to and fro about the streets of the city.

He, I say—I cannot say, I. That child of Hell had nothing human; nothing lived in him but fear and hatred. And when at last, thinking the driver had begun to grow suspicious, he discharged the cab and ventured on foot, attired in his misfitting clothes, an object marked out for observation, into the midst of the nocturnal passengers, these two base passions raged within him like a tempest.

He walked fast, hunted by his fears, chattering to himself, skulking through the less-frequented thoroughfares, counting the minutes that still divided him from midnight. Once a woman spoke to him, offering, I think, a box of lights. He smote her in the face, and she fled.

When I came to myself at Lanyon's, the horror of my old friend perhaps affected me somewhat: I do not know; it was at least but a drop in the sea to the abhorrence with which I looked back upon these hours. A change had come over me. It was no longer the fear of the gallows, it was the horror of being Hyde that racked me. I received Lanyon's condemnation partly in a dream; it was partly in a dream that I came home to my own house and got into bed.

I slept after the prostration of the day, with a stringent and profound slumber which not even the nightmares that wrung me could avail to break. I awoke in the morning shaken, weakened, but refreshed. I still hated and feared the thought of the brute that slept within me, and I had not of course forgotten the appalling dangers of the day before; but I was once more at home, in my own house and close to my drugs; and gratitude for my escape shone so strong in my soul that it almost rivalled the brightness of hope.

I was stepping leisurely across the court after breakfast, drinking the chill of the air with pleasure, when I was seized again with those indescribable sensations that heralded the change; and I had but the time to gain the shelter of my cabinet, before I was once again raging and freezing with the passions of Hyde.

It took on this occasion a double dose to recall me to myself; and alas! Six hours after, as I sat looking sadly in the fire, the pangs returned, and the drug had to be re-administered.

In short, from that day forth it seemed only by a great effort as of gymnastics, and only under the immediate stimulation of the drug, that I was able to wear the countenance of Jekyll. At all hours of the day and night, I would be taken with the premonitory shudder; above all, if I slept, or even dozed for a moment in my chair, it was always as Hyde that I awakened.

Under the strain of this continually-impending doom and by the sleeplessness to which I now condemned myself, ay, even beyond what I had thought possible to man, I became, in my own person, a creature eaten up and emptied by fever, languidly weak both in body and mind, and solely occupied by one thought: the horror of my other self.

But when I slept, or when the virtue of the medicine wore off, I would leap almost without transition (for the pangs of transformation grew daily less marked) into the possession of a fancy brimming with images of terror, a soul boiling with causeless hatreds, and a body that seemed not strong enough to contain the raging energies of life.

The powers of Hyde seemed to have grown with the sickliness of Jekyll. And certainly the hate that now divided them was equal on each side. With Jekyll, it was a thing of vital instinct. He had now seen the full deformity of that creature that shared with him some of the phenomena of consciousness, and was co-heir with him to death: and beyond these links of community, which in themselves made the most poignant part of his distress, he thought of Hyde, for all his energy of life, as of something not only hellish but inorganic.

This was the shocking thing; that the slime of the pit seemed to utter cries and voices; that the amorphous dust gesticulated and sinned; that what was dead, and had no shape, should usurp the offices of life. And this again, that that insurgent horror was knit to him closer than a wife, closer than an eye; lay caged in his flesh, where he heard it mutter and felt it struggle to be born; and at every hour of weakness, and in the confidence of slumber, prevailed against him and deposed him out of life.

The hatred of Hyde for Jekyll, was of a different order. His terror of the gallows drove him continually to commit temporary suicide, and return to his subordinate station of a part instead of a person; but he loathed the necessity, he loathed the despondency into which Jekyll was now fallen, and he resented the dislike with which he was himself regarded.

Hence the ape-like tricks that he would play me, scrawling in my own hand blasphemies on the pages of my books, burning the letters and destroying the portrait of my father; and indeed, had it not been for his fear of death, he would long ago have ruined himself in order to involve me in the ruin.

But his love of life is wonderful; I go further: I, who sicken and freeze at the mere thought of him, when I recall the abjection and passion of this attachment, and when I know how he fears my power to cut him off by suicide, I find it in my heart to pity him.

It is useless, and the time awfully fails me, to prolong this description; no one has ever suffered such torments, let that suffice; and yet even to these, habit brought—no, not alleviation—but a certain callousness of soul, a certain acquiescence of despair; and my punishment might have gone on for years, but for the last calamity which has now fallen, and which has finally severed me from my own face and nature.

My provision of the salt, which had never been renewed since the date of the first experiment, began to run low. I sent out for a fresh supply, and mixed the draught; the ebullition followed, and the first change of colour, not the second; I drank it and it was without efficiency. You will learn from Poole how I have had London ransacked; it was in vain; and I am now persuaded that my first supply was impure, and that it was that unknown impurity which lent efficacy to the draught.

About a week has passed, and I am now finishing this statement under the influence of the last of the old powders. This, then, is the last time, short of a miracle, that Henry Jekyll can think his own thoughts or see his own face (now how sadly altered!) in the glass.

Nor must I delay too long to bring my writing to an end; for if my narrative has hitherto escaped destruction, it has been by a combination of great prudence and great good luck. Should the throes of change take me in the act of writing it, Hyde will tear it in pieces; but if some time shall have elapsed after I have laid it by, his wonderful selfishness and Circumscription to the moment will probably save it once again from the action of his ape-like spite.

And indeed the doom that is closing on us both, has already changed and crushed him. Half an hour from now, when I shall again and for ever re-indue that hated personality, I know how I shall sit shuddering and weeping in my chair, or continue, with the most strained and fear-struck ecstasy of listening, to pace up and down this room (my last earthly refuge) and give ear to every sound of menace.

Will Hyde die upon the scaffold? Or will he find courage to release himself at the last moment? God knows; I am careless; this is my true hour of death, and what is to follow concerns another than myself. Here then, as I lay down the pen and proceed to seal up my confession, I bring the life of that unhappy Henry Jekyll to an end.

The End

Chapter Summaries and Analysis

Chapter 1: The Story of the Door

Mr Utterson is a wealthy lawyer, respected for his unemotional mind, loyalty to friends, and apparent lack of vices. This makes him pretty boring, as Stevenson points out.

We begin chapter 1 by discovering his friendship with a cousin, Mr Enfield, who is also a London gentleman. They walk together every Sunday, regardless of how little they have to say to each other, or perhaps because of it.

When Enfield tells Utterson about his strange encounter with Mr Hyde, he is very careful not to reveal the identity of the man he believes Mr Hyde is blackmailing. This is typical of how Stevenson sees society in its praise of the Victorian gentleman: avoiding scandal, protecting the reputation of others, and preserving a front which is morally upstanding.

The more interesting reading will be to ask whether Stevenson views this pursuit of a moral facade as both pointless and damaging. Does he believe that the strict moral behaviours expected by society actually make us worse as human beings? Does he believe a gentleman's life is in fact a life worth living?

As Utterson and Enfield pass a particularly dilapidated looking building, Enfield tells Utterson about a walk late one night when he was coming back from "the end of the world" and saw a small figure of a man walking with purpose. Suddenly, a young girl ran into him, fell in front of him, while the man completely ignored her pain, stepping over her and carrying on his journey. We soon discover this man is Mr Hyde.

The conventional view is that this shows his evil nature and lack of remorse or empathy for the pain of others. **However, Enfield catches up with this man who does not resist. Enfield grabs hold of him, and takes him back to the scene of the collision.**

Meanwhile her family arrive (they have been out looking for a doctor). A doctor is found, and he and Enfield, being gentleman, take charge. On first seeing Hyde they're overwhelmed with a desire to kill him. They don't see this as an indication of evil in themselves. Instead they see this as an indication of the terrible evil emanating from Hyde. Yes, 'we want to kill you, and it is all your fault!'

However, murder being illegal in Victorian London, (as it still is today) they decide to blackmail him instead which was, and still is illegal. They "screw him" out of £100, more than a year's wages for the average Victorian worker. If Hyde doesn't pay, they threaten to cause a scandal, presumably by suggesting that he has sexually assaulted the young girl.

The implication is that they can complain about anything they want: there does not need to be any factual crime, his reputation would be damaged by association. But, the justification goes, because Hyde is so evil, he deserves it, right?

Sophisticated readers might well ask why Hyde should care about a scandal? Presumably, everything he does is worthy of scandal, and consequently the fear of scandal would not intimidate him. This therefore suggests what Hyde most fears is not scandal, but the physical violence threatened by the family, Enfield and the doctor. Stevenson might be Implying that society is far worse than Hyde because, you know, they want to kill him!

Hyde gives the family £10 in gold guineas, then enters the door and returns with a cheque for £90 written by a famous gentleman who is known for his good deeds (and who we later find out is Dr Jekyll). Enfield assumes that Mr Hyde has obtained this cheque by blackmailing Dr Jekyll. Interestingly, he refuses to tell Utterson the name of the man who he believes is being blackmailed, because this would damage his reputation as a gentleman.

Utterson realises it is Dr Jekyll when Enfield names the short figure as Hyde. He has seen this name on Jekyll's will. And he knows that this doorway is to the back of Jekyll's house. He also keeps this a secret from Enfield.

Enfield is unable to describe Mr Hyde's facial features. This suggests that Hyde is not physically ugly, rather it is the ugliness of his evil, which can be sensed by others, because no other soul is truly evil.

However, this deformity of the soul doesn't seem to cause any deformity of the body. On the one hand, this might suggest that anybody could be entirely evil and still look normal. This plays to the Victorian fear of the criminal, the murderer, or the middle-class gentlemen hiding secret, evil vices.

Another possibility, however, is that Stevenson does not believe in the concept of evil. He wants to point out that this is simply an artificial construct, dreamt up by society. Because it is abstract and artificial, rather than real and tangible, Enfield is not able to describe it. Utterson will also be unable to describe it in the next chapter. Therefore the only criminal acts in this chapter are the threat of violence and the blackmail carried out by Enfield, the doctor, and the girl's family.

Stevenson is simply pointing out that society is much more corrupt than the individual. Whatever Hyde is up to, it is simply pleasure. The worst proof Stevenson gives about him is that a young girl ran in to him, she wasn't particularly hurt, and Mr Hyde ignored her. I mean, he didn't even hurt her on purpose, and took no pleasure in her pain, he just "calmly" kept on walking. The most evil human being in the world? I think we need a bit more proof than that.

Chapter 2: The Search for Mr Hyde

In the search for Mr Hyde Jekyll decides he must know more about Edward Hyde, because his friend Dr Jekyll has written a will in which Hyde will inherit everything Jekyll owns, even if Jekyll only disappears for three months. Utterson assumes this means Hyde will want to murder Jekyll, or find a way to force him to move away, perhaps abroad.

This is a logical conclusion for Utterson to reach. However, Mr Utterson knew all this the moment he read the will. Enfield's story should not change anything, because it simply confirms what he already knows.

The sophisticated reader will therefore ask why Utterson now wants to see Edward Hyde? It could be that he now realises Hyde is not blackmailing Jekyll for some past event. Instead it seems Hyde has a key to visit Jekyll in secret. What could that secret be? The logical reason for these secret night time visits is that Hyde is Jekyll's homosexual lover. So, another possibility is that Utterson is jealous of Jekyll's relationship with Hyde, that this imagined relationship heightens Utterson's own repressed homosexual desires.

He visits Dr Lanyon, because he, Jekyll, and Utterson were all at school together. On the one hand this marks them out as old and firm friends. However, the British public school being what it is, the suspicion of childhood homosexual relationships is obvious. This is also alluded to by Enfield in chapter 1, when he hypothesises that Jekyll is being blackmailed because of the "capers of his youth".

But Dr Lanyon has never heard of Hyde. He tells Utterson that he and Dr Jekyll have drifted apart after a disagreement over his scientific experiments, which Dr Lanyon describes as "unscientific balderdash". Utterson does not ask what this means.

Utterson has nightmares, in which he imagines a strange figure, Mr Edward Hyde, striding through the streets of London and knocking over girls at every corner. At the same time he transports this figure into Dr Jekyll's bedroom, where Edward Hyde summons the sleeping Jekyll to stand and "do his bidding".

On the one hand this symbolises the evil power Edward Hyde has over Dr Jekyll. On the other hand, it implies that this power is sexual, which is why he commands Jekyll from his bed. Utterson has placed Jekyll in his bed in the imagination of his own dream. Utterson is therefore dreaming of Jekyll in his bed. The astute reader will see this as an allusion to Utterson's own homosexual attraction to Jekyll, and therefore understand his obsession with seeing the face of Edward Hyde, the man whom Dr Jekyll appears to have chosen as a sexual partner, who is now, in Utterson's imagination, blackmailing him.

Now of course, we don't have to interpret this as homosexual symbolism. Utterson might be dreaming of Dr Jekyll in his bed in an entirely random way, and he may have dreamed of Hyde having the power to enter this bedroom and summon Jekyll simply as a metaphor for the power he has over Jekyll's life, and this could have happened in the parlour, the study, the theatre, the laboratory and it just so happens that he chooses the bed. You can play the 'it's just a coincidence card, he didn't mean anything by it really' card if you want, but that don't butter no parsnips.

Utterson becomes obsessed by Edward Hyde, and keeps watch on the door for several days and nights, until eventually he spots Hyde. He introduces himself, and asks if he can see Edward Hyde's face. Although Utterson is threatening in his manner, Edward Hyde is unfailingly polite.

Utterson has the same dislike of Hyde as Enfield, confirming to Victorian readers that the poisonous evil of Edward Hyde's soul is somehow making itself felt physically by the morally Christian and good observer, Utterson. **However, knowing that Stevenson is an atheist, who does not believe in the existence of a soul, we can also infer that Utterson's reaction is also a result of prejudice. This is why he contrasts Utterson's rudeness with Hyde's politeness. Hyde is being judged unfairly.**

Utterson describes Edward Hyde as being like a troglodyte, what we would call a Neanderthal man. Although he is unable to describe Hyde's features, this allusion refers to Darwin's theory of evolution, and the survival of the fittest. On the one hand, this illustrates Victorian society's fear that civilisation is vulnerable, and that Christian morality is the only hope of saving mankind from reverting to an earlier, primitive form. The Christian interpretation is that we are brutish and animalistic by nature, and can only be saved by a Christian God.

However, the existence of Neanderthal man, and troglodytes, suggests that the Biblical story is just that, a story and that the origins of mankind are far older than the 6500 years suggested by the Bible. Here Stevenson is pointing out the science, which says that the fittest will survive. This implies that those who are best adapted to their environment will survive.

When Christians have to treat the story of Genesis as an allegory, rather than historical fact, they need to be able to explain evolution. One way to do this is to see mankind as evolving into an ever improved form: we become more enlightened, more civilised, more moral and, of course, more Christian.

However, Stevenson could also be proposing the opposite to this vision of improvement. Because Victorian society is inherently immoral and corrupt, the inherently immoral and corrupt Edward Hyde will survive longer than the less in moral do-gooder, Henry Jekyll. This is in fact what happens in the novel. Christian morality, he might argue, is weak, which is why Hyde triumphs.

A Christian reader will read this differently. They would argue that man's true nature is evil, as we all carry Original Sin. (This is the belief that Adam and Eve first sinned against God in eating the forbidden fruit from the Tree of Knowledge of Good and Evil. Because we are all descended from them, we all carry this

Original Sin with us. Of course, we know that Stevenson was an atheist, and we also know that his allusions to Darwin's theory of evolution all discredit the idea of Original Sin and the creation story of Genesis).

This Christian interpretation of evil will fit the interpretation of Hyde's motiveless killing of Sir Danvers Carew. However, this is not the only way to interpret Edward Hyde. As we shall see, Stevenson doesn't name any criminal activity, or indeed any sin that Hyde commits before the killing Danvers Carew. This strongly suggests that Hyde is not inherently savage. Indeed, when he speaks to Enfield, and later to Utterson, he is unfailingly kind and polite. He even fears them, suggesting that they have more power than he does, that they are more savage than he is.

This presents us with the possibility that earlier versions of man were less savage than modern humans. It implies that the earlier versions of man were simply eradicated by the murderous impulses of modern man, practising genocide. Because this is the obvious question: if Neanderthal man was so much more savage and so much more physically powerful than modern man, Homo Sapiens, how did Homo Sapiens survive while Neanderthals completely died out? How did an entire species disappear? An obvious conclusion is that Homo Sapiens was simply much better at killing. This is what survival of the fittest means.

So, the irony here is that Victorians feared this kind of regression – that mankind might evolve backwards into some earlier, or primitive form. Stevenson creates Hyde to give the readers a version of that primitive form. But, until the killing of Carew, Hyde just doesn't do anything that evil – while those around him do. Hyde simply responds to everyone meekly and politely. Here, Stevenson suggests it is modern man, Christian man, that is more dangerous and savage.

As you will see later, Hyde's killing of Carew actually makes no sense until we consider that he is acting for Jekyll. Jekyll has a reason for killing Carew, but hides this from Utterson, and therefore from the reader. Again, it will suggest that modern man rather than the regressive Hyde, is the real villain. This reason is connected to theme of homosexuality in the novella.

Hyde also tells Utterson his private address in Soho, telling Utterson that he might need it. **This implies that when Jekyll disappears, and Hyde inherits everything, he will not want to deal with Utterson in Dr Jekyll's house in Leicester Square, but would instead prefer to live in the much smaller accommodation in Soho, because Soho is associated with sin, depravity, and the availability of any vice.**

Utterson next goes to visit Dr Jekyll, and we find out that his house is the same one that Edward Hyde entered through the back door. It was easy not to realise this because the house is so long that the back door is actually on a separate street to the front door.

Jekyll's Butler, Mr Poole, tells Utterson that Jekyll is not at home, but that Hyde has a key to the laboratory, which is entered from that back entrance. All the servants have instructions to obey Mr Hyde. Utterson supposes that Hyde is blackmailing Jekyll, perhaps for some wrongdoings that Jekyll committed in his youth, which again invites us to consider homosexuality as the likely cause.

The more astute reader might also see the metaphor for Hyde always entering at the back of the house as a symbol of sodomy, again alluding to the Victorian fear of homosexuality.

This will be even more relevant when we discover that Jekyll has a theatre at the centre of his house. This of course is a medical theatre, because the house is based on that of the famous surgeon John Hunter. But a second reason for having the theatre in the house is that the theatres in Soho are also a shorthand for homosexual society. We will find out later that Utterson used to enjoy going to the theatre in his youth, but has denied himself this pleasure for the last 20 years. This again implies that Utterson also had a homosexual past. Because everything else about Utterson is repressed, it suggests that his own homosexual desire was not realised.

Chapter 3: Dr Jekyll was Quite at Ease

Two weeks later, Jekyll throws a dinner party. Utterson stays late to ask Jekyll about Edward Hyde. Jekyll appreciates Utterson's concern, but tells him that the situation with Hyde is not a problem Utterson can solve, and one that cannot be talked through. He claims that he can be rid of Edward Hyde whenever he wants to, but also points out that he takes a great interest in Edward Hyde and wants to continue to provide for him. He makes Utterson promise that he will carry out the will.

This will be important later, because it shows us how far Dr Jekyll identifies with Hyde. We might expect that Henry Jekyll would simply cease to be once he can no longer transform from Edward Hyde's body. However, Dr Jekyll will still experience everything that Edward Hyde experiences, and consequently he is already preparing for the day when he knows that he will not be able to change back. This means that Jekyll does not feel Hyde is entirely evil – he looks forward to experiencing everything that Hyde experiences. He loves being Hyde because Hyde ignores society's moral values: he can enjoy his pleasures because he does not feel guilty.

What we need to know here is that Hyde, at this stage in the novel, has never had the power to appear on his own. He has always needed Dr Jekyll to take his drugs first. This means that Jekyll was always planning to disappear – he always knew that Hyde would become more powerful, and take over both his personality and his body. Jekyll never admits this, but his will proves it.

Remember this – the existence of the will proves that Jekyll always intended to become Hyde permanently.

Chapter 4: The Carew Murder Case

About one year later we witness the savage and apparently motiveless murder of Sir Danvers Carew. Stevenson deliberately withholds any first-hand account, so that we cannot really be sure why the murder happened. **This is actually the central mystery of the novel, because the answer to the other mystery – who is Hyde, and what does he have to do with Jekyll – are fully answered at the end of the novella.**

He places the witness, a maid, in the same position as the Victorian reader who enjoys the sensationalism of news stories, Penny Dreadful books, and Gothic fiction. Consequently, her narrative follows those sensationalist and Gothic conventions. It is very likely that Stevenson does this to associate his readers' interest in this kind of story with the uneducated working classes. It is another way for him to peel back the mask of respectability, and suggest to his middle class, respectable readers that they revel vicariously in other people's sins, just like Utterson appears to do, and a bit like Jekyll.

He implies that all his Victorian readers might well share Jekyll's desires, and would take a similar advantage of the scientific ability to create a doppelgänger, an alter ego, to experience all those forbidden pleasures without fear of society's disapproval. 'You like this stuff, he seems to say, because if it weren't for society's rules and the fear of being caught, it is exactly what you would be doing. You think you are socially and morally superior to a mere maid? Think again!'

She describes Sir Danvers Carew as looking both beautiful and innocent. The way he steps back when Edward Hyde becomes angry is probably intended to be comic, as though Stevenson is amused at the

thought of beating him to a pulp, which Hyde now does, for the delightful shock and entertainment of Stevenson's readers.

The improbability of Carew's body bouncing up and down on the pavement while Hyde is both standing on it and beating it with his cane also adds to the comedy. To the Victorian reader, salacious and eager to hear details of the murder, this scene only points to Edward Hyde's evil savagery – it isn't comic at all. **To a more logical reader, the impossibility of these simultaneous actions happening at the same time reveals Stevenson's purpose, to ridicule this interest in violence and crime. Perhaps he is also pointing out that such random attacks, without any motive, are so rare as to be entirely fictitious – they only exist in books.**

Once we realise this, Stevenson asked us to consider what the real motive might have been. He drops several clues, but refuses to help us solve it.

Clue number one:

Sir Danvers Carew is out walking near the Houses of Parliament, where he works, yet the police have assumed he doesn't know where to post a letter: unlikely. Much more likely that he was out walking with a different purpose.

Clue number two:

The letter is addressed to Gabriel Utterson. Why? What confidential matter might Sir Danvers want the lawyer to keep secret? Utterson refuses to tell us, and so we are left with the coincidence that the one man Utterson is obsessed about, Edward Hyde, has chosen to kill only once, and to pick the one man brandishing a letter addressed to Utterson. What might his motives be? Jekyll refuses to tell Utterson what the motives are when he writes his confession. Instead he says that Hyde had no motive at all, he simply saw an opportunity to murder someone, and excitedly took it.

This is entirely unlikely, given his night-time travels, through the fogs of London. He could easily have murdered dozens of people without choosing a bright night under the light of the silvery moon. There are any number of back alleys in which he could murder someone in complete darkness, with no available witnesses. Instead he chooses an open street, with great visibility, opposite a house where a maid is sitting at a window.

Instead, it is far, far more likely that something was said by Sir Danvers which enraged Hyde. But Stevenson refuses to tell us what it is – only that a conversation took place.

Clue number three:

The maid recognises Edward Hyde as a visitor to her master. This strongly suggests a connection between Hyde's desire to commit sins and the master of the house. After all, the whole point of Hyde's existence is to seek his illegal or immoral pleasure: Hyde is here on purpose. As for Carew, let's face it, who tries to post a letter at nearly midnight? Which MP couldn't simply ask his butler to do it for him? In fact, Utterson lives just a few hundred meters south of the Houses of Parliament, at Gaunt Street. It would be just as easy to deliver the letter to Utterson by hand!

On the other hand why might an older man be out cruising "in a very pretty manner" in the middle of the night? Why might he stop the young man and proposition him in some way? Why might that young man suddenly decide to beat him to death?

The implication is that Hyde is enraged by the older man propositioning him for sex, or moved to violence when he discovers Carew is an MP and represents the repressive laws which prohibit the expression of his sexual desires, or is overcome at discovering a connection to Utterson or it is just entirely both a random encounter and a motiveless crime. Which one seems more likely?

When we consider that the law criminalising homosexuality was written in the same year as the novel, 1885, we can see a direct connection between the two. Stevenson attacks the law by having one of its creators killed!

This also gives Jekyll a motive – he has had to create an alter ego, Hyde, specifically because his homosexual desires are illegal. And now he has met an MP who not only made that law, but also has done so while being homosexual himself. He is therefore killed for his hypocrisy.

The police come to Utterson because the letter Carew was carrying was addressed to him, and they would like him to identify the dead body. Utterson still has Edward Hyde's address, and so takes the police immediately to Soho, where they discover Hyde has left. **They do find the other half of the murder weapon, a cane given to Henry Jekyll by Utterson.**

Another coincidence links Utterson to the murder, and also links Utterson to Hyde in Jekyll's mind: symbolically, he has given Hyde Utterson's gift.

What is Jekyll's reason for linking Hyde with Utterson? Does he believe that Utterson's desires are the same as Hyde's desires?

And why does Stevenson decide that all roads should lead back to Utterson? There is, after all, no need in the plot to give Hyde this murder weapon – it could imply have been a cane bought by Jekyll himself.

Instead, this is another clue. Stevenson refuses to tell us what it means. You can come up with your own solution – for me, the logical explanation is that Jekyll understands Utterson's repressed homosexual desires. He has created Hyde in order to live out his own homosexual desires, so that he no longer has to repress them or hide them.

The police also find the burnt remains of Hyde's cheque-book, and assume that he will need to visit the bank in order to finance his escape. They stake out the bank, but Hyde never appears (because, as we will later discover, he has simply transformed back into Jekyll, who has no intention of returning to the form of Hyde.)

Chapter 5: Incident of the Letter

Utterson calls round to Jekyll's house and finds him very ill. Jekyll claims that Hyde has disappeared, and that he has written a letter to say that he will never return. Jekyll apparently shows this letter to Utterson because he doesn't know whether to give it to the police. He wishes to avoid a scandal, and so he asks for Utterson's advice.

Anyone who knows Utterson's respect for secrecy as we do will suspect that he will not give this to the police, but will instead choose to avoid scandal and keep the letter secret. Perhaps Jekyll is also counting on this.

However, as we shall see later, Utterson immediately recognises the handwriting as Jekyll's. He does not want to admit this to himself, and consequently he shows it to his clerk, Mr Guest, who does indeed guess immediately that the handwriting belongs to Dr Jekyll. Utterson is also suspicious that Dr Jekyll has burned the envelope in which the letter has arrived, because there is now no evidence that this was indeed written by Edward Hyde. Instead, it appears to have been written by Dr Jekyll in order to protect his friend and possible lover.

The final thing Utterson wants to discover is whether Edward Hyde forced Dr Jekyll to write the terms of his will. This suggests that Hyde has a powerful hold over the doctor, which Utterson will use as a reason to loyally support his friend.

Dr Jekyll knows that if he tells Utterson he willingly wrote the terms of the will, Utterson will assume there is a homosexual relationship between Dr Jekyll and his young lover Hyde. The horror of this relationship would probably encourage Utterson to take the letter to the police. Consequently, Dr Jekyll lies, and tells Utterson that he was indeed forced to write to the will. There is no other reason for Jekyll to lie about this!

On his way out, Utterson asks the butler, Poole, to describe the man who delivered the letter. Poole, however, says no one had arrived to deliver the letter.

So Stevenson wants us to think carefully about why Utterson continues to protect Henry Jekyll. Are we supposed to imagine that he is simply being loyal to another gentleman, and that this loyalty should be more important than the law?

Or, is Stevenson asking us to question the impartiality of the law? After all, he has deliberately chosen Utterson to be a lawyer. Or, is Stevenson suggesting that Utterson is so loyal to Dr Jekyll because he wants to replace Edward Hyde in the doctor's affections?

To the Victorian reader, Utterson's protection of his friend might even seem noble and gentlemanly. That doesn't mean that the author views Utterson in the same way.

Stevenson makes very clear that the letter is a forgery, and that Utterson's silence is a cover-up. Utterson deliberately shows the letter to Mr Guest, and Mr Guest guesses that it is Jekyll's handwriting immediately. He says nothing, but when a message arrives from Dr Jekyll, he asks permission to compare the handwriting and immediately tells Utterson that they appear to have been written by the same person. In Hyde's handwriting the letters are only "differently sloped". **Utterson knows that Dr Jekyll has forged this letter for a murderer, but still swears his clerk to secrecy, and locks the letter in the safe "where it reposed from that time forward". Stevenson wants us to know that, even after the events of the novel are over, Utterson still protects his friend's guilty secret.**

In this way Stevenson prepares the ground for Utterson's silence about the origins of Hyde which will also continue even after the events of the novel. Does Henry Jekyll's reputation need defending even after he is dead?

Only Utterson can profit from this. Jekyll has no relatives, and therefore there is no one who will be affected by the scandal of the truth coming out, except for Utterson who has gained everything, Dr Jekyll's home and his entire fortune.

You will notice that Stevenson doesn't give Utterson any staff. He has no maid, nor a Butler, nor it appears a cook. Stevenson takes great trouble to describe all the servants in Dr Jekyll's house when Poole brings Utterson to break down the door into his master's study. We therefore know that Jekyll's wealth far exceeds Utterson's, providing another motive for Utterson's continued silence and to secrecy after the death of his generous friend.

Chapter 6: Remarkable Incident of Dr Lanyon

With the disappearance of Hyde, Jekyll appears to become healthier looking and more sociable. He carries out more good works, presumably giving to charity. After two months, Jekyll holds a dinner party which even Dr Lanyon attends.

But a few days later when Utterson visits, he finds that Jekyll is refusing to have any visitors at all. Puzzled by this, he goes to visit Dr Lanyon. Amazingly Dr Lanyon looks very ill, and explains that he expects to die soon. He does not appear saddened by his death, saying that he no longer enjoys life: "I sometimes think if we knew all, we should be more glad to get away."

Stevenson makes him describe death as a holiday, "to get away". Remember that Stevenson was an atheist, and did not believe in a heaven or hell. To him life was precious, because life is all there is. Moreover, Stevenson was living with the idea of death every day, because his lungs were weak: he died very early at the age of 44. He took any number of drugs in order to try and preserve life as long as possible. He would be disgusted by Dr Lanyon's attitude.

However, as a committed Christian, Dr Lanyon expresses the blind faith of most of his Christian readers. They too would rather reject a world full of simple, yet forbidden pleasures, choosing instead the perfection of death, and the certain knowledge that their souls would go to heaven. This idea appals Stevenson, which is why he gives Dr Lanyon such a ridiculous phrase.

He plants a clue that Dr Lanyon's giving up on life is deeply connected to Dr Jekyll, because Dr Lanyon refuses to speak about his old friend.

Jekyll writes to Utterson to say that he is no longer receiving visitors, but still values Utterson's friendship. He explains that he is suffering from a punishment that he cannot describe.

Lanyon dies a few weeks later. After the funeral, Utterson sits with an envelope addressed to him from Dr Lanyon. He considers not opening it, because he instinctively knows it will implicate Dr Jekyll, and he doesn't want to lose a second friend. When he does open the envelope, he finds another envelope inside which is not to be opened until the death or disappearance of Dr Henry Jekyll.

Like the reader, Utterson is struck by the coincidence that this has the same wording as Dr Jekyll's will. Although he is desperately curious to open up the envelope, he follows his dead friend's instructions, and returns it to his safe. This emphasises his noble restraint, and his ability to keep a secret at all costs. It is why it is so easy to interpret Utterson as a good man (although for a top grade I will keep showing you in the guide how to question this simplistic view).

Although Utterson keeps trying to see his friend, Dr Jekyll, he only ever speaks to Poole. Over time, his visits become less frequent, and Stevenson suggests that Utterson is secretly glad not to speak to Dr Jekyll.

Chapter 7: Incident at the Window

On a Sunday, Utterson and Enfield are again walking, as they did at the beginning of the novel. They are passing the door at the back of Jekyll's house. Enfield remarks that he has now worked out that the house belongs to Jekyll. He is pleased that Hyde has disappeared. He assumes this is because Hyde is on the run from the police.

In a free society, Stevenson might expect Enfield to ask Utterson about the connection between Edward Hyde and Dr Jekyll, but he doesn't. Enfield says it was partly Utterson's fault that Enfield found out that Hyde's house was the back of Jekyll's house. **This remark is not commented on. It is as though Enfield has** suspected some connection between Utterson and Dr Jekyll's interest in Hyde. It is a clue that Utterson is connected to Hyde in Enfield's mind. This is another clue that Stevenson plants to suggest that Utterson has homosexual desires. This is the connection Enfield senses.

Finding that he doesn't have to keep the connection between Hyde and Jekyll secret, Utterson decides to take Enfield into the courtyard at the back of the house, hoping to catch sight of his friend Dr Jekyll. Surprisingly, he does see Dr Jekyll sitting at an upstairs window. They invite him to come for a walk, and Dr Jekyll says he would like their company, but is not yet well enough to go for a walk.

At that moment Jekyll's expression changes to "abject terror and despair." However, Stevenson also adds "they saw it but for a glimpse" and they react to it by turning "pale" and feeling a sense of "horror" themselves. Utterson says "God forgive us, God forgive us". This strongly implies that he has seen much more than Jekyll's feeling of terror. As we later discover, this is a moment when Jekyll involuntarily transforms into Hyde. The two men have seen this transformation, but their minds refuse to accept it. Enfield insists in walking on in silence.

To the Victorian reader this suggests an element of supernatural horror which is so shocking to the men that they cannot speak of it even to each other.

To Stevenson, however, their silence is also deliberate ignorance. They have seen an amazing scientific discovery, but they would rather suppress it, just as they have suppressed anything else which is out of the norm.

Chapter 8: The Last Night

Jekyll's butler, Poole, calls on Utterson to say he suspects Dr Jekyll has been the victim of a crime, and perhaps he has been murdered. Utterson goes with him to Jekyll's house. There, the servants are gathered in the main hall, full of fear. Utterson and Poole go to the door of Jekyll's laboratory, but they are greeted by a strange voice which sounds nothing like Dr Jekyll. It tells Poole that it can receive no visitors.

Poole tells Utterson that his master has sent instructions to many chemists, desperate for some chemical ingredients that cannot be found. He explains that the man who has been writing these instructions is in fact Edward Hyde, as Poole has seen him coming out of the laboratory.

Both men suspect this means that Dr Jekyll is dead. Utterson decides they must break down Jekyll's door with an axe. Mr Hyde's voice begs Utterson for mercy from the other side of the red door. Oh the symbolism. Danger, blood, sexual desire.

However, when they have smashed open the door they find Edward Hyde's body still twitching, clutching a vial of poison (smelling like arsenic) dressed in clothes which are far too big for him. Utterson describes this as the "body of a self-destroyer", meaning that Hyde has committed suicide.

There is no trace of Dr Jekyll.

Jekyll has left behind a large envelope addressed to Utterson that contains three items. It is on a side table. **Hyde, of course, knows exactly what is in them. But amazingly, he has not destroyed them, but left them for Utterson to find. An astute reader will need to come up with a motive for this.**

The first is Jekyll's will, which now leaves everything to Utterson, and nothing to Hyde. The second is a note written this very day, which tells Utterson to read the letter Jekyll knows Dr Lanyon gave him to be opened in the event of Dr Jekyll's death. The third envelope contains Dr Jekyll's confession.

So, the story is over, but the Victorian reader still does not know the answer to any of the mysteries, in particular, where is Jekyll, and what is his relationship to Hyde?

Rather than turn any of these over to the police, Utterson decides to take them home. He promises Poole that he will return that night and send for the police.

This means, of course, that the dead body and Mr Hyde will remain in Jekyll's house for several hours without the police being informed. Once more, Utterson is breaking the law.

Chapter 9: Dr Lanyon's Narrative

This is Dr Lanyon's letter in which he describes receiving instructions from Henry Jekyll. Jekyll has asked him to visit his house, where Poole will introduce him to a locksmith. Together, they are to go to Jekyll's cabinet, open a precise cupboard, and bring a specified drawer and its contents back to Lanyon's house. Jekyll writes that he will then appear at midnight to claim the contents. Oh the Gothic symbolism.

Lanyon does as he is instructed, and describes a white chemical and a red (yes, there is that Gothic and sexual symbolism again) liquid as ingredients in the drawer, together with a notebook recording a series of experiments. He is so convinced that Dr Jekyll has gone mad, that he arms himself with a gun.

On the one hand this will prove to the Christian reader that Lanyon's faith has armed him with foresight – Jekyll's creation of Hyde, the embodiment of evil, is truly the act of a mad man.

On the other hand, Jekyll has shown no tendency towards violence at all, and hosted Lanyon at a dinner party only days before. Why does he need a gun? This suggests a level of insanity in Lanyon. It prepares the ground for what Stevenson would see as his insane decision to give up on life and choose death. It is a gentle nudge to his Christian readers that their preference for heaven over life is insane.

Just after midnight, Hyde arrives, saying he has been sent from Dr Jekyll. Lanyon does not describe Hyde as evil or deformed. Instead he says being near him causes a "subjective disturbance". This precise use of language is the opposite of scientific objectivity – to be "subjective" is to be biased, to see only partial truths. Stevenson wants us to know that the perception of Hyde as wholly evil is not a fact, but also "subjective".

It means that Edward Hyde's appearance is not disturbing in himself, but that other people view him this way. He then says that he does find Edward Hyde "revolting" and then feels "horror" at his visitor, but remember this is a "subjective" view.

Hyde offers Lanyon the choice of leaving the room, so that he does not see the effect of the drug. However he suggests that Lanyon's "greed" and "curiosity" will be satisfied if he stays. He suggests that staying will give him "a new province of knowledge and new avenues to fame and power".

Although Lanyon pretends that this is not his reason for staying, we might think differently. After all, if Hyde's appearance is so shocking and horrifying to the soul, why would Dr Lanyon stay? The answer would appear to be that Lanyon's desire for fame and power is greater than his revulsion at Hyde.

Lanyon describes how Hyde changes into Jekyll as though becoming Jekyll is a deformity. His face "seemed to swell" and "became suddenly black and the features seemed to melt and alter". **To Lanyon, Jekyll appears more evil than Hyde.**

Once again Stevenson leaves us with secrets. Jekyll stays with Lanyon for a full hour, deep in conversation. But Lanyon refuses to "set on paper" what he heard. He is desperate for any kind of denial, saying "I ask

myself if I believe it, and I cannot answer". The science he has seen is so beyond what he thought was possible, that he cannot bring his scientific mind to accept it. This is because of the interference of his Christian faith: "my soul sickened at it".

Stevenson rejects this, and indicates his disgust at Lanyon with his final words "yet I shall die incredulous". He portrays Lanyon's ignorance as deliberate and wilful, and the opposite of what a rational, scientific mind should do.

Lanyon's final revelation is that Dr Jekyll had transformed from a "creature" whose name was Hyde, the man who had murdered Sir Danvers Carew!

Chapter 10: Henry Jekyll's Full Statement of the Case

This is Jekyll's brief autobiography. He explains that he was born with "a large fortune", was hard-working, and sought to please. However, he sees a fault in his younger self as being interested in life, having "gaiety of disposition". These pleasures in life are ones that he believes an ordinary man might be happy to be known for, but because he sought high social status, he keeps this frivolous side of his nature secret, which leads to "a profound duplicity of life".

He next admits that the pleasures he sought out left him "plunged in shame" but he refuses to tell us what these are. **He appears to be critical of religion, saying that at its "root" is "one of the most plentiful springs of distress". This juxtaposition of the kind of imagery we find in praise of nature, coupled with "distress" suggests that religion takes what is natural and pure, like a spring, and makes us view it as corrupt and evil.**

He describes this state as "man's dual nature" and for himself "a dreadful shipwreck". **This realisation comes to him before he creates Edward Hyde. In other words, society's views of pleasure and sin are at the "root" of Jekyll's tragedy. Society creates man's dual nature. Without Christian rules, he would be able to live freely, simply expressing his nature without fear of being judged.**

He imagines that other scientists will follow and "outstrip me on the same lines". We can see that his confession is also written for posterity: he wants his scientific discoveries to be developed, even though he does not leave behind a precise record of how to do so. He tells us that he doesn't want to leave a proper scientific record of his experiments in case future scientists recreate another Edward Hyde, rather than a more angelic version of themselves.

He creates Edward Hyde so that he can experience pleasure, without being "exposed to disgrace and penitence". It isn't just that he does not want people to know what pleasures he seeks out, he particularly doesn't want to feel guilty about them, and of course it is society's repression which makes him feel this guilt and "shame".

He explains that when taking the drug for the first time he risked death. **The first time he took the potion he felt agonising pain, but he describes becoming Edward Hyde as "I came to myself as if out of the great sickness". The symbolism suggests that Hyde, the pleasure seeker, is his more natural state, while Dr Jekyll, the product of society, is a kind of sickness. This is another attack on society's moral values.**

He describes the sensation of being Hyde in a very sensual language, as "not an innocent freedom of the soul". The reader might well ask what the soul needs freedom from? Perhaps it suggests the soul needs freedom from Christianity, and the moral codes of 19th-century British society. He equates this with wickedness.

Although other people in the novel apparently react with horror at Hyde's presence, they are unable to describe his face. Jekyll gives us a clue that it is attractive. He deliberately buys a large mirror, so that he can see himself in the form of Hyde. This is true, even though he feels that evil is written on Hyde's face, while good is written on Dr Jekyll's. Of course, this is a façade – he points out that Jekyll is not wholly good. The juxtaposition invites us to ask if Hyde is therefore wholly evil. Even though Jekyll states that he is, his description of Hyde calls this into question.

Jekyll supposes that Edward Hyde is younger and smaller than Dr Jekyll because Jekyll's evil desires have been kept under check for so much of his life: they haven't had time to grow.

Jekyll points out that his new identity is "natural and human". Instead of God looking down on him, he imagines being judged by "the constellations" who would observe him "with wonder". These are the pagan constellations of the Greeks, whose Gods did not have the same moral views as Christian theology. Just as all men are "commingled out of good and evil" so were the Greek Gods. In other words, standards of morality were very different then. Homosexuality was celebrated, as every male middle and upper class reader would know – they would have studied such stories in the original Greek while at school.

The idea of "pure evil" embodied by Edward Hyde is a Christian construct. While Jekyll appears to agree with this view of Edward Hyde, his actions, and choice of imagery suggests that he doesn't accept this Christian definition.

Stevenson needs Jekyll to conform to a Christian perspective in order to satisfy his Christian readers. However, his more astute readership will read a different story behind Dr Jekyll's words. As we shall see in this chapter, Dr Jekyll can only describe one truly evil act, the killing of Sir Danvers Carew. This is hardly "pure evil", or the act of somebody "alone in the ranks of mankind". If this were the case, Sir Danvers Carew's murder would be only the first murder in history, never mind the only murder Hyde commits.

He imagines that if he had drunk the potion for the first time when he was in a different mood, the new identity created might have been "an angel instead of a fiend". He points out that the drug just creates a different being, it doesn't dictate the character or personality of that being: that is produced by the emotional state, or the moral state of the drinker. Some readers feel this is Jekyll's delusion. They feel he has become corrupted by the evil of Hyde. Other readers believe that he is correct. Stevenson is pointing out that scientific progress is always progress: how people use it dictates whether it is good or evil.

Stevenson describes the secret pleasures of his life as "undignified" as though he struggles to find them horrifying, while society describes them as evil. He also suggests that they were more difficult to enjoy because he was "growing towards the elderly man". This is another hint that the pleasures might be physically strenuous, needing a young man's energy. Alternatively, they may require the cooperation of other young people, who would not be attracted to "the elderly" Dr Jekyll. This is another prompt that the secret pleasures are sexual, but also consensual. Hyde doesn't have to pay for them. If he did, his age would not matter.

He describes furnishing a house in Soho for Hyde, and introducing him to his servants. He now describes the "undignified" pleasures as turning "towards the monstrous". However, his language contradicts this kind of morality, referring to Hyde's doing "his good pleasure". Although he speaks of "any degree of torture to another" he is unable to give us any examples. Added to this, he gets tremendous vicarious pleasure from Hyde's actions. Again we wonder if these are simply pleasures society rejects, but which at the level of the individual are entirely acceptable.

Jekyll explains that he did not feel guilt at these monstrous acts, because they were performed by Edward Hyde. On the one hand, this suggests that Jekyll is deceiving himself, because after all he created Hyde for the sole purpose of carrying out these monstrous acts. But on the other hand, his lack of guilt strongly suggests that he does not believe these acts were monstrous, but were instead "good pleasures", simply judged as evil by a repressed, Christian society.

Interestingly, he writes about the first incident of the novel, where Hyde bumped in to the young girl. **He describes it as "one accident" but his principal memory is that "I feared for my life". This again suggests that Hyde was not behaving in any evil manner at this point, and was instead a victim**. It is at this point that Jekyll decides to open a separate bank account in Hyde's name, so Jekyll will no longer have his name publicly traceable to Hyde on a cheque.

He explains that two months before the murder of Sir Danvers Carew he woke up for the first time as Edward Hyde after having taken the potion to go to sleep as Dr Jekyll. He claims that from this moment he realised that Edward Hyde would become stronger than Dr Jekyll, his wholly evil personality overcoming Jekyll's which was "commingled" out of good and evil. **However, we remember that he drew up the will long before this: becoming Edward Hyde was always part of the plan.**

He reveals that over time he has had to take larger and more frequent doses of the drug in order to turn back into Dr Jekyll. He tells Utterson that in the form of Edward Hyde he is able to remember and experience everything Dr Jekyll experiences, and the same is true in reverse. However, when he is Edward Hyde he does not take any pleasure in being Dr Jekyll, because Dr Jekyll does not seek pleasure when he is in that form.

When he views himself as the doctor it is as "elderly and discontented", while as Edward Hyde he felt "liberty, the comparative youth, the light step, leaping impulses and secret pleasures." This is the full list in his comparison. Astute readers will notice the absence of evil. This is another clue that Jekyll's life as Edward Hyde is not in fact full of evil deeds, but simply the freedom to pursue pleasures which are rejected by Christian society.

He manages to repress Hyde for two months, but because Hyde has been imprisoned inside Jekyll for so long, "he came out roaring". He now describes how he killed Sir Danvers Carew, which he says was done with "so pitiful a provocation" and compares it to a child breaking "a plaything". **As we have seen earlier, this lack of a motive makes no sense. Sir Danvers Carew cannot have been the first person Hyde met on his walk. Nor is Hyde lying in wait, hoping to murder the first person who comes along. This strongly suggests a motive.**

Jekyll's description of the murder does not tally with the maid's. Instead of clubbing him to death with a cane and stamping on his body, he describes it much more intimately as "with a transport of glee, I mauled the unresisting body, tasting delight from every blow". Animals maul with teeth and claws, and the use of "tasting" to describe his delight similarly suggests different actions. In Victorian times mauling also held these sexual connotations (which you can hear on Audible, in episode 3 of Stephen Fry's Victorian Secrets).

This doesn't invite the reader to disbelieve the maid – after all, the cane is clearly the murder weapon, and half of it is left at the scene, and the other half in Edward Hyde's house. Instead, the language suggests an alternative, sexual motive for the killing. To the Christian reader, the animalistic imagery simply suggests Jekyll and Hyde's primitive nature. The Christian fear of science would argue science is propelling us towards an earlier, more savage, pre-Christian form of humanity.

To the more astute reader it is the suppression of homosexual desire which has led to this great rupture and violence, so that Dr Jekyll remembers the killing in sexual language. Of course, Jekyll cannot confess any of this to Utterson, who represents society's repressed, Christian morality.

Next, Jekyll describes Edward Hyde as destroying his papers, while toasting the dead victim, gloating about his crime, and planning to carry out other murders in the future. **Again, the astute reader will notice that he doesn't commit any future crimes. Consequently, he does not appear in his actions to be motivated by evil, but by pleasure.**

Although he describes feeling guilty at this murder, once he realises that he cannot be caught, simply transforming himself back into Dr Jekyll, he describes only feeling "joy". He is struck not just that the murder was "a crime, it had been a tragic folly". It was a mistake because it means that he can no longer risk transforming into Edward Hyde. His greatest regret is that he can no longer indulge in his pleasures, and not that he has ended Carew's life. This involves the Christian narrative, which sees Hyde's growing power as a warning that all men should be vigilant against their evil impulses. To give in even a little bit, will corrupt with greater power, as symbolised by Hyde's return.

Dr Jekyll decides to spend the rest of his life doing good works in order to "redeem the past".

He permanently locks the back entrance to his house and destroys Hyde's key, as a way to ensure that he will never again take the potion to become Hyde.

However, Edward Hyde is finally able to overcome Jekyll's resistance, without requiring the potion, after Dr Jekyll indulges in one of his secret pleasures "in my own person", rather than in the form of Hyde. The symbolism here is that once he accepts himself for who he is, and owns these pleasures, Hyde takes over. He transforms into Hyde while sitting in Regents Park.

To the Christian reader this is clear evidence that he has abandoned Christian morality, with the consequence that his soul has been lost forever. He has forever become the evil Edward Hyde, and his soul will now go to hell.

To the astute reader Dr Jekyll's fate is more complicated. The killing of Sir Danvers Carew, a member of Parliament, is now symbolic of an attack on the laws in society. This suggests that Edward Hyde is driven to crime through society's criminalisation and condemnation of his more innocent pleasures. This suggests that true evil is created by society: it is the constant repression which has led to this violent outburst, rather than a growing evil.

Another possibility is that there is a more real motive which Jekyll has for killing Carew. We remember that Hyde is created solely for living out Jekyll's desires. There is a strong hint that Jekyll has a particular reason for wanting to kill Carew, but he refuses to tell us what this is.

Unfortunately, Hyde no longer has access to Jekyll's back door. Jekyll tells us that he is impressed with Hyde's resourcefulness, especially under pressure. He comes up with a plan, writing to Poole to get a locksmith and to expect Dr Lanyon, and then writing to Dr Lanyon with instructions about how he should break into Dr Jekyll's laboratory and retrieve the drawer containing the ingredients necessary for the transformative potion.

He writes these letters at a hotel in Portland Street. **Despite being angered by the driver of his cab, and wanting to attack him, he doesn't. This is another puzzle given that he has recently murdered Sir Danvers Carew, yet he is able to resist even swearing at the driver. He only manages to snarl; he "gnashed my teeth", hardly the act of the most evil human being to walk the planet. Stevenson mentions this to force us to question Jekyll's Christian perspective on Hyde's narrative.**

While waiting for Lanyon to carry out his instructions, he cannot bear to remain in the hotel, and spends time travelling the streets in a cab. When the driver grows suspicious, he decides to get out and walk. He commits another terrible and astonishing crime. **Yes, a woman selling matches tries to persuade him to** buy. Being the most evil man who has ever lived, he … punches her in the face. However, this punch is apparently so feeble that she is able to turn around and run to escape him. Again, the more astute reader will try to find an explanation for this rather feeble anger. Yes, it is highly unpleasant, but evil? Why is it directed at a woman? Why does it cause so little harm? What does this tell us about the single act of rage which led to him murdering Sir Danvers Carew?

He very briefly explains going to Dr Lanyon's and transforming into Jekyll. But he does not tell us how he tempted Lanyon, or how he wanted to attack his "unbelief". **This strongly suggests that, as Hyde, he carries out Jekyll's revenge on Dr Lanyon. As Jekyll, he glosses over this, and doesn't want Utterson to know how much control Jekyll appears to have over Hyde's actions. It shows us that Jekyll is in the habit of hiding facts from Utterson. We are not being given the definitive truth. This also makes us doubly curious to know what he has concealed from us about the motive for killing Carew. Stevenson effectively challenges us to return to Jekyll's motives and desires.**

Jekyll also refuses to tell us what he said to Dr Lanyon, and what Dr Lanyon said to him after the transformation. He claims that he now feels "the horror of being Hyde", although whether this is because being Hyde is evil, or whether being Hyde means being hunted by society and the police, is not clear.

However, the next morning, having awoken as Dr Jekyll, he transforms into Edward Hyde without the aid of drugs, while crossing his courtyard. Despite doubling the dose to return to Jekyll, Edward Hyde spontaneously appears six hours later. Jekyll realises that he can no longer go to sleep, because he will always wake up as Edward Hyde.

Jekyll now comes to see Hyde as "hellish" and "inorganic" as though to distance himself from the fleshy presence of Hyde's body. He cannot bring himself to admit that he himself is Edward Hyde.

Hyde, on the other hand, is disgusted by Dr Jekyll's "despondency" and lack of "life". He attacks Jekyll by scrawling "blasphemies" in his books, attacking Jekyll's Christian faith. **This implies that he blames Christian morality for the "dislike" others feel for him. He burns Jekyll's letters from his father, and his father's portrait. In this way he symbolically attacks Dr Jekyll's parent, the authority figure who has made him feel so guilty about the pleasures he has pursued in secret.**

This also foreshadows Edward Hyde's decision not to destroy the documents that Henry Jekyll wants to leave behind for Utterson. So the astute reader will therefore have to work out Hyde's motive. If Hyde wants to attack Dr Jekyll, then leaving these documents for Utterson must be another kind of attack. But how will this damage Jekyll? Perhaps he knows that Utterson will keep them secret, and so Jekyll's work will be suppressed. He will never find fame or acceptance.

Dr Jekyll contrasts himself with Hyde's "love of life" which "is wonderful". This appears to be a much more real description of Hyde, addicted to the pleasures of living, than the description of him as the ultimate evil in mankind. Even before he is about to cease to be Dr Jekyll forever, he realises the great joy in being Edward Hyde. The tragedy now seems that Dr Jekyll has not been allowed to be himself by society, and has not been allowed to enjoy his pleasures openly. The tragedy is that society has forced him to create Edward Hyde to enjoy these pleasures.

Then a final tragedy is that he has to destroy Hyde's "love of life", when Hyde decides to commit suicide.

Jekyll now writes urgently, because he no longer has any supply of the salt necessary as the final ingredient in his potion. He describes trying to find this salt in every chemist, and realising that his original batch must have been contaminated with some unidentified impurity, which he can no longer recreate. This confession is therefore a note written before his inevitable death.

Christian readers will link the impurity of the salt to the impurity of Hyde.

His final comment on Edward Hyde is that he suggests suicide would be an act of "courage". This courage would be to "release himself". This strongly suggests that Jekyll does not believe in the notion of hell, because that could not be a "release". As even atheists will know, eternal damnation is a prison that lasts for eternity (which is a very, very, very, very long time!) Dr Jekyll can only use this language if he ultimately rejects Christianity, and the concept of hell. Of course, he can't tell us this, as it would alienate Stevenson's Christian readers. But Stevenson leaves enough clues that he rejects Christian views for the astute reader to work this out for themselves.

It suggests that Jekyll's Christian language, the duality between good and evil, the despair at his own sin, the claim that Hyde is the most evil of men, has all been a posture, a pose, a façade. It is the message he believes Christian society wants to hear, presented in terms which Utterson will understand. But Jekyll doesn't really believe it.

This is why death can be a "release", and why the description of Hyde's ultimate evil is so unconvincing. It is why his last words about Hyde contain a note of admiration.

And what is he releasing himself from? Not from death, obviously. Instead the release is from public condemnation, a public death on "the scaffold". He is being released from society's moral condemnation of his pursuit of pleasure. Dr Jekyll clearly sees Edward Hyde's crime in killing Sir Danvers Carew as a result of social repression, not the result of Edward Hyde's innate evil.

Consequently, we are left to ask the question why Edward Hyde allows Utterson to receive the documents left to him by Dr Jekyll, and why he allows Utterson to inherit Dr Jekyll's estate and fortune.

It could be that he knows Utterson will suppress Dr Jekyll's scientific discoveries. This might be his ultimate revenge, burying Dr Jekyll's science and making sure that no one else can follow in his footsteps. There will be no posthumous fame, no recognition.

Stevenson also uses it to point to the corruption in society, so that even its apparently most upstanding member, Gabriel Utterson, who refuses to indulge many pleasures, is still presented as a self-interested criminal. By extension, the law is criminal, protecting the interests of rich men. He hides the truth from the police in order to protect the reputation of a man who is already dead, and who leaves no family to be affected by that reputation: it is only to preserve Utterson's inheritance.

The added introduction of Jekyll's house as the John Hunter house also throws up how posterity judges people differently, how what once seemed criminal later comes to be a great benefit to humanity. Ultimately, Stevenson rejects the Christian morality of his own story, but it takes a sophisticated reader to realise this dual nature in the narrative.

On the one hand, it is a Christian allegory, warning faithful readers not to be tempted by their evil impulses, not to seek out hedonistic and sexual pleasures, not to embrace scientific discoveries as though they offer hope for a better future.

On the other hand, it presents Christian society as hypocritical and repressive, turning violence upon itself because repression of desire does not lead to moral behaviour, it leads to rage and increased temptation and sin.

Perhaps Stevenson could not make his true feelings any clearer than by abandoning Britain for ever, and choosing the much more primitive Samoa where, like Hyde, he might experience "not an innocent freedom of the soul" without fear of social condemnation.

Context

Biography of Stevenson

Robert Louis Stevenson (1850 – 1894)

Stevenson's best known novels are **Treasure Island** and **The Strange Case of Doctor Jekyll and Mr. Hyde.**

In Long John Silver and Doctor Jekyll he gives us two anti-heroes. They are a fascinating combination of good and evil. Stevenson specialised in characters whose moral compass is different from our own. They are ambiguous. We don't know whether they are more good than evil. He even asks us to question what evil is.

He was born in Edinburgh in 1850. Stevenson was an only child. He had weak lungs from birth, and was often bedridden. From the age of two, he was looked after by a nurse, Alison Cunningham.

From an early age he was interested in the **Bible**. He wrote a prize winning history of Moses when he was 6. At 16, he wrote about a Protestant uprising. His devoutly Christian father paid for it to be published.

But by the age of 22 he had given up Christianity. Going to university at 16, he enjoyed the seamy side of Edinburgh, smoking hashish (cannabis) and visiting brothels.

He trained as a lawyer to please his father, but never actually practised. Instead, he trained himself to write by imitating great writers he admired, (which I encourage you to do if you buy the **Mr Salles Guide to Awesome Story Writing**, where I show you how it is done).

He coupled this with a longing to travel. Partly this was medical, to find warmer climates where he could breathe better, and he turned his travels into books.

In 1876, he met Fanny Van de Grift Osbourne at an artists' colony in Paris, with her two children. She was 11 years older than him, but he appears to have fallen in love with her.

She returned to California, and her husband in 1878, but then wrote to Stevenson and he decided to visit her. The journey almost killed him, but he reached California. She divorced her husband and, in 1880, she and Robert were married.

He persuaded her to return to Scotland with him in 1881. There he was inspired by drawing with his 12 year old stepson, to draw the map of an Island, and **Treasure Island** was born.

He wrote it as a serial, to be published in a magazine. It is fair to say it revolutionised children's fiction, which had previously been more concerned with teaching children how to behave and make moral choices. The rejection of Christian moral choices is very relevant to Jekyll and Hyde, and suggests he does not believe in society's view of morality.

In 1882 he moved the family to the South of France, but had a stroke. He wasn't able to write novels, but found he could write poetry for children. Then came two children's novels, **The Black Arrow** and **Kidnapped** in 1884, when he had now moved to Bournemouth.

Here he had a nightmare. Fanny woke him, and he told her off for disturbing the story of his dream: "I was dreaming a fine bogey tale," he said. He claims to have written the 40,000 word first draft of **The Strange Case of Doctor Jekyll and Mr Hyde** over the next 3 days. Historians report that he was taking cocaine while he wrote it, as the drug helped alleviate the symptoms of his lung disease. The Guardian describes it as a "cocaine binge". Drugs were not illegal in the 19th century.

Fanny didn't like the novel, believing it was too sensational. In her letters she describes burning it. He rewrote it as an allegory in 3 days, then redrafted it for 6 weeks. You will see that it works as a Christian allegory, for his Christian readership. But it also has a dual nature, hidden beneath the surface, which rejects Christianity.

Stevenson later claimed it was the worst book he had ever written, probably because it was only understood for its Christian message, with readers not understanding its dual purpose. But it ironically sold 40,000 copies in the first 6 months, and made him famous.

Soon after writing the novel he left Britain for ever, settling in Samoa. You can easily find pictures of him online, in a family setting, together with half naked locals. He was appalled at their treatment by European governments who occupied different parts of the islands. We can easily see parallels with the hypocritical, civilised Jekyll imposing rules on the more natural Hyde.

How Would You use This?

The obvious conclusion is to suggest that Stevenson did not believe in the Christian message of his novel. He introduced it to cater to the demands of his audience. This also invites us to think of his dislike for the views of many of his readers. We can add to that, perhaps, his attitude to the sensationalism in his book. We can read in this a mockery of people like the "maid" and Hyde's "landlady" who delight in the misfortune of others. This is exactly the sort of reader, delighting in the misfortune of Jekyll. It is also the delight that Utterson must share, being the last friend to "downward going men".

The knowledge that he rejected law, and had only taken it up to please his father, will help us be critical of Utterson, who represents the law Stevenson has already rejected. Utterson seems morally upstanding to a Christian readership, but to Stevenson he represents the full extent of Victorian hypocrisy and repression.

We can also infer some sympathy for Jekyll, who is trying to create an alter-ego. Is this perhaps a metaphor for the author himself, creating alternative version of himself in his books, or reinventing himself abroad? Perhaps too we can see a parallel between his own ill health and Dr Jekyll's, and his addiction to powerful drugs – not to criticise the addict – but to celebrate the power to escape reality.

Interestingly, The Guardian also suggests that Stevenson was using cocaine as a medication against his lung disease at the time. This gives us a drug induced dream as the origin of the story. It also allows us to see the drug taking of Jekyll in a new light. Stevenson might well see it as necessary for promoting life. This suggests that he sees Jekyll's death as a tragedy, one brought about by a society which did not let him live freely as himself, but necessitated the creation of the destructive alter-ego Hyde. It is a death which his readers demand, because it reflects God's justice. He might have hated having to give them what they want!

Life After Britain

Next Stevenson moved to New York in 1887, where they met up with Fanny's mother. Then they toured the South Pacific.

We might read into this a strong desire to escape the corruption of cities and even of western society.

Deciding to live in Samoa is an attempt to enjoy a pastoral innocence. It is free from a Christian idea of sin and moral behaviour. Although Christianity was practised, women and men still spent their days unashamedly topless (although women covered their breasts in the formal photographs with Stevenson's family). Although friendly with some of the missionaries spreading Christianity on the island, he was very critical of them.

Samoan society appears free of the need to hide from one's passions and interests. In Samoa, Dr Jekyll would have no need of creating Hyde – we might argue that he would simply be able to be himself, without worrying about society's disapproval of his desires.

Stevenson had a house built in 1890, and remained in Samoa until his death in December 1894, aged only 44. Many critics feel he wrote his best novels while in Samoa, and he also wrote extensively campaigning for the rights of Samoan people.

How Would You Use This?

It allows you to read the novel as a rejection of western civilisation and its Christian morality. We can also see it as a very strong rejection of British society, represented by Utterson's and Jekyll's desires for secrecy.

In his writing of novels and campaigning for the rights of 'primitive' and exploited people we can also infer a pursuit of intellectual freedom which Dr Jekyll so craved, in contrast to the "hidebound pedant" Dr Lanyon, and the Christian society he represents.

The Origins of the Novel

Gothic Fiction

Gothic fiction grew in popularity at the same time as Romantic poetry. These novels shared many similarities: strange and unexplained events; buildings which had a presence or persona, like a character; passionate and intense feelings; a rich or noble villain or anti-hero and anxious characters.

The genre gradually became extreme and dramatic – my favourite plot description comes from Professor John Mullan, "Matthew Lewis's *The Monk* (1796), was an experiment in how outrageous a Gothic novelist can be. After a parade of ghosts, demons and sexually inflamed monks, it has a final guest appearance by Satan himself." This theme of evil being embodied by a Satanic character is one which Stevenson draws on.

In 1817, Jane Austin wrote a satire of the Gothic genre, *Northanger Abbey*. There are elements of this satiric tradition carried on by Stevenson in his treatment of the violence in his novel.

As if timed to bring something new to the genre, Frankenstein, written by Mary Shelley in 1818, introduced the idea of a double or doppelgänger, and this was picked up as a tradition in future Gothic novels, which we can again trace in Jekyll's creation of Hyde.

By the 1840s many of the uncanny elements and heightened emotions of the Gothic had entered mainstream fiction. Some of the most famous novels – Jayne Eyre, Wuthering Heights – are heavily influenced by it and both published in 1847.

The Strange Case of Dr Jekyll and Mr Hyde is not just a Gothic novel. It's title strongly alludes to the conventions of detective fiction, which became popular in American fiction in the 1840s before gaining popularity in Britain in the 1860s. The Sherlock Holmes stories were first published 6 years after Jekyll and Hyde, in 1891 and borrow the idea of the ignorant narrator who, like Utterson, sees everything, and understands so little.

Victorian Statistics

In the 19th century London had become the largest city in the world, and had grown from around 1 million in population in 1800 to over 6 million by 1900.

All the action in Jekyll and Hyde takes place in the centre of London, which had already been well established in 1800, which is why the male characters represent the establishment, the ruling classes.

London was also the centre of the British Empire, so it was full of immigrants. We get a sense of the fear of foreign immigration in the description of Utterson's trip to Hyde's Soho lodgings. Hyde himself is described as "swarthy", as though part of his unnatural appearance reminds the reader of immigrants from which we can infer an element of fear of cultural change. This same fear is echoed by the reaction to Darwin's theory of evolution and the threat this makes to the dominant Christian culture.

Because houses were heated by coal or wood burning, London experienced terrible air pollution which often resulted in orange, grey or black fog, which would often cause an extra 700 Londoners to die each day. The crime rate would also rise, as criminals found it easier to escape detection. Stevenson setting of the fog is not just a Gothic convention, but a real fear Londoners faced.

Drug Use in Victorian England

Opium and cocaine could be bought at any chemist in London. Patients would take these as medicines, as well as recreationally. It isn't known how widespread this use was, but even medicines given to children contained opiates.

By the time Stevenson was writing, other writers were including unflattering descriptions of addicts, which implies that drug taking was becoming viewed differently, with the beginnings of a view which saw drug addiction as a moral weakness, rather than an addiction for which we should have sympathy.

At the time Stevenson was writing, however, the medical benefits were seen to far outweigh the dangers of addiction, and it is widely assumed that Stevenson wrote this novel while taking cocaine as a medicine.

Literacy in Victorian England

It is difficult for us to imagine now, when even an adult with the reading age of a ten year old can read The Sun newspaper and understand every word in it, but we are living in a golden age of literacy.

In 1840, 50% of brides could not write their own name, and neither could 35% of grooms. For women, this represented a 10% improvement since 1800, while there had been no improvement for men.

But by 1885, over 90% of men and women could read and write, and in 1900 over 95% could do so. There are many explanations for this incredible revolution, but it also explains why there are so many brilliant novels written in the 1900s – books are pretty much the only game in town. Even the explosion in magazines was just another way to consume books in smaller chunks, as novels were often serialised, and readers eagerly waited a week for the next chapter.

We can also see that the group who benefited most were women. The other factor dramatically increasing the number of female readers is the rise of the middle class. One way of defining the Victorian middle class is any household which had a servant. Women with servants had leisure time. Books were Hollywood, TV,

YouTube, Amazon and Netflix all rolled in to one, and the Victorian readers were the first in history to have the leisure time for a huge number of the population to simply read.

But, just as modern audiences will binge watch through a series, Victorian readers would binge read through a genre.

Stevenson was riding the crests of these waves, the established Gothic genre, the newly popular Penny Dreadfuls, and the recent development of detective stories. But this also means he was writing for a mass market he didn't necessarily respect.

We get a strong sense in Jekyll and Hyde of the struggle Stevenson had in writing the story he wanted to write, about the political and moral corruption of middle class men, and giving the public what they want – a whodunit, with fear, violence and supernatural or uncanny horror. This struggle is particularly strained in dealing with the readers' Christian viewpoint, while Stevenson is an atheist. We might also sense the struggle in his unflattering portrayal of women, in particular the maid and her vicarious enjoyment of the murder of Sir Danvers Carew, as a rejection of his female readers, or the controlling influence of his wife Fanny, who burned his first draft of the novella!

Victorian Scandals

Victorian newspapers did not have to worry about a person's right to privacy – such a law did not exist. The desire to keep family and personal secrets was not seen as wrong, but a natural way to protect the family. A Victorian reader would understand and applaud the need for cover up, where our own modern audience would see it as hypocritical.

For this reason Stevenson does not give any of the men families: they have no one to protect but themselves. Their desire for secrecy is therefore more suspect and self-interested.

The huge growth in newspapers coincided with the huge improvements in literacy. But it also coincided with the changes in divorce law. Up until 1857, only the church could grant divorce. In the preceding 200 years there had been only around 300 divorces in the country. After this date, there were 1200 a year!

Another feature of the divorce law was that you had to be rich to pay for the court proceedings. So, each divorce was the equivalent of a celebrity scandal. To make things even more exciting for the newspapers, women couldn't divorce men simply because they were repeatedly unfaithful. There had to be special cruelty, or incest or bestiality. Well you can imagine this made quite an impression in the newspapers.

There were also many famous newspaper stories associated with the theatre: actors murdering each other, female actresses faking suicide, numerous affairs of course, drag queens cited as love rivals, homosexual affairs, etc. This resonates when we learn that Utterson forbids himself to return to the theatre, though he had much enjoyed its pleasures before he learned to see them as sins.

The Geography of London

Leicester Square and Soho

Hyde and Jekyll live side-by-side, the first in Soho, the second in Leicester Square, both of which seem diametrically opposed. However, a study of the geography of London would let every reader know that Soho runs into Leicester Square, the two are like sides of the same coin. By implication, the corruption of Soho is next door to the gentility of Leicester Square. This is because gentlemen were corrupt, and wanted easy access to the secret, forbidden pleasures and vices they could satisfy next door. Every London reader would know this.

Hyde Park and Regents Park

You'll understand the symbolism of the parks in the section on names. They represent the status of Jekyll and Hyde as gentleman, but also the primitive instinct of human nature. Both parks were created as a hunting ground of Henry VIII. Having London Zoo in Regents Park also links Jekyll to our primitive, animalistic nature. It is also a reference to Darwin's Theory of Evolution.

The John Hunter House

Jekyll's house was historically the house of a famous surgeon, John Hunter, who infamously advanced scientific knowledge of anatomy and surgery. However, he could only do so by paying grave robbers to illegally obtain corpses for him. His infamy of 100 years ago had turned to fame and celebration in Stevenson's day.

This symbolises the importance of scientific discovery, and minimises the importance of social convention and moral values.

Homosexuality: "The Love That Dare Not Speak Its Name"

Section 11 of the Criminal Law Amendment Act 1885 made "gross indecency" a crime in the United Kingdom. In practice, the law was used mainly to prosecute male homosexuals. The date of publication of Jekyll and Hyde is 6th January 1886!

In Claire Harman's biography of Robert Louis Stevenson, she mentions his enjoyment of prostitutes, and suggests that there is no evidence of his being homosexual. However, she does point out he had a style of dress which suggested homosexuality. She quotes a scholar of the time, Andrew Lang, who commented that Stevenson "possessed, more than any man I ever met, the power of making other men fall in love with him".

Lang himself was homosexual, and at the very least Stevenson played with his affections, even writing a poem to him, which begins with a physical description: "Dear Andrew, with the brindled hair/ Who glory to have thrown in air" and ends by comparing him to Mount Helicon: "And your ink sings of Helicon." This is the home of the Muses – Greek women in myth who inspired the poets. As Stevenson's muse, Lang's homosexuality may well be the inspiration for the novel.

The link to Greece is of course suggestive of homosexuality, and the likening of "Andrew" to the home of female Muses also makes him feminine.

Harmon observes of Stevenson that he "can't have been unaware of the homoerotic forcefield he generated".

John Singer Sergent, a famous painter (and also a homosexual) painted Stevenson in 1885, the year he wrote Jekyll and Hyde. The portrait with his wife, Fanny, shows them far apart, separated by an open door. Stevenson wrote about the painting that it was:

"… too eccentric to be exhibited. I am at one extreme corner; my wife, in this wild dress, and looking like a ghost, is at the extreme other end… all this is touched in lovely, with that witty touch of Sargent's; but of course, it looks dam [sic] queer as a whole."

The open door at the centre of the picture asks to imagine what world Stevenson enjoys, that separates him from his wife. It could simply be fiction, books, the world of the imagination. But Stevenson also sees his wife as 'like a ghost', perhaps suggesting that Sergeant is suggesting the marriage itself, or Stevenson's sexual desire for his wife, is also dying or dead. We don't know if Sargent is suggesting the distance between them is due to Stevenson's sexuality, but many scholars have wondered.

The use of "queer" to mean homosexual is very probably referenced here deliberately by Stevenson. It definitely meant homosexual nine years later, when it appears in a letter from John Douglas, 9th Marquess of Queensberry.

His eldest son, Francis, died in a shooting accident, which may have been suicide. He was rumoured to have been the homosexual lover of the then Prime Minister, The 5th Earl of Rosebery. Wikipedia states that "Queensberry believed, as he put it in a letter, that "snob queers like Rosebery" had corrupted his sons, and held Rosebery responsible for Francis's death.[10]"

The other son in question was his third, Alfred, who famously was Oscar Wilde's lover. This was an extraordinary case. Queensbury accused Wilde of being a "sodomite", publicly exposing him. Wilde, a married man, sued to protect his reputation (though he was indeed homosexual, and Alfred's lover) and sued Queensbury for libel. Queensbury tracked down male prostitutes who would testify to having sex with Wilde, so he dropped the libel action.

Queensbury counterclaimed, and fighting this bankrupted Wilde. Then Queensbury handed over his evidence to the police who prosecuted him for "gross indecency" under the "Criminal Law Amendment Act 1885". He was sentenced to two years' hard labour, and when released, fled to France, rather than face the scandal in London.

It is probably no coincidence that Stevenson wrote his novel, with the secret of homosexuality at its heart, at the same time as this act was passed, 1885.

It also gives Stevenson a motive for choosing his one murder victim, Sir Danvers Carew. As an MP, he represents Parliament. We can go a step further. The symbolism in his description of Carew paints him as a homosexual who, by implication, has hypocritically voted for a law which criminalises his own sexuality.

This is even more probable when we consider Queensbury's attack on Archibald Primrose, 5th Earl of Rosebery, who was Foreign Secretary at the time Stevenson wrote his novel, and at the time the law was passed. He is exactly the kind of hypocrite who would criminalise homosexuality rather than face the public scandal of being known to be homosexual.

Obviously, this gives Stevenson a motive for making his death the centrepiece of his novel. It also gives Jekyll a motive for the murder, one that he won't even admit to himself perhaps, but certainly not to Utterson. Carew is part of the Parliament which has passed this same law in 1885, making it even harder for society to accept Jekyll's sexuality. Society's lack of acceptance has led to Jekyll feeling compelled to create Hyde, which is a motive for Jekyll to use Hyde as his murder weapon. It also explains why Hyde appears to experience the murder in sexual imagery, as you have already seen.

The Significance of Names

"In a novel, names are never neutral". David Lodge, Professor of Literature

Doctor Henry Jekyll

Although Jekyll describes himself as a scientist, Stevenson also describes him as a doctor.

Doctors symbolise better health and help for mankind. He exists in juxtaposition to Doctor Lanyon, who chooses to die, in comparison to Jekyll who fights to live. Jekyll's experiments, we might argue, are intended to make life worth living, while Lanyon rejects life because it does not conform to his Christian world view.

The other doctor in the novel, the "Sawbones", experiences the desire to kill Hyde, and blackmails him out of £100. Stevenson unsettles us, and asks us what makes society better? Is it Christian morality, is it science, is it personal liberty?

Henry derives from both Latin and German, carrying the meaning of 'ruler', 'ruler of the house'. He therefore symbolises the ruling classes. The name is most obviously associated with King Henry VIII, who is both a powerful ruler, famously tall and strong, and also famously violent, cruel and revolutionary. He executed three of his wives. He attacked the church, abolishing the rule of the Pope and Catholicism, and replacing it with the Anglican church, frequented by over 90% of Stevenson's readers. Here he represents the dual nature of good and evil quite clearly, and also symbolises how Jekyll overturns Christian belief.

Jekyll is clearly a homophone for 'I kill'. The 'Je' at the start is French for 'I'.

This is quite interesting, because it strongly suggests that Jekyll is the murderer, not Hyde. It tells us that Jekyll wanted Sir Danvers Carew murdered. This is even more likely when we consider that Hyde doesn't kill anyone else, despite Jekyll's claim that he is "pure evil". This is another way Stevenson unsettles us, and forces us to wonder why Jekyll would want to kill Sir Danvers Carew.

Edward Hyde

Edward is also a royal name. There have been eight Edwards as kings of England. This clearly shows him, even numerically, as the alter-ego of Henry – an exact match. It also symbolises how Hyde is also a representation of the ruling classes, the gentlemen of Victorian society. Stevenson implies that they all share Hyde's sinful desires.

It also derives from the Old English Eadweard, meaning the guardian of wealth. This reminds us of course of Jekyll's will, and suggests a symbolic meaning. The wealthy are more like Hyde than they are like Jekyll – they are more evil.

Hyde derives from a large unit of land, a hyde, up to 100 acres needed to keep an extended family in food. This symbolises again how Hyde is natural and human. Again, this unsettles us: the family unit is a bedrock of society, not something we associate with evil.

It is also a homophone for 'hide', symbolising Jekyll's hidden desires. We never find out for certain what these are. But we do know they are common desires which Jekyll is ashamed of because they do not fit with his reputation as a gentleman. Here Stevenson is asking us if they should be hidden, or socially accepted.

The most famous Hyde in London is of course **Hyde Park**. In Stevenson's day it was the centre of London, chosen as the venue of the 1851 Great Exhibition, symbolising Britain's conquest of its Empire. The nobility, the rich, the great and good, would ride there, or visit in their carriages – it symbolises the ruling classes.

It was also created by Henry VIII, again symbolising the link to Henry Jekyll.

But, it was best known perhaps for Speaker's Corner. This part of the park was the centre for free speech, for challenging the establishment, for pursuing the truth. This symbolises Hyde as an uncomfortable truth. The comfortable truth is that we are all sinful, but Christian belief can save us. The uncomfortable truth Stevenson subtly promotes is that there is no God, and we need a different, more tolerant moral code by which to judge human nature and desire.

When Hyde first transforms from Jekyll in daylight it is significantly not at home, but in **Regent's Park**. This is a strong hint that Stevenson wants us to think symbolically, not just with the obvious homophone of 'hide', but through the actual parks. Regent's Park is again royal, created by Henry VIII. Again, it is symbolic of wealth and power in society.

Both parks were created in order to preserve an area of land in which Henry VIII could indulge one of his favourite pastimes, hunting and, of course, killing. This again symbolises man's dual nature as essentially violent.

The park is also famous, even in Stevenson's day, for London Zoo. It is no coincidence that the moment Jekyll loses control and transforms into Hyde is described:

"I sat in the sun on a bench; the animal within me licking the chops of memory".

Victorian readers would be very alert to this symbolism, that we are all descended from animals. This is reinforced geographically, where Jekyll is pretty much as close to animals as a man can get: he is literally next door to the zoo!

Doctor Hastie Lanyon

Hastie is obviously a homophone for 'hasty', suggesting that he acts impulsively. This strongly symbolises Stevenson's disapproval of his choice to die. But it also suggests that his initial split with Jekyll over his "unscientific balderdash" was impetuous and later proved by Jekyll to be wrong.

As a surname, **Hastie** derives from an insult in French, 'hastif', describing someone impulsive. As a forename, it is older, deriving from Old English, meaning "son of the austere man". The dictionary offers these versions of austere: 'severe, stern, strict, harsh, unfeeling, stony, steely, flinty, dour, grim, cold, stiff, stuffy, reserved, remote, distant, unsmiling, unsympathetic, unforgiving, uncharitable' which definitely fit Jekyll's description of him as a "**hide-bound** pedant".

Jekyll calls him a "pedant" three times, and we can perhaps infer that Stevenson shares this view.

However, did you notice the deliberate pun of "hide-bound" which appears twice? The primary meaning is being 'unwilling or unable to change because of tradition or convention'. This is the very society which Stevenson is attacking.

However, bound here also means covered by – it suggests that Lanyon is covered in Hyde – he is just as much a mix of good and evil as Jekyll, and his evil is giving up on life and denying scientific change and progress. Another meaning of "bound" is to move toward, or to jump. Here, Lanyon is moving toward Hyde (an encounter which will lead to his death), but also, in Stevenson's view, leaping toward it, embracing evil by rejecting science.

Lanyon is used ironically. It is an Ancient British name, predating Christianity. Here Stevenson symbolises how Christianity is only a more modern social convention, which he rejects. Giving his most Christian character a non-Christian name is a humorous way of showing this.

Lanyon also derives from London, meaning someone who comes from London. In this way Stevenson again symbolises the corruption, and his own rejection, of London society. The novel attacks this society.

Richard Enfield

Richard derives from German, 'ric' meaning ruler or king, and 'hard' meaning strong and brave. He clearly represents the ruling classes, as Henry and Edward do. There have been three English kings called Richard.

Enfield derives from Old English, meaning open field. This is a symbol for freedom, and our first meeting suggests he enjoys the same freedom as Hyde: they are both coming back from "the end of the world".

But since the 1850s, Enfield is also associated with killing and the expansion of Empire, in the form of the 'Enfield rifle', which enabled British military dominance. This clearly links him symbolically to his desire to kill Hyde, and suggests the violence of the British ruling classes.

Gabriel John Utterson

Gabriel is a Hebrew name, meaning 'God is my strength'. This clearly represents his Christian symbolism in the novel. In Luke's Gospel he also appears to the Virgin Mary, Jesus's future mother, to foretell the births of John the Baptist and Jesus.

He clearly symbolises Christian goodness. However, his role in Christianity is to spread the word, to break secrets, to show a new truth. This is used ironically, because it is the exact opposite of Utterson's behaviour, which is to suppress the truth, and keep it hidden.

Just in case we miss this irony, Stevenson introduces it again with his middle name, John.

John is an obviously Christian name. John the Baptist is a saint, who prepared the way for Jesus, and another John is one of the four disciples who wrote the Gospels, the New Testament of the Bible. Again, his role was to reveal truth, rather than hide it, so it is an ironic name for Utterson.

Since the 1700s John Bull was also a popular personification of England in particular – the name John symbolises Englishness. To a Christian reader, he symbolises all that is good about the rational, loyal, respectable English. To Stevenson he also represents their attraction to sin, to their practice of corruption and hypocrisy, and their suppression of their own desires and pleasures.

Utterson could derive from several different sources, none of which really help us. 'Otter farm' was my favourite one of these, as it links to the animal imagery of the novel, and Utterson as an Otter sneaking around after Hyde would make a great meme. But in the end, I think Utterson appears for its sound.

He is an "utter son" of England – he represents true Englishness and, as a 'son', true male Englishness. So, his goodness and his moral corruption are both symbolic of all English men.

Another interpretation of the surname is ironic, as by now you should expect! If we read it as 'utters on', Stevenson again emphasises the need to "utter", to speak, which links us to the roles of Angel Gabriel and John the Baptist, and John, the writer of the Gospel. Their defining role is to speak, to reveal, to "utter".

Stevenson implies that this ***should*** be Utterson's role. He alone has all the details of Jekyll's life and experiments, but he refuses to pass this on.

The very existence of the novel is an attack on Utterson's behaviour, because it reveals what he would keep secret.

So, he is not the good guy that he seems! When you know that Stevenson has also rejected Christianity, you can also see how he intended us to reject Utterson.

Mr Guest

Guest is of course a homophone for 'guessed'. He has guessed that Jekyll has forged the letter for Hyde, a pun which Stevenson enjoys. However, he indicates that he guesses much more: Utterson remarks that he doesn't keep as many secrets from him as he would like. Nevertheless, he maintains the social convention of keeping a gentleman's secrets. He may guess, but the knowledge is useless to society, because it stays secret.

Mr Poole

Poole had been one of the country's biggest ports in the 1700s, but by the 19th century, its merchants had pretty much ceased trading. It was no longer a great hive of industrial activity or wealth. Perhaps this symbolises the decline of England in Stevenson's mind. Poole, as part of the servant class, is also a symbol of social decline, forced to live a life of servitude rather than independence.

Motifs, Themes and Symbols

Man's Dual Nature

The whole novel is constructed around duality. Obviously, Hyde represents Jekyll's dual nature. Jekyll's house reflects the dual nature of the two men. However, it also reflects the duality of science, where what was once considered immoral now seems like scientific progress for the benefit of mankind .

This suggests that history, like the John Hunter house and story, also has a dual nature, with what is experienced by people living at the time is changed by the perceptions of future generations.

The novel itself has a dual nature. Stevenson the atheist writes a Christian fable, in which the embodiment of evil, Hyde, is punished and killed, and Dr Jekyll, who has created this evil is first tortured by fear, and then punished by death as a sinner who could not resist temptation. He is a warning to us all.

However, beneath the surface we realise that the tragedy of the novel is created by a repressive, Christian society, which Stevenson ultimately rejects. Stevenson wants Jekyll to be able to live a full life of pleasure without social disapproval. Society is so disapproving, however, that Jekyll feels he has to create Hyde.

The Dual Nature of the Detective Story

Stevenson has followed the conventions of a detective story, and the final solution, where all the clues are put together, occurs in the final chapter, through Dr Jekyll's confession. On the other hand, Stevenson refuses to tie up these clues in a neat ending – the opposite of a traditional detective story. We are left instead with troubling questions:

- What secret pleasures did Dr Jekyll want to enjoy when he created Edward Hyde?
- Why does he refuse to tell us what these are, but is happy to narrate the shocking details of the murder of the Danvers Carew?
- What was Hyde's motive in this murder?
- If Hyde exists to experience Jekyll's pleasures for him, what motive might Jekyll have had for the murder?
- If Hyde is the embodiment of evil, why do his assaults on other people leave them unblemished and unharmed (particularly the young girl he supposedly trampled on, and the match seller whom he punched in the face)?
- Why does Hyde not destroy Jekyll's confession or his new will, citing Utterson as a beneficiary?
- Why does Utterson keep Jekyll secrets even after death?

These questions ensure a duality to the detective story, where the mystery appears to be resolved, only to present us with many new mysteries which demand a unifying theory.

My theory, as you will see, is that these questions can all be answered by seeing the novel as a protest against society's legal and moral repression of homosexuality.

I realise that this is culturally quite difficult for some readers to accept. They will have to interpret the novel from a Victorian, Christian perspective. They would argue that Jekyll's explanations have to be accepted as exactly factual – Hyde's illogical behaviour is the consequence of his evil nature, acting on instinct, unable to control his own impulses unless he is controlled by fear of his own capture and death.

But this will inevitably lead to a less rich interpretation of the novel: these readers will have to argue that there is no dual purpose to the novel as a whole, that it is simply a Christian fable, spun in Gothic imagery to match its readers' interests.

All readers will have to decide if Stevenson believed we are all commingled out of good and evil, or that these moral descriptions are merely a convention? Could Victorian society be better if it had different values?

Another duality concerns human nature itself.

- Are we, in evolutionary terms, troglodytes, still animals, or have we evolved beyond this as civilised human beings?
- Is civilised behaviour just a thin veneer, hiding our true, primitive natures underneath?
- Does Stevenson value this kind of civilisation, or does he seek to escape it, as his final years in Samoa suggest?

Silences

These silences are portrayed as a symptom of a corrupt society, thriving on secrecy, where the law does not exist impartially, but to the benefit of the rich and those connected to power.

1. No one can describe Hyde's features, yet Dr Jekyll enjoys them so much that he installs a large mirror in his laboratory so that he can see Edward Hyde when he transforms.

2. The society of the novel is almost exclusively male, but no explanation is given as to why there are no wives or fiancées, no sisters or mothers. (A homosexual theme would explain this).

3. There is no proper explanation for Hyde's motives in killing Carew.

4. Nor why Hyde did not destroy the new will, or Jekyll's letter for Utterson.

5. Why Stevenson also gave Edward Hyde a murder weapon provided by Utterson.

6. Nor is there an explanation why Sir Danvers had a letter for Utterson, and what Stevenson wanted us to understand by these connections.

7. Enfield and Utterson refuse to disclose the identity of Dr Jekyll as the writer of Hyde's cheque. Utterson remains silent about the forgery Jekyll has written in order to protect Hyde. Utterson swears Mr Guest to secrecy, and tells the butler Poole to say nothing while he leaves Hyde's dead body behind in the laboratory.

8. Enfield and Utterson witness Jekyll begin to transform, or perhaps fully transform, into Hyde at his window, but agree never to speak of it.

9. Dr Lanyon also refuses to disclose what Dr Jekyll said to him, and he refuses, as Dr Jekyll does, to leave behind any instructions as to how the scientific experiments which created an alter ego could be repeated by others.

10. Utterson refuses to tell the police about Jekyll's forged letter for Hyde, and he suppresses the details of Jekyll's confession.

Indeed, the whole tragedy of Jekyll's life is that he cannot enjoy his pleasures in public, as others can, because it is not deemed socially acceptable by society. Society's instructions that these pleasures should be hidden, and silence are the root cause of the creation of evil in the novel.

Ultimately Hyde's revenge is to ensure that Utterson preserves a silence around Dr Jekyll's discoveries. Society is not allowed to make this possible scientific advance, which a Christian reader will find to be a just punishment and just precaution against evil. A scientific reader would have the opposite view.

As you have seen, I believe that the solution to all of these is the theme of repressed homosexuality. You don't have to accept that solution at all. However, your grade 9 will be secured by your own explanations for all these silences and questions.

Doors

The novel starts with "The Story of the Door". This would make a brilliant title for Sergent's portrait of Stevenson. When he writes "with that witty touch of Sargent's" we can see that that touch is the open doorway which separates Robert from Fanny. It is literally at the visual centre of the paining, almost as though it is the subject.

Sergent's wit might also allude to the popular meaning of 'Fanny' in English to mean female genitalia. The door represents an escape from 'Fanny', through the doorway, perhaps to another sexuality.

In the novel, the door represents duality – it is the door which admits Hyde into Jekyll's house. But it also allows Jekyll to leave and explore a world of pleasure. It is "blistered and distained", to symbolise Hyde's evil nature.

The "doors" of London's "theatre" are also introduced on the first page, as a symbol of the pleasures which Utterson has refused himself for "twenty years". Perhaps he is in denial of his own dual nature.

When Utterson dreams of Hyde summoning Jekyll to do his bidding, he states "the door of that room would be opened" as though it has not been opened by a person, but by the power of a mysterious force, a desire. It is possibly the sexual desire that Jekyll, Hyde and Utterson all share.

When Hyde has murdered Carew, Utterson finds his half broken walking stick "behind the door". Stevenson could have decided it should be half burned with the papers, or dropped anywhere else in the house, but instead he places it symbolically behind the door for Utterson to find. This links us directly to Utterson who "haunted" the door at Jekyll's rear entrance, and is again symbolic of Utterson's repressed homosexual desires.

The final door is the one smashed down by Utterson and Poole to get to Hyde, a "door covered with red baize". The symbolic "red" suggests the evil of Jekyll and Hyde – remember it is Jekyll's room, only now inhabited by Hyde. It symbolises the imminence of death, but perhaps the natural violence of Poole and Utterson. 'Red' is also symbolic of love and sexual desire. Utterson bursts in hoping to satisfy his desire to find Jekyll. But he is unsatisfied!

In Jekyll's confession, the door also represents the social need for secrecy. Notice that Utterson therefore refuses to smash it in – symbolically, he cannot go against society's desire to keep gentlemen from scandal. Instead, the "elderly" Poole is made to do it.

And of course, the final, implied door is the one to Utterson's safe, where all the documents remain. They preserve Jekyll's secrets, but also save Utterson from association with scandal, so that he can enjoy his inheritance without social disapproval.

It also symbolises his continued repression of his own homosexuality, to keep him "safe" from social disapproval. Perhaps the horde of wealth is also a representation of the size of the void in his emotional life which he is trying to fill. We infer that these riches will make Utterson no happier.

The Structure of the Novel

Understanding why Stevenson introduces information in a particular order will help you answer any question on *tension, mystery, or suspense*.

Chapter 1. The Story of the Door.

This chapter is used to introduce us to the rational but ignorant viewpoint of Gabriel Utterson, from whom we find out what happens in the first 8 chapters. This creates the premise of a detective story, seen from a similar point of view as the ignorant reader. It is a device to help us see all the right clues, but not understand what they mean.

It also introduces the novel's main villain, Mr Edward Hyde, and establishes the Christian theme of the novel, the battle between good and evil.

Through the actions of Enfield and a doctor, Stevenson also introduces the idea that human nature is inherently evil, and that civilised society is only prevented from turning murderous by social customs. It suggests that these customs are weak.

Finally, it serves to introduce the theme of respectability through the secrecy preferred by Enfield and Utterson, the gentlemen, and the vulnerability of gentlemen to blackmail in order to keep their secrets hidden.

Chapter 2. Search for Mr Hyde.

This chapter continues the detective form, as Utterson tries to discover the identity of Hyde and the reason that Jekyll has left him everything in his will.

It also adds a psychological element, by suggesting that Utterson's dreams are worth interpreting.

The setting and subject matter of the dreams serves to give clues as to the nature of the possible blackmail – Jekyll's sexual adventures have probably been homosexual.

This is a red herring, of course, as Jekyll is not being blackmailed by Hyde. However, introducing the theme of homosexuality invites the reader to consider what Stevenson is criticising in society.

The fact of Utterson's dream and his obsession also raises the mystery of Utterson's sexuality.

It introduces Doctor Lanyon, the third doctor in two chapters. This signposts that the novel is deeply concerned with the idea of medical and scientific progress. This is highlighted by the revelation that Lanyon and Jekyll have fallen out over the nature of Jekyll's scientific research.

Utterson's meeting with Hyde is also intended to make the mystery of his relationship with Jekyll a more urgent mystery, because it seems that Hyde intends to murder Jekyll.

Chapter 3. Dr Jekyll Was Quite At Ease.

Utterson at last asks Jekyll about Hyde. However, Jekyll implies that he is not being blackmailed, that he can be rid of Hyde whenever he wants, but that he still wants the terms of the will to be honoured. This invites the reader to wonder if Jekyll and Hyde are in fact secretly lovers, and there is no blackmail at all.

It is anti-climactic in that it suggests there is no mystery to be solved, and perhaps this is not a detective novel after all.

Chapter 4. The Carew Murder Case.

This chapter acts as a sudden shock. A new mystery is introduced, revealing that Hyde has killed a prominent Member of Parliament in an unprovoked, brutal attack. It asks us to consider what Hyde's motive is. Interestingly, Stevenson will never give us this motive – he forces us to come up with our own hypothesis. He will force us to be detectives, without confirming whether we have read the clues correctly.

He also introduces us to another mystery: what has this got to do with Utterson? We find out that the murder weapon was a cane given by Utterson to Jekyll. We also learn that the murdered man was carrying a letter to be posted to Utterson, and Utterson was the victim's lawyer. This is Hyde's only murder victim, and so the connection to Utterson must be an important clue.

Chapter 5. The Incident of the Letter.

Two further mysteries are introduced here. The first is the discovery that Jekyll has forged a letter from Hyde, which claims that he has fled and will never return. We assume even more strongly that Jekyll is in love with Hyde. He also appears very sick, as though Hyde's absence has caused this.

The second is that though he knows Jekyll is covering the tracks of a murderer, he decides not to take this letter to the police, but lock it up forever in his safe. It invites us to wonder if what connects Utterson to Jekyll to Hyde to Sir Danvers Carew is in fact the theme of homosexual love.

By now we have met every major character in the novel: Jekyll, Hyde, Utterson, Lanyon, Enfield, and they are all explicitly single. At this half way point in the novel Stevenson wants us to question why he has done this. It is another clue which he refuses to answer, forcing us to become detectives. It is a clue that the unspoken theme is homosexuality.

Chapter 6. The Incident of Dr. Lanyon.

Although we are expecting a chapter which will concentrate on finding the murderer, Stevenson now confuses us by turning to Doctor Lanyon. It is a way to build suspense.

Jekyll appears to recover for two months but then refuses to receive any visitors. When Utterson tries to find out why from Lanyon, he finds Lanyon has given up on living and is looking forward to death. He refuses to talk about Jekyll.

Within three weeks Lanyon is dead, and has left Utterson a letter to be opened only in the case of Jekyll's death or disappearance.

This introduces a totally new mystery. The disappearance of Jekyll was also a clause in his will. Why does Jekyll imagine disappearing and giving away all his wealth? Why has Lanyon decided to die?

Jekyll has now also locked himself in his house and refuses to see any of his friends, including Utterson.

This is much greater than a murder mystery now. It asks us if there is something more powerful at work, that causes the murder of Carew, the pseudo-suicide of Lanyon and the self-imposed imprisonment of Jekyll. It suggests a more supernatural or gothic solution to the mysteries.

Chapter 7. The Incident At the Window.

This appears to be a very minor incident, especially for a whole chapter. Again, we are expecting a return to the detective genre, and the mystery of Hyde, but there is no mention of him. We get the impression that Stevenson is toying with us.

Instead Enfield and Utterson witness Jekyll transform at the window. We are told he has an expression of "terror". But rather than rush to his aid, Enfield and Utterson walk away quickly, with Utterson repeating "God forgive us" and Enfield refusing to speak.

This strongly points to some supernatural and evil explanation. We are asked to wonder what they have both seen. As usual, Stevenson refuses to tell us.

The mystery of Hyde has now been fully replaced by the mystery of Jekyll.

Chapter 8. The Last Night.

The story appears to end. Poole asks Utterson to help him. He suspects that Jekyll has been killed, and that the murderer is still in the house, locking himself in Jekyll's rooms.

He and Utterson return, and demand entry. The voice which replies is Hyde's. Smashing down the door, they find Hyde's still twitching body. He has taken cyanide to commit suicide. But a further mystery is the disappearance of Jekyll.

At the end, Utterson has completely failed as a detective. However, Jekyll has left a new will giving everything to Utterson, and also leaving a letter of explanation for him to read after Doctor Lanyon's. So we are left with all those unresolved questions:

1. Who was Hyde?
2. Where is Jekyll?
3. What was the reason for the will?
4. Why did Hyde kill Sir Danvers Carew?
5. Why did Jekyll forge a letter for him?
6. Why did Lanyon choose to die?
7. Why did Jekyll stop seeing any of his friends?
8. Why did he decide to give everything to Utterson?

Chapter 9. Doctor Lanyon's Narrative

We read this hoping for an explanation to these questions, especially Lanyon's despair of life and choice to die.

Lanyon narrates how he received a letter from Jekyll with specific instructions about breaking into his cabinet, with the assistance of Jekyll's butler, Poole, and a locksmith, to retrieve a drawer with certain chemicals, and await him at midnight.

Instead of Jekyll, a short, young man arrives. Lanyon admits him, eventually noticing that he feels uncomfortable in the man's presence. However, he offers Lanyon the opportunity to see new scientific knowledge which will make him famous and powerful, or, if he has no wish to do this, the young man advises Lanyon to leave the room.

Lanyon chooses to stay and is astonished to find that when the young man drinks the potion, he transforms in to Doctor Jekyll.

This revelation is sensational. Having seen the case through Utterson's eyes up until now, we expect some reaction from him, but Stevenson refuses to give us this. Again, he forces us to play detective about each character's motive.

Lanyon doesn't fully explain his choice to die. Nor does he tell us what Jekyll and he talked about for an hour. Partly this is to keep us ready for the final chapter, which we will read in Jekyll's own words.

However, it is also to show us that Lanyon is prepared to censor scientific truth. As a scientist he should find out from Jekyll exactly how the science of his experiment worked. It asks us to judge the morality of Lanyon's choices.

Chapter 10. Henry Jekyll's Full Statement of the Case

Doctor Jekyll tells us everything.

However, there are significant gaps. We find out why he created Hyde, and how Hyde came to develop the ability to transform from Jekyll without the aid of drugs.

We find out that Jekyll believes that Hyde is wholly evil, the most evil human being ever created.

We discover Jekyll created Hyde in order to act out his secret vices, but we are never told what these are. We are never told why he really killed Sir Danvers Carew and why he refused to kill anyone else.

And new questions are presented. Why did Hyde leave the new will for Utterson, rather than destroy it? Will Utterson now go to the police?

This device is used to force us to look at the novel much more deeply, and to question the portrayal we have been given. It forces the reader to turn back to the novel and try to read the symbolism of "dual nature" and to question the Christian reading of events which Jekyll promotes. We begin to look for Stevenson's real viewpoint. This viewpoint will give you grades 7 and above.

How to Write Top Grade Essays

What Essay Questions Might You Get?

Is **Jekyll** a tragic hero?

Why is **Hyde** a frightening character?

How does Stevenson present **Utterson**, and what does he represent?

How does Stevenson use **Setting** to captivate the reader? (You can substitute the Gothic genre and Horror for Setting)

How does Stevenson use **Violence** in the novella?

How does the novel explore the **Dual Nature** of man?

How does Stevenson explore the **Conflict between Christianity and Science**? (which will include Lanyon)

How to Plan Your Answer

This is a bit like getting dressed in the morning. I could tell you the most efficient way to do this, having researched whether it is quicker to put your shirt on before your trousers (yes) or your socks on before your underwear (no), but that won't help you.

If you already have a routine, my method will slow you down, because you will have to think about it.

The same is true of planning – keep a method that works for you.

But How Do You Know What Works?

Your plan earns you no marks. None! So, it only serves as a very quick pause in which you think about which ideas will get you most marks.

So, no matter what the question, your plan has to include:

- The writer's purpose or purposes
- The key themes
- Then some notes on how to use these to answer the question
- Then some quotations or events which link to these themes

All this has to be done quickly, in no more than 3 minutes, preferably 2.

To show you how important that is, let me illustrate it with a question.

"How does Stevenson create an atmosphere of fear, or mystery, or suspense in The Strange Case of Doctor Jekyll and Mr Hyde?"

Nothing in that question asks you to write about the author's point of view. And nothing asks you to write about the themes. Many excellent students will write the whole essay, saying nothing which will get them into the top band. WTH. As you can see, this makes me really angry.

One way of looking at this is that the exam board expect you to be able to work this out for yourself – if you are good at literature, you will, and get a high mark, and if you are bad at literature, you won't, and your lower mark will be fair.

That is how the exam board look at it.

Another way of looking at it is it stops too many students getting really high marks, so it is easier to find the top 17% who are going to get a grade 7 and above. Because the exam board are not allowed to give you a top grade just because you have top grade skills.

That's right. The exam board have to give around 17% of students a grade 7 or above. If 30% of students got in the top band, they couldn't all get grade 7 and above even though their skills were good enough! To make grading easier, the exam boards need fewer students to write well enough to get in the top band.

But this guide will make sure you can be one of the 17%!

Let's apply the question above to Jekyll and Hyde.

It's All About the *Why*!

My plan will start with Stevenson's purposes and themes (which are in bold):

1. To entertain a gullible readership.
2. To educate the more intelligent readers about the **hypocrisy of middle class men**.
3. To challenge the **idea of a God**.
4. To allow the gullible readership to read it as a story of God punishing the wicked.
   *I've deliberately left out the theme of homosexuality here, so you can see it is possible to get a top grade without it.

Those are the "why".

So now I try to apply the types of fear to these purposes.

- I can write about Dr Lanyon's fear of a world without God, so that he chooses to die.
- Jekyll's fear of discovery as a hypocrite, with secret desires and habits which would cause a scandal if discovered, so he creates Hyde to live them for him.
- Hyde's fear of death and punishment.
- The reader's fear of scientific discovery, which might suggest the death of God.
- The reader's fear of drug addiction, which is punished in the novel.
- Any sense of fear in the extract, which leads to the reader wondering about any of those things.
- The readers feeling a sense of suspense about what is likely to happen next.

If I don't think about the author's purpose, I am very likely to write mainly about the last bullet point. I will write about **how** fear is presented, but nothing about **why**.

How to Write a Thesis

If you start with a thesis, you will always remember to write about the author's purpose.

Grade 6 Example

Stevenson wrote Jekyll and Hyde in order to explore the dual nature of man's conflict between the evil impulses of his soul, and the Christian desire to do good.

Grade 7 Example

Stevenson exploits the Gothic form in Jekyll and Hyde to dramatise the nature of man's conflict between the evil impulses of his soul, and the Christian desire to do good, and to explore contemporary fears of science.

Grade 8 and 9 Example

Stevenson exploits the Gothic form in Jekyll and Hyde to dramatise the nature of man's conflict between the evil impulses of his soul for his Christian readership. But he subtly suggests that the Christian world view is damaging to society and better replaced by scientific insight and a more liberal morality.

You don't have to have such a detailed thesis, because these are about the whole novel. But a detailed thesis will force you to write a well sequenced argument.

An argument that has more than one viewpoint in it is at least grade 6, as you can see.

Remember, you can memorise each thesis and each essay to use for yourself in the exam. You won't remember it word for word, and it won't be plagiarism. It will just be knowing what to write for any question which comes up.

How to Write an Essay on an Extract

The essays you will read in this guide will work, no matter which exam board you study.

However, most of you will have a question which involves you writing about an extract, and then the rest of the novel.

In the AQA exam, the question asks you to write about the extract first. However, the mark scheme doesn't ask for that: you can write about the novel in any order, with just a couple of references to the extract, or twenty – it doesn't matter, so long as you relate it to the rest of the novel.

You Can Write About the Novel Before the Extract

Why do the examiners not make this clear? Well, they want to do you a favour. They imagine that someone who doesn't know the novel well will be able to score marks by finding something in the extract to write about.

However, this causes lots of problems for students who have studied the novel, but find the language of the extract difficult (60-70% of 16 year olds perhaps!) This kind of student would be much better off ignoring the extract, and making a quick list of everything they know which will answer the topic of the question.

- Number the ideas in your list in the order you want to put them to build an argument.
- 2-3 minutes spent doing this will mean that when you read the extract, you will automatically see links to the ideas you jotted down.
- Write numbers on the extract which correspond to your list.

So, when you get to that part of your essay you know you can add in a quotation and idea from the extract.

If you are already getting grade 7 or more in your essays, you can ignore the method I've outlined. The extract is not a barrier for you.

But, if you are getting grade 6 or below, there is a strong chance that you spend too long reading the extract and wondering what on earth you are going to write about. If that sounds like you, you must try the method I've described.

Write the essay, mark it yourself using the mark scheme in this guide, and then give it to your teacher to mark as well.

Checklist of How to Write a Literature Essay

As you go through the guide, you will notice that I keep reproducing the marks scheme, based around the three assessment objectives. This is to give you practice in how the examiner and your teacher will grade your essay.

But this page is my personal favourite. The mark scheme outlines the skills you must use. This takes the mark scheme and says, "**Ok, but what do I actually have to do? What do these skills look like?**"

Re-read each essay, and see how it has done each of these 12 things. Then you will be able to do them in your own writing.

Mr Salles 12 Step Guide to Getting Grades 7, 8 and 9

1.   Begin an introduction linking the words of the question to the writer's purpose.

2.   Keep exploring the writer's wider purpose – what does his novel suggest about their society?

3.   Always refer to society, as this will always involve the writer's purpose.

4.   Use tentative language to show you are exploring interpretations – e.g. "perhaps".

5.   Use connectives which tell the examiner (and remind you!) that you are dealing with alternative interpretations: although, however.

6.   Embed your quotations within the sentence.

7.   Use words such as suggests, implies, emphasise, reveals, conveys etc, instead of 'shows'.

8.   Use literary language that students of literature at university would also use.

9.   All novels deal in contrast and juxtaposition, or pointing out similarities – use these words.

10.   Always quote from the ending and interpret the ending – this is where the author makes their purpose most clear.

11.   Write a conclusion which deals with how the author wants us to view or change society.

12.   Try to include a quotation in your last sentence.

Analysis and Model Essays

I've structured this part of the guide by chapter, which is why Hyde comes first and Jekyll comes last.

For each Chapter, I have tried to find the extract which is most likely to come up in the exams. With each one, I've given you an exam answer at grade 9, or an essay plan.

For several, I have also given you a grade 6 answer, so that you can see how to progress from grade 6 to grade 9.

How Evil is Edward Hyde?

Read the following extract from Chapter 1 and then answer the question that follows.

In this extract…

"Well, it was this way," returned Mr. Enfield: "I was coming home from some place at the end of the world, about three o' clock of a black winter morning, and my way lay through a part of town where there was literally nothing to be seen but lamps. Street after street, and all the folks asleep — street after street, all lighted up as if for a procession and all as empty as a church — till at last I got into that state of mind when a man listens and listens and begins to long for the sight of a policeman.

All at once, I saw two figures: one a little man who was stumping along eastward at a good walk, and the other a girl of maybe eight or ten who was running as hard as she was able down a cross street.

Well, sir, the two ran into one another naturally enough at the corner; and then came the horrible part of the thing; for the man trampled calmly over the child's body and left her screaming on the ground. It sounds nothing to hear, but it was hellish to see.

It wasn't like a man; it was like some damned Juggernaut. I gave a view-halloa, took to my heels, collared my gentleman, and brought him back to where there was already quite a group about the screaming child. He was perfectly cool and made no resistance, but gave me one look, so ugly that it brought out the sweat on me like running.

The people who had turned out were the girl's own family; and pretty soon, the doctor, for whom she had been sent, put in his appearance. Well, the child was not much the worse, more frightened, according to the Sawbones; and there you might have supposed would be an end to it.

But there was one curious circumstance. I had taken a loathing to my gentleman at first sight. So had the child's family, which was only natural. But the doctor's case was what struck me. He was the usual cut-and-dry apothecary, of no particular age and colour, with a strong Edinburgh accent, and about as emotional as a bagpipe.

Well, sir, he was like the rest of us; every time he looked at my prisoner, I saw that Sawbones turn sick and white with the desire to kill him. I knew what was in his mind, just as he knew what was in mine; and killing being out of the question, we did the next best. We told the man we could and would make such a scandal out of this, as should make his name stink from one end of London to the other. If he had any friends or any credit, we undertook that he should lose them.

And all the time, as we were pitching it in red hot, we were keeping the women off him as best we could, for they were as wild as harpies. I never saw a circle of such hateful faces; and there was the man in the middle, with a kind of black, sneering coolness — frightened too, I could see that — but carrying it off, sir, really like Satan.

'If you choose to make capital out of this accident,' said he, 'I am naturally helpless. No gentleman but wishes to avoid a scene,' says he. 'Name your figure.'

Well, we screwed him up to a hundred pounds for the child's family; he would have clearly liked to stick out; but there was something about the lot of us that meant mischief, and at last he struck. The next thing was to get the money; and where do you think he carried us but to that place with the door? — whipped out a key, went in, and presently came back with the matter of ten pounds in gold and a cheque for the balance on Coutts's, drawn payable to bearer and signed with a name that I can't mention, though it's one of the points of my story, but it was a name at least very well known and often printed.

The figure was stiff; but the signature was good for more than that, if it was only genuine. I took the liberty of pointing out to my gentleman that the whole business looked apocryphal, and that a man does not, in real life, walk into a cellar door at four in the morning and come out of it with another man's cheque for close upon a hundred pounds.

But he was quite easy and sneering. 'Set your mind at rest,' says he, 'I will stay with you till the banks open and cash the cheque myself.' So we all set off, the doctor, and the child's father, and our friend and myself, and passed the rest of the night in my chambers; and next day, when we had breakfasted, went in a body to the bank. I gave in the check myself, and said I had every reason to believe it was a forgery. Not a bit of it. The cheque was genuine."

Question

Using the extract as a starting point, how is the character of Hyde presented and developed?

Approach to the Question

The length of this extract is a good clue that it is packed with quotations to analyse.

Normally I recommend thinking about the rest of the novel first, but in this case there is enough in the extract to start there if you wish.

Analysis

Thesis:

Stevenson portrays Hyde very subtly. He gives his Christian readers an embodiment of evil, which will be apparent in the hyperbole of his language. However, he will ask his more alert readers to realise that Hyde is almost blameless in his early actions, while everyone else behaves in truly evil ways. The real evil is therefore society.

We meet Hyde in the context of Enfield's night time expedition at "three o'clock" in the morning "**from some place at the end of the world**". Stevenson signals that whatever sinful activity Hyde has been up to, Enfield has probably matched him. His attempt to distance himself from this, "at the end of the world" suggests that his vices are so shocking, he places himself as far from them as possible.

Next, we find Hyde is portrayed as an innocent and unthreatening, as "**a little man**" who is moving awkwardly, "stumping" and whose speed is moderate, "at a good walk". Stevenson contrasts this with his apparent victim, who is "running hard". The collision is therefore clearly not his fault.

When she falls, he simply walks on. This can only mean one of his feet lands on her in a single step. However, Enfield describes him hyperbolically. To Stevenson's Christian audience, Enfield's description that Hyde is "**like some damned Juggernaut**" portrays him as essentially evil. But the juxtaposition of "Juggernaut" is clearly ridiculous. A juggernaut is a reference to massive size, which we already know is the opposite of Hyde. Consequently, Stevenson immediately asks us to question the portrayal of Hyde as evil.

Far from being evil, when Enfield restrains him, he "**made no resistance**", and the worst he did, was give Enfield a "look". He is utterly unthreatening.

Now Stevenson describes the astonishing reaction of each of the onlookers, in ways that are absolutely and unquestionably evil. Enfield and the "girl's family" had taken an instant "**loathing**" to Hyde. However, Enfield confesses he is of the same "mind" as the doctor, who turned "**sick and white with the desire to kill**" Hyde.

Because killing is socially unacceptable, they do the "**next best thing**" and blackmail Hyde with the threat of "**scanda**l". An evil man would laugh at such a threat, but a "**gentleman**" would feel vulnerable, because he would have a reputation to uphold. Consequently, at the beginning of the novel, Hyde is the victim of extreme prejudice and abuse.

Next Enfield's own words condemn him in comparison to Hyde, confessing he and the doctor were "**red hot**" in their treatment of him. This allusion points to the idea of torture of Hyde. It is picked up with the image of the women of the family being like "**harpies.**" It's worth looking at the Greek myths to see what this implies. Harpies were sent by Zeus to torment King Pitheus for using his gift of prophecy, seeing into the future. This suggests a divine punishment is being given to Hyde, because he is Jekyll's vision of the future. However, the harpies are symbols of evil, and are eventually driven away by a Greek hero, Jason. Pitheus's punishment is seen as unjust. In this way, Stevenson questions everyone's reaction to Hyde as totally disproportionate and unjust. Their actions become the much greater evil.

Enfield's opinion of him now looks ridiculous. He physically describes Hyde as a victim, "— **frightened too, I could see that — but carrying it off, sir, really**" and we might admire the fact that Hyde is trying not to show his fear. However, astonishingly, Enfield ends that sentence with "**like Satan.**" This is laughable, as though Satan is well known for both being afraid, and being unable to hide the fact that he is afraid.

Stevenson does this to satisfy the Christian reader, who will follow Enfield's language choice as clear proof of Hyde's satanic nature. However, he must expect his more educated readers to see through Enfield's portrayal, and recognise that he and the others are far more evil. This is immediately made obvious when he confesses "**we screwed him out of a hundred pounds**" which was much more than an average worker's annual wages.

And what terrible injuries did this huge sum compensate for? Absolutely none. Stevenson makes sure we know the doctor diagnoses that "**the child was not much the worse**".

Stevenson makes us realise this at the start so that we will be vigilant as the story unfolds. He wants us to keep questioning each observer's account, and concentrate on the known facts.

Consequently, when Utterson wants to meet him, Hyde's reacts to Utterson's request for "a favour" with complete generosity, "**With pleasure.**" His next response is to deceive Hyde, who is astonished, ""**I did not think you would have lied.**" The emphasis on "you" implies again that others are more evil than Hyde. Stevenson does this to point out who is the true gentleman here. It is Hyde.

Utterson's view of Hyde is very different. He remarks, "**the man seems hardly human! Something troglodytic, shall we say**?" Stevenson explores the Christian anxiety around the challenge Darwin's theory of evolution made to Christian faith. But he is also pointing out that Darwin says evolution is only interested in the survival of the fittest. So mankind could easily become "**troglodytic**" again if the environment made this an advantage. Consequently, Stevenson perhaps suggests that the apparent civilization of London does not represent an advance. It is corrupt and hypocritical, and therefore more suited to a brutish kind of man.

Alternatively, he may be holding up a "**cheval glass**" to modern man, pointing out that the "**handsome**" exterior of modern man is a mask. Our more primitive ancestor may have been a better version of ourselves.

This is certainly a plausible interpretation given Stevenson's rejection of western culture and Christian values, which made him choose a more primitive but liberal society to live in when he settled in Samoa.

However, for his Christian audience, Stevenson has to present Hyde as essentially evil. Consequently, Utterson focuses on his appearance, "**I read Satan's signature upon a face**". These readers will trust Utterson. The more discerning readers will find all sorts of ways Stevenson discredits Utterson. Here, we notice his inability to describe Hyde's face. Stevenson points out that it is like a blank canvass on which society paints its own prejudices. Alternatively, it suggests that society refuses to see Hyde for what he is – a version of ourselves. Consequently we refuse to see what is before our eyes.

Hyde also attacks the hypocrisy of Christianity through Doctor Lanyon. Lanyon would rather die believing in an illusion of Christian faith, rather than face the truth that we are not created by God. Stevenson dramatises this by showing Lanyon that Hyde is created by man, in this case Jekyll. It is also a way of dramatising a belief that scientific discovery will one day explain how life was created. He offers Lanyon this knowledge, "**a new province of knowledge and new avenues to fame and power shall be laid open to you**". On the one hand this is a generous act. He is offering up Jekyll's great scientific discovery so that he, not Jekyll, can achieve "**fame and power**".

Hyde is very aware that his power is overtaking Jekyll's right at the start of the novel, when he first meets Utterson. This is why he offers, "**you should have my address**", because he knows Jekyll will soon be unable to transform back from Hyde. Yet still he wants to preserve Jekyll's scientific work for him at this stage.

On the other hand, Stevenson's Christian readers are invited to see this as an exercise in spite. It's Jekyll's professional resentment at Lanyon's earlier dismissal of his scientific discoveries that Hyde, as an evil character, is using to destroy Lanyon. Here Hyde is tempting him with dangerous "**knowledge**" in the same way that Eve tempted Adam with 'the knowledge of good and evil'. To them, Lanyon's desire to escape this view of the world, and choice to die is somehow noble. But whose revenge is it? Not Hyde's. Again, he is carrying out Jekyll's revenge for him.

To Stevenson, it is ludicrous, and he uses Lanyon's death to point out how repressive Christian faith is. In this case, it literally destroys life. Again, Stevenson can't point this out to the majority of his readers who would reject his attack on their faith.

Our most vivid descriptions of Hyde come at the end of the novel from Jekyll, and they are worth an essay of their own. His first transformation into Hyde was:

"**incredibly sweet. I felt younger, lighter, happier in body; within I was conscious of a heady recklessness, a current of disordered sensual images running like a mill-race in my fancy, a solution of the bonds of obligation, an unknown but not an innocent freedom of the soul**".

Nothing in this description sounds evil. The "**sensual images**" are delightful. They also appear natural, like a "**current**". They are "**incredibly sweet**" and like a lost youth, which leaves him feeling "**happier**". The absence of Christian morality makes him feel "**lighter**" and to have "**not an innocent freedom of the soul**". Here he challenges us to think of "**knowledge**" as a way to attain a freedom which is not "innocent". Stevenson here equates innocence with ignorance. In this perspective, Adam and Eve's existence in Eden was bland, "innocent" but without "knowledge". There was nothing "sweet" in it.

Hyde's freedom is also from the "**bonds of obligation**". He portrays society's values as a form of bondage. Another way of interpreting this description of Hyde is to notice how exactly it matches the mind of a writer. "**The disordered sensual images running like a mill-race**" is exactly how he has structured his novel, around vivid "**images**". He has deliberately disrupted the natural order, where the beginning of the story is not revealed until the final chapter. He doesn't allow us to discover that Jekyll and Hyde are the same man until the previous chapter. It shows how he identifies with Hyde.

Jekyll's description of Hyde is contradictory. For the Christian readership, Stevenson makes him describe Hyde as wholly evil, "**Evil besides (which I must still believe to be the lethal side of man) had left on that body an imprint of deformity and decay**."

But the brackets reveal Stevenson's detachment from this view – we are listening to Jekyll trying to convince himself that the Christian division of the world into good and evil is real. This panders to a Christian readership, but also reveals Stevenson's disagreement with it. Jekyll reveals this when he describes seeing Hyde for the first time, "**I was conscious of no repugnance, rather of a leap of welcome. This, too, was myself. It seemed natural and human.**"

This is exactly Stevenson's point. Hyde's desires are "**natural and human**". It is only society which portrays them as evil, whatever they are. This is emphasised further in Jekyll's description of how others respond to Hyde, "**at first**" with "**a visible misgiving of the flesh. This, as I take it, was because all human beings, as we meet them, are commingled out of good and evil: and Edward Hyde, alone in the ranks of mankind, was pure evil**."

Although this conforms to the Christian view, notice how he says this happens only "**at first**". Notice again the strange contrast in the words "pure" and "evil". Again, Stevenson asks us to question if the concept of an "evil" nature actually exists.

This brings us to the evil act of killing Sir Danvers Carew. This is the most fascinating incident in the novel, because it is wholly unexplained. Hyde's attack seems entirely without motive. This fits entirely with the Christian narrative. He kills because he is "**pure evil**". Further proof of this evil is the contrast with Sir Danvers, who appears "**innocent**", "**beautiful**", perhaps angelic. Hyde's attack is presented as unprovoked, "**And then all of a sudden he broke out in a great flame of anger**". The metaphorical "**flame of anger**" invites a Christian readership to associate Hyde with the "great" fires of hell.

I'll analyse this passage separately when we consider the theme of homosexuality in this novel. For now, however, we can ignore that.

We can clearly see that Stevenson is challenging us to provide a motive. The Christian reader doesn't need to – killing without a motive is the very definition of "pure evil". But Stevenson hints at it at the beginning of the chapter, "**NEARLY a year later, in the month of October, 18—-, London was startled by a crime of singular ferocity and rendered all the more notable by the high position of the victim.**" This strongly hints at the probability that this was an attack both the ruling classes and parliament, as the makers of law. These, like the Church, are the guardians of what is socially acceptable and moral. Hyde attacks Carew perhaps because he is appalled at what society and parliament consider to be moral.

There is also a real clue to motive in the timing, "**nearly a year later.**"

Moreover, it is worth remembering that Hyde has spent nearly a year *not* killing anyone. This strongly implies that it is the 1885 'gross indecency' Act which has changed Hyde's behaviour.

For two months, Hyde has been in worse than solitary confinement. He has been imprisoned, isolated from the world, inside Jekyll. Much worse than this, he has been forced to experience life as Jekyll, denying his own true nature. It is with great rage at this injustice, perhaps even a madness, that he is now released.

The murder, of course, cannot be justified – murder is always an evil act. However, it is not the act of a person who is "pure evil". If it is Hyde's choice alone, it is the act of someone who has been broken by his treatment at the hands of Jekyll. Jekyll feels "**pity**" for Hyde for that very reason, writing that when Hyde has to escape by becoming Jekyll, it is "**temporary suicide**", a total loss of the "**self**". And of course, the only reason Jekyll has imprisoned him, is his fear of society. Hyde lives out the experiences Jekyll longs to have, but cannot because social morality says he can't.

We must also consider why Hyde was created: to live out and experience Jekyll's secret desires. This strongly suggests, as we shall see later, that the murder of Carew may not be a random act, but one that satisfies Jekyll, not just Hyde.

This also explains why Hyde attacks Jekyll's Christian texts, "**scrawling in my own hand blasphemies on the pages of my books.**" Christians will see this as further proof of his "**pure evil**". But keener readers will notice Jekyll's real fear, that this is written in his "**own hand**". In other words, these "**blasphemies**" are exactly what he should think. In this way, Stevenson is pointing out that Hyde is just like Jekyll. Like him, he can't publicly attack Christian faith, because this will alienate the vast majority of his readers. Instead, like Jekyll, he can only express his true desires through Hyde.

Stevenson doesn't finally deny that Hyde becomes evil. But his point is that society has driven Hyde to it, and in particular a Christian society which sees the world falsely as a battle between good and evil, "**God**" and "**Satan**". We can point to this in all sorts of biographical ways, including his choice to live away from London, and his final choice to live in the more "**primitive**" but much less restrictive Samoa. Stevenson, like Hyde, knew he was trying to escape "**the gallows**". For Stevenson it was his brain aneurism and his lung disease. Stevenson could be described by the very words Jekyll uses to describe Hyde, "**But his love of life is wonderful.**" This is a strong clue that Stevenson sympathises with Hyde.

This is his ultimate challenge to the reader. Is a love of life a definition of evil? If it is, perhaps society has got its definition of evil wrong. Perhaps Victorian society is the "**self-destroyer**", and the dying Hyde represents society's true "**face**".

What are the Key Events Involving Hyde?

This analysis comes from the following extract. You can use these to test your understanding of the analysis, and to make your own notes.

From Chapter 2 SEARCH FOR MR. HYDE

Hyde and Utterson, the first meeting.

"On your side," said Mr. Utterson, "will you do me a favour?"

"With pleasure," replied the other. "What shall it be?"

"Will you let me see your face?" asked the lawyer.

Mr. Hyde appeared to hesitate, and then, as if upon some sudden reflection, fronted about with an air of defiance; and the pair stared at each other pretty fixedly for a few seconds. "Now I shall know you again," said Mr. Utterson. "It may be useful."

"Yes," returned Mr. Hyde, "it is as well we have met; and a propos, you should have my address." And he gave a number of a street in Soho.

"Good God!" thought Mr. Utterson, "can he, too, have been thinking of the will?" But he kept his feelings to himself and only grunted in acknowledgment of the address.

"And now," said the other, "how did you know me?"

"By description," was the reply.

"Whose description?"

"We have common friends," said Mr. Utterson.

"Common friends?" echoed Mr. Hyde, a little hoarsely. "Who are they?"

"Jekyll, for instance," said the lawyer.

"He never told you," cried Mr. Hyde, with a flush of anger. "I did not think you would have lied."

...

God bless me, the man seems hardly human! Something troglodytic, shall we say? or can it be the old story of Dr. Fell? or is it the mere radiance of a foul soul that thus transpires through, and transfigures, its clay continent? The last, I think; for, O my poor old Harry Jekyll, if ever I read Satan's signature upon a face, it is on that of your new friend."

From Chapter 9 DR. LANYON'S NARRATIVE

Hyde tempting Dr Lanyon into seeing him transform.

"And now," said he, "to settle what remains. Will you be wise? will you be guided? will you suffer me to take this glass in my hand and to go forth from your house without further parley? or has the greed of curiosity too much command of you?

Think before you answer, for it shall be done as you decide. As you decide, you shall be left as you were before, and neither richer nor wiser, unless the sense of service rendered to a man in mortal distress may be counted as a kind of riches of the soul.

Or, if you shall so prefer to choose, a new province of knowledge and new avenues to fame and power shall be laid open to you, here, in this room, upon the instant; and your sight shall be blasted by a prodigy to stagger the unbelief of Satan."

From Chapter 4 THE CAREW MURDER CASE

Hyde's Soho home.

Mr. Hyde had only used a couple of rooms; but these were furnished with luxury and good taste. A closet was filled with wine; the plate was of silver, the napery elegant; a good picture hung upon the walls, a gift (as Utterson supposed) from Henry Jekyll, who was much of a connoisseur; and the carpets were of many plies and agreeable in colour.

From Chapter 4 THE CAREW MURDER CASE

Hyde's killing of Carew

When they had come within speech (which was just under the maid's eyes) the older man bowed and accosted the other with a very pretty manner of politeness. It did not seem as if the subject of his address were of great importance; indeed, from his pointing, it sometimes appeared as if he were only inquiring his way; but the moon shone on his face as he spoke, and the girl was pleased to watch it, it seemed to breathe such an innocent and old-world kindness of disposition, yet with something high too, as of a well-founded self-content.

Presently her eye wandered to the other, and she was surprised to recognise in him a certain Mr. Hyde, who had once visited her master and for whom she had conceived a dislike. He had in his hand a heavy cane, with which he was trifling; but he answered never a word, and seemed to listen with an ill-contained impatience.

And then all of a sudden he broke out in a great flame of anger, stamping with his foot, brandishing the cane, and carrying on (as the maid described it) like a madman. The old gentleman took a step back, with the air of one very much surprised and a trifle hurt; and at that Mr. Hyde broke out of all bounds and clubbed him to the earth.

And next moment, with ape-like fury, he was trampling his victim under foot and hailing down a storm of blows, under which the bones were audibly shattered and the body jumped upon the roadway. At the horror of these sights and sounds, the maid fainted.

From Chapter 10 HENRY JEKYLL'S FULL STATEMENT OF THE CASE

Jekyll's first impression of Hyde

There was something strange in my sensations, something indescribably new and, from its very novelty, incredibly sweet. I felt younger, lighter, happier in body; within I was conscious of a heady recklessness, a current of disordered sensual images running like a mill-race in my fancy, a solution of the bonds of obligation, an unknown but not an innocent freedom of the soul. I knew myself, at the first breath of this new life, to be more wicked, tenfold more wicked, sold a slave to my original evil; and the thought, in that moment, braced and delighted me like wine. I stretched out my hands, exulting in the freshness of these sensations; and in the act, I was suddenly aware that I had lost in stature.

There was no mirror, at that date, in my room; that which stands beside me as I write, was brought there later on and for the very purpose of these transformations. The night, however, was far gone into the morning—the morning, black as it was, was nearly ripe for the conception of the day—the inmates of my house were locked in the most rigorous hours of slumber; and I determined, flushed as I was with hope and triumph, to venture in my new shape as far as to my bedroom.

I crossed the yard, wherein the constellations looked down upon me, I could have thought, with wonder, the first creature of that sort that their unsleeping vigilance had yet disclosed to them; I stole through the corridors, a stranger in my own house; and coming to my room, I saw for the first time the appearance of Edward Hyde.

I must here speak by theory alone, saying not that which I know, but that which I suppose to be most probable. The evil side of my nature, to which I had now transferred the stamping efficacy, was less robust and less developed than the good which I had just deposed.

Again, in the course of my life, which had been, after all, nine-tenths a life of effort, virtue, and control, it had been much less exercised and much less exhausted. And hence, as I think, it came about that Edward Hyde was so much smaller, slighter, and younger than Henry Jekyll.

Even as good shone upon the countenance of the one, evil was written broadly and plainly on the face of the other. Evil besides (which I must still believe to be the lethal side of man) had left on that body an imprint of deformity and decay. And yet when I looked upon that ugly idol in the glass, I was conscious of no repugnance, rather of a leap of welcome. This, too, was myself. It seemed natural and human. In my eyes it bore a livelier image of the spirit, it seemed more express and single, than the imperfect and divided countenance I had been hitherto accustomed to call mine. And in so far I was doubtless right.

I have observed that when I wore the semblance of Edward Hyde, none could come near to me at first without a visible misgiving of the flesh. This, as I take it, was because all human beings, as we meet them, are commingled out of good and evil: and Edward Hyde, alone in the ranks of mankind, was pure evil.

From Chapter 8 THE LAST NIGHT

Hyde's fear of death and desperation for drugs.

All this last week (you must know) him, or it, or whatever it is that lives in that cabinet, has been crying night and day for some sort of medicine and cannot get it to his mind.

From Chapter 10 HENRY JEKYLL'S FULL STATEMENT OF THE CASE

Hyde's taunting of Jekyll and his Christian texts.

The hatred of Hyde for Jekyll, was of a different order. His terror of the gallows drove him continually to commit temporary suicide, and return to his subordinate station of a part instead of a person; but he loathed the necessity, he loathed the despondency into which Jekyll was now fallen, and he resented the dislike with which he was himself regarded.

Hence the ape-like tricks that he would play me, scrawling in my own hand blasphemies on the pages of my books, burning the letters and destroying the portrait of my father; and indeed, had it not been for his fear of death, he would long ago have ruined himself in order to involve me in the ruin. But his love of life is wonderful; I go further: I, who sicken and freeze at the mere thought of him, when I recall the abjection and passion of this attachment, and when I know how he fears my power to cut him off by suicide, I find it in my heart to pity him.

From Chapter 10 HENRY JEKYLL'S FULL STATEMENT OF THE CASE

Hyde's suicide.

Right in the midst there lay the body of a man sorely contorted and still twitching. They drew near on tiptoe, turned it on its back and beheld the face of Edward Hyde. He was dressed in clothes far too large for him, clothes of the doctor's bigness; the cords of his face still moved with a semblance of life, but life was quite gone; and by the crushed phial in the hand and the strong smell of kernels that hung upon the air, Utterson knew that he was looking on the body of a self-destroyer.

Edward Hyde Essay

It is a good idea, even if your exam board bases the question around an extract, to practise writing revision essays as proper essays, just considering the novel as a whole.

How does Stevenson present Mr Hyde as a frightening character?

Stevenson presents Hyde as a frightening character in several ways. The language used to describe Hyde portrays him as fundamentally '**evil**' and '**unhuman**'. Stevenson also uses contrast throughout the novella, emphasising Hyde's '**savage**' nature. Most prominently, a key motif throughout is the duality of man, represented by Hyde being part of Jekyll. This makes Hyde even more frightening as Stevenson reminds the readers that '**evil**' is a part of all of us.

When Utterson first comes face to face with Hyde, he uses sibilance to describe Hyde's laugh as he '**snarled…a savage laugh**'. This sibilance implies Hyde's sinister nature. The word '**savage**' further emphasises Hyde's threatening persona and portrays Hyde as uncivilised. Throughout this extract, Stevenson refers to Mr Utterson most often, as '**the lawyer**'. Lawyers were well respected men and the height of sophistication. By referring to Utterson as "**the Lawyer**", he creates a sharp contrast with Hyde, who '**gave an impression of deformity**'. This further portrays Hyde as an outsider, someone who does not conform to the rules of society, which would have been particularly frightening to Victorian gentlemen at the time.

Furthermore, Utterson suggests Hyde's darkness is more deep-rooted than the '**flush of anger**' or the '**savage laugh**'. He describes Hyde's face bearing '**Satan's signature**'. This reference to the devil implies Hyde's innate evil. However, the signature which is later associated with Hyde is recognised as forged by Dr Jekyll. As Jekyll later explains, the only physical aspect Hyde retains from Jekyll is '**my own hand**', his handwriting. Therefore, '**Satan's signature**' is that of Dr Jekyll's. Perhaps Stevenson is suggesting that Jekyll too is truly '**evil**', as he creates a '**creature**' who he is a '**rare luxury**', carrying out his '**secret pleasures**'.

These '**pleasures**' are often uncivilised and sinful. During the rising action in the novella, Hyde performs his most sinful act yet, he murders. The account of the murder is delivered to us by the maid who describes the victim as full of '**old-world kindness**' and the murderer as a '**madman…with ape-like fury**'. This '**old-world kindness**' highlights the innocence of the victim and subsequently emphasises Hyde's frightening character and the monstrosity of his cruel act. The reference to '**ape-like**' is consistent with the '**creature**' which Hyde is often referred to as. It also suggests that he is not as evolved as his upper-class counterpart, Dr Jekyll. In fact, Victorian upper-class gentlemen often believed that they were more evolved than the rest of society. This reference to Hyde as '**ape-like**' supports the common misconception, made by the Upper-class gentlemen, that the lower classes and those who commit crime, are less evolved.

After the murder, Hyde returns to his '**dark and dingy**' residence in Soho. Not only does Stevenson use alliteration to accentuate the darkness of Hyde's house, reflecting his '**dark**' character, he also deliberately notes that Hyde resides in Soho. In the 1800s, Soho was associated with poverty and immorality. Thus, for people reading the novella at the time it was published, this association with the immoral Soho, would have portrayed Hyde as even more frightening.

Ultimately, Hyde is most frightening because Stevenson reminds us that evil resides in all of us, just as Hyde resides in Jekyll. Jekyll's biggest revelation, and the one that encourages him to create Hyde, is the belief that **'man is not truly one, but two'**. This suggests the duality of man, the belief that man is both good and evil.

In Jekyll's letter, he creates the image of an internal **'war'** describing his **'two natures that contended on the field'**. The **'field'** implies a battlefield in which no man shall prosper. Although both sides of Jekyll technically die simultaneously, Jekyll eventually succumbs to Hyde's will and brings his own **'unhappy life...to an end'**.

Hyde would then be free to act **'centred on self'**, to think about no others and do only what pleases him. Stevenson is suggesting that as we let our **'devil**(s)**'** grow, we lose control of our **'gentle'** nature and submit to the temptations of selfish **'pleasures'**. This is what makes Hyde particularly frightening, the suggestion that there is a Hyde in all of us, that we too can succumb to our innate immoral drives.

In conclusion, Stevenson presents Hyde as a particularly frightening individual through using contrasting language. Not only is there a contrast between the victim and the murderer (Hyde) but the most obvious contrast is between Hyde and Jekyll. Furthermore, Hyde's actions are unlawful and do not conform to the Upper-class circles he is surrounded by. Perhaps most notably, Hyde is particularly frightening because he represents the evil part of man, which Stevenson suggests dwells in even the most respected of individuals.

776 Words

Grades 7, 8 and 9

AO1

1. A well-structured argument which begins with a thesis.
2. Each paragraph is ordered to build the argument to prove your thesis.
3. Explores at least two interpretations of the character or the author's purpose.
4. You pick really good evidence, or quotations, to back up your argument or interpretations.
5. You write about the full task, which always includes the ending of the text.

AO2

6. Your interpretations of quotations look at individual words and phrases.
7. You sometimes find more than one interpretation of the same quotation.
8. You interpret how the form of the text shapes the way the author wants readers to understand it.
9. You interpret how the structure of the text shapes the way the author wants readers to understand it.
10. You use just the right terminology a student of literature needs to explain ideas.

AO3

11. You write about more than one interpretation. So your thesis argues why one interpretation is better than another.
12. You use details from the author's life, or society, or literature at the time to back up your interpretation.
13. Your conclusion sums up why you have picked one interpretation as more convincing than another. It shows why your thesis is correct.

Student Reflection

I think my understanding and knowledge of how to answer a question to meet exam criteria has developed significantly. Whilst writing this essay, I had in mind the importance of commenting on *structure, purpose and context.*

Although I think I struggled with commenting on structure, I did succeed in combing context into my answer and noting the author's purpose/effect on the reader. I think I have gotten significantly more confident in writing these answers than I was when writing the 'Lord of the Flies' essay. I am now able to complete an essay in less time also, just as I would be asked to do in the exam.

Additionally, since the beginning of the course I think my use of literary terms has improved; I would have not even considered using terms like 'novella' or 'motif' in an essay before.

You can see from this self-assessment, that I think it is the best way to improve in your essays.

Examiner's Comments: Your Turn

I'm not going to write these for you in the exam, so this is a really useful essay for you to practise on. Use the mark scheme above to work out how to grade the essay. It will certainly get into the top band.

Find which bullet points are done less well. If you can mark it, you can write an even better essay, and nail these skills in the exam.

You should notice that this student has not read my guide, and has not been taught this text by me. This means she includes nothing about Stevenson's dual purpose, or his atheism. She treats the novel entirely at face value, as a Christian allegory promoting good and challenging evil in the English upper classes.

The good news is that you can get a top grade doing that. The even better news is that you can see how including the ideas from this guide are going to blow the examiner away, and suggest you have a far deeper understanding of the novel than a normal top grade student!

Grade 6 Essay

Grade 6 Mark Scheme

1. **All your explanations are clear**
2. Focus on the full task, everything in the question
3. Make a range of points
4. Choose relevant references (examples and quotations)
5. Link these to your explanations
6. Comment on a range of methods which the writer uses
7. Show how this affects the reader's thoughts and ideas about a character or a theme
8. Use **relevant and appropriate** terminology to discuss literature, with a greater number
9. Explain **several** relevant contextual factors.
10. **Link these to the writer's perspectives and ideas**

In 2018, Grade 6 started at 61%.

(Bold indicates the difference between grade 5 and grade 6)

Question

Using the extract as a starting point, how is the character of Hyde presented and developed?

Stevenson portrays Hyde for his Christian readers as an embodiment of evil, through hyperbole. Because Hyde is a gentleman's alter ego, Stevenson suggests that all Victorian gentleman share the same vices as Hyde.

Stevenson tells us Enfield has come from "the end of the world" which implies he has given in to similar vices as Hyde.

Hyde appears innocent, "a little man" who is only, "stumping" along when a girl collides with him, "running hard". It is clearly not his fault.

However, Enfield describes him hyperbolically "like some damned Juggernaut." This doesn't fit with his smallness, nor with the lack of damage to the girl: "the child was not much the worse". Therefore we assume it is not his size, but Hyde's enormous evil which causes others to hate him.

Enfield confesses he and the doctored shared "the desire to kill" Hyde. They do the "next best thing" and blackmail Hyde with the threat of "scandal".

The women are compared to "harpies" who torture people who deserve punishment in Greek myth. Enfield makes us aware of his extreme evil by describing Hyde as "like Satan."

Christian readers would understand Enfield's blackmail of Hyde: "we screwed him out of a hundred pounds" and see this great sum as a reflection of how evil Hyde must be to appear so terrible at first sight.

Stevenson links his evil nature to evolution when Utterson describes him as "hardly human! Something troglodytic..?" Here Stevenson explores Christian anxiety around the challenge Darwin's theory of evolution made to Christian faith. Many Christian's would view these apparent scientific discoveries as evil.

Stevenson also uses Dr Lanyon to reinforce the Christian message. Consequently, Lanyon would rather die than live in a world where science can create a Hyde. He fears that scientific discovery is going too far, and "new province of knowledge" will, like Hyde, make us all more evil. Horrified, Lanyon simply gives up on life.

Jekyll presents Hyde's desires are "natural and human". Stevenson is therefore reinforcing the message of Original Sin, suggesting that only Christian faith can prevent us from giving in to all our innate and universal sinful desires. He might be arguing that the turn away from Christianity, and the acceptance of scientific explanations for life, is a terrible danger and will make us behave in sinful ways.

This is symbolised by the evil act of killing Sir Danvers Carew. Hyde's attack seems entirely without motive. To Christians, he kills because he is "pure evil". He also describes the murder as carried out "with ape-like fury" to remind us that, without Christianity, we can so easily revert back to primitive savagery. This warns us that if evolution is true, preserving Christian morality is even more important in guarding against our primitive desires.

Because of this, Hyde is punished in the novel and becomes a "self-destroyer". This also punishes Jekyll, who loses his life to Hyde, defeated by his own dangerous and immoral scientific experiments. This is a warning that society should turn away from scientific discovery, and embrace Christian values.

506 words

Question

Using the extract as a starting point, how is the character of Hyde presented and developed?

Thesis

Stevenson portrays Hyde for his Christian readers as an embodiment of evil, through hyperbole. However, sophisticate readers will see through this, and recognise Hyde is almost blameless in his early actions, while everyone else behaves in truly evil ways. Consequently Stevenson blames society for any evil in Hyde, showing that he is created by its Christian oppression of natural desire.

At first, Stevenson signals that Hyde's sinful activity is probably matched by Enfield who has come from "**the end of the world**".

Hyde appears innocent, "**a little man**" who is only, "**stumping**" along when a girl collides with him, "**running hard**". It is clearly not his fault.

However, Enfield describes him hyperbolically "**like some damned Juggernaut.**" This juxtaposition is clearly ridiculous compared to Hyde's smallness. When Enfield restrains him, he "**made no resistance**", giving him only a "**look**". He is utterly unthreatening. Stevenson even points out "**the child was not much the worse**" and completely unharmed.

Now Stevenson describes the onlookers as unquestionably evil. Enfield confesses he and the doctored shared "**the desire to kill**" Hyde. They do the "**next best thing**" and blackmail Hyde with the threat of "**scandal**". An evil man would laugh at such a threat, but he is clearly a victim of a real crime.

The women are compared to "**harpies**" who were evil and inhuman torturers in Greek myth, suggesting they are far more evil than Hyde.

Enfield actually describes Hyde as a victim, "**— frightened too, I could see that — but carrying it off, sir, really**" and we might expect a note of praise. However, astonishingly, Enfield continues with "**like Satan.**" This is laughable. Satan has no history of showing fear.

Stevenson does this to satisfy the Christian reader, who will follow Enfield's language choice as clear proof of Hyde's satanic nature. However, sophisticated readers will see Enfield as evil, as he confesses "**we screwed him out of a hundred pounds**", which astonishingly was much more than an average worker's annual wages.

Even Utterson lies to Hyde, who is only doing him a favour, "**with pleasure**". Hyde's shock, "**I did not think you would have lied**" suggests Hyde is more moral. Yet Utterson describes him as "**hardly human! Something troglodytic..?**"

Here Stevenson explores Christian anxiety around the challenge Darwin's theory of evolution made to Christian faith. Stevenson's rejection of western culture and Christian values, which made him choose a more primitive but liberal society to live in when he settled in Samoa, suggests he prefers the "**troglodytic**" Hyde to the veneer of civilization presented by Jekyll and Utterson.

However, for his Christian audience, Stevenson has to present Hyde as essentially evil. Consequently, Utterson focuses on his appearance, "**I read Satan's signature upon a face**". But to other readers, he has already discredited Utterson, and Stevenson implies that Hyde's face is a blank canvass on which Christians can paint their prejudices.

Stevenson instead presents Hyde in his own lodgings as having "**good taste**" and the instincts of "**a connoisseur**". This obviously suggests his other tastes may not criminal or immoral vices, or not more so than any other gentleman.

Alternatively, Stevenson may use this description to point out that all middle class men hide behind this veneer of respectability, even Hyde. This will help a Christian narrative, which is trying to root out immoral behaviour in everyone, no matter what their social status.

Hyde also attacks the hypocrisy of Christianity through Doctor Lanyon. Lanyon would rather die believing in an illusion of Christian faith, rather than face the truth that we are not created by God. Stevenson dramatises this by showing Lanyon that Hyde is created by man, offering "**a new province of knowledge**". Horrified, Lanyon simply gives up on life.

Stevenson contrasts this with Hyde's sense of joy. His "**sensual images**" are delightful and natural. The absence of Christian morality makes him feel "**lighter**" and to have "**not an innocent freedom of the soul**". Here he challenges us to think of "**knowledge**" as a way to attain a freedom which is not "**innocent**". Hyde's desires are "**natural and human**". It is only society which portrays them as evil.

This brings us to the evil act of killing Sir Danvers Carew. Hyde's attack seems entirely without motive. To Christians, he kills because he is "**pure evil**". But Stevenson is challenging us to provide a motive. The Christian reader doesn't need to – killing without a motive is the very definition of "**pure evil**". But Stevenson tells us Hyde has been imprisoned inside Jekyll, which is a "**temporary suicide**". This inhumane imprisonment is caused by Jekyll's fear of society's morals.

In refusing to give Hyde a motive for this killing, Stevenson invites us to see it as a symbolic attack on Parliament which had in that same year, 1885, published an Act attacking homosexuality.

Stevenson suggests Christian society has driven Hyde to act this way, by repressing his desires. Stevenson therefore rejects this Christian society, choosing "**primitive**" but much less restrictive Samoa. Just like Hyde, Stevenson's "**love of life is wonderful**."

This is his ultimate challenge to the reader. Is a love of life a definition of evil? If it is, perhaps society has got its definition of evil wrong. Perhaps Victorian society is the "**self-destroyer**", and the dying Hyde represents society's true "**face**".

877 words

How Good is Utterson?

From Chapter 1 STORY OF THE DOOR

"MR. UTTERSON the lawyer was a man of a rugged countenance, that was never lighted by a smile; cold, scanty and embarrassed in discourse; backward in sentiment; lean, long, dusty, dreary, and yet somehow lovable. At friendly meetings, and when the wine was to his taste, something eminently human beaconed

from his eye; something indeed which never found its way into his talk, but which spoke not only in these silent symbols of the after-dinner face, but more often and loudly in the acts of his life.

He was austere with himself; drank gin when he was alone, to mortify a taste for vintages; and though he enjoyed the theatre, had not crossed the doors of one for twenty years. But he had an approved tolerance for others; sometimes wondering, almost with envy, at the high pressure of spirits involved in their misdeeds; and in any extremity inclined to help rather than to reprove.

"I incline to Cain's heresy," he used to say quaintly: "I let my brother go to the devil in his own way." In this character, it was frequently his fortune to be the last reputable acquaintance and the last good influence in the lives of down-going men. And to such as these, so long as they came about his chambers, he never marked a shade of change in his demeanour.

No doubt the feat was easy to Mr. Utterson; for he was undemonstrative at the best, and even his friendship seemed to be founded in a similar catholicity of good-nature. It is the mark of a modest man to accept his friendly circle ready-made from the hands of opportunity; and that was the lawyer's way. His friends were those of his own blood or those whom he had known the longest; his affections, like ivy, were the growth of time, they implied no aptness in the object.

Hence, no doubt, the bond that united him to Mr. Richard Enfield, his distant kinsman, the well-known man about town. It was a nut to crack for many, what these two could see in each other, or what subject they could find in common. It was reported by those who encountered them in their Sunday walks, that they said nothing, looked singularly dull, and would hail with obvious relief the appearance of a friend. For all that, the two men put the greatest store by these excursions, counted them the chief jewel of each week, and not only set aside occasions of pleasure, but even resisted the calls of business, that they might enjoy them uninterrupted."

Analysis

Utterson's physical appearance foreshadows his dual nature, so that his face "**was never lighted by a smile**". His personality is also "**cold**" and "**dreary, and yet somehow loveable.**" This feels both like a contradiction and highly unlikely. It puts the reader on alert to find what could make him "**loveable**".

We find that it is in his actions which, Stevenson hints, may be corrupt. Consequently, "**it was frequently his fortune to be the last reputable acquaintance and the last good influence in the lives of down-going men**". The alliterative "**frequently his fortune**" reveals how he must seek out such down going men, and he counts himself fortunate to have found them. In fact, we can assume his fascination with Jekyll is a fascination with the most "**downward going**" of all men, through his creation of Hyde.

So frequently is he attracted to this immoral behaviour of others, that he has developed a catch phrase for the occasion, ""**I incline to Cain's heresy," he used to say quaintly: "I let my brother go to the devil in his own way."**"

Although others in this society seem to admire him for his tolerance, Stevenson might want us to react differently. Cain jealously murdered his more preferred brother, Able. This is a direct parallel in Hyde, symbolically, murdering Jekyll. Or, of Jekyll, through Hyde, murdering an even more respected Sir Danvers Carew. Stevenson may want us to be highly critical of this tolerance of others' immoral behaviour and their crimes.

From Chapter 2 SEARCH FOR MR. HYDE

That evening Mr. Utterson came home to his bachelor house in sombre spirits and sat down to dinner without relish. It was his custom of a Sunday, when this meal was over, to sit close by the fire, a volume of some dry divinity on his reading-desk, until the clock of the neighbouring church rang out the hour of twelve, when he would go soberly and gratefully to bed.

On this night, however, as soon as the cloth was taken away, he took up a candle and went into his business-room. There he opened his safe, took from the most private part of it a document endorsed on the envelope as Dr. Jekyll's Will, and sat down with a clouded brow to study its contents. The will was holograph, for Mr. Utterson, though he took charge of it now that it was made, had refused to lend the least assistance in the making of it; it provided not only that, in case of the decease of Henry Jekyll, M.D., D.C.L., LL.D., F.R.S., etc., all his possessions were to pass into the hands of his "friend and benefactor Edward Hyde," but that in case of Dr. Jekyll's "disappearance or unexplained absence for any period exceeding three calendar months," the said Edward Hyde should step into the said Henry Jekyll's shoes without further delay and free from any burthen or obligation, beyond the payment of a few small sums to the members of the doctor's household.

This document had long been the lawyer's eyesore. It offended him both as a lawyer and as a lover of the sane and customary sides of life, to whom the fanciful was the immodest. And hitherto it was his ignorance of Mr. Hyde that had swelled his indignation; now, by a sudden turn, it was his knowledge. It was already bad enough when the name was but a name of which he could learn no more. It was worse when it began to be clothed upon with detestable attributes; and out of the shifting, insubstantial mists that had so long baffled his eye, there leaped up the sudden, definite presentment of a fiend.

"I thought it was madness," he said, as he replaced the obnoxious paper in the safe, "and now I begin to fear it is disgrace."

With that he blew out his candle, put on a great-coat, and set forth in the direction of Cavendish Square, that citadel of medicine, where his friend, the great Dr. Lanyon, had his house and received his crowding patients. "If any one knows, it will be Lanyon," he had thought.

Analysis

Thesis

Utterson, like so much in the novel, is constructed on the principle of *"dual nature"*. Stevenson wants his readers to understand that Christian ideas of sin is only a social construct, and the Victorian gentleman's desire for secrecy leads to a morally corrupt society.

Initially, he is presented as a very positive figure. He conforms to the Victorian idea of goodness, reading a **"divinity"** each **"Sunday"**. He seems to represent Christian values and notes that **"the mark of Satan"** is written on Hyde's **"face"**, warning us of his evil nature. Stevenson also chooses his name, **"Gabriel"** as a deliberate echo of the Bible's most famous and noble angel.

However, Stevenson himself was an atheist. He also uses this portrayal of Utterson ironically. We will see that he is secretive, a hypocrite, withholds evidence from the police, helps a murderer escape in order to protect Jekyll's reputation and also acts in his own self-interest rather than reveal the truth to the police. We might see him as the true symbol of Victorian corruption, because, unlike Jekyll who is torn apart by the battle between his good and evil desires, Utterson appears to see no corruption in his own actions.

So his part in the novel ends with the antithesis of this extract. Hyde is no longer the beneficiary, instead **"in place of the name of Edward Hyde, the lawyer, with indescribable amazement, read the name of Gabriel**

John Utterson." We can only imagine the "**disgrace**" which would be attached to Jekyll's name if his scientific experiment in creating Hyde, and his responsibility for the murder of Sir Danvers Carew came out.

Similarly, this would expose Utterson's part in keeping his knowledge of Jekyll forging for Hyde secret. In order to inherit Jekyll's property and substantial fortune, he needs to suppress the truth and Jekyll's confession.

Now we can see the change in the will as deeply symbolic. The "**name**" of Hyde is replaced by Utterson not just because he has inherited Jekyll's property. This is also Stevenson's way of saying that Utterson would also bring forth a Hyde if he had taken the potion. He is just as corrupt as Jekyll, and has symbolically, through the will, just become Hyde.

His name is also symbolic of Christianity. "**Gabriel**" is the name of the angel who announces the births of John the Baptist and Jesus. His role is to proclaim. Utterson, in his dual nature, sees his role as the opposite, to suppress knowledge, and preserve secrecy. Stevenson uses this irony to criticise Utterson.

Stevenson also highlights Hyde's name as "**Edward**" and Utterson's as "**John**". This clearly suggest normality, but above all, Englishness. At the time, the name and character which most personified England was "John Bull". Here Stevenson suggests that the corruption exhibited by Hyde and Utterson are typical of English gentlemen. It is another way he attacks the hypocrisy of this rich, male society.

Another unsettling aspect of Utterson's personality is his refusal to embrace life. When we meet Jekyll's confession, Jekyll speaks with awe at Hyde's lust for life: "**his love of life was wonderful**". Utterson's personality is the dual opposite of this. "**He was austere with himself; drank gin when he was alone, to mortify a taste for vintages.**"

On the one hand this sounds sober, refusing to drink the wines which give him pleasure. However, he is also replacing wine with gin, with four times the alcohol content. Is Stevenson suggesting Utterson drinks to excess? He suggests that Utterson's avoidance of pleasure is literally damaging to his health, as a parallel to the way Jekyll's health is damaged by avoiding pleasure in his own form.

Stevenson asks us what is Utterson trying to blot out of his mind through his gin drinking? The obvious answer will be to suppress his homosexual desires.

We are also invited to wonder if this is connected to his last reported pleasure, "**though he enjoyed the theatre, had not crossed the doors of one for twenty years**". We want to know what happened at the theatre "**twenty years**" ago that prevents him now from returning?

The theatre is shorthand to a Victorian reader, symbolising sexual promiscuity, possibly heterosexual, but probably homosexual.

In this way Stevenson gradually presents us with a man in denial, and he invites us to read as detectives, to find out the cause.

From Chapter 2 SEARCH FOR MR. HYDE

"*Six o'clock struck on the bells of the church that was so conveniently near to Mr. Utterson's dwelling, and still he was digging at the problem. Hitherto it had touched him on the intellectual side alone; but now his imagination also was engaged, or rather enslaved; and as he lay and tossed in the gross darkness of the night and the curtained room, Mr. Enfield's tale went by before his mind in a scroll of lighted pictures.*

He would be aware of the great field of lamps of a nocturnal city; then of the figure of a man walking swiftly; then of a child running from the doctor's; and then these met, and that human Juggernaut trod the child down and passed on regardless of her screams.

Or else he would see a room in a rich house, where his friend lay asleep, dreaming and smiling at his dreams; and then the door of that room would be opened, the curtains of the bed plucked apart, the sleeper recalled, and lo! there would stand by his side a figure to whom power was given, and even at that dead hour, he must rise and do its bidding.

The figure in these two phases haunted the lawyer all night; and if at any time he dozed over, it was but to see it glide more stealthily through sleeping houses, or move the more swiftly and still the more swiftly, even to dizziness, through wider labyrinths of lamplighted city, and at every street-corner crush a child and leave her screaming.

And still the figure had no face by which he might know it; even in his dreams, it had no face, or one that baffled him and melted before his eyes; and thus it was that there sprang up and grew apace in the lawyer's mind a singularly strong, almost an inordinate, curiosity to behold the features of the real Mr. Hyde. If he could but once set eyes on him, he thought the mystery would lighten and perhaps roll altogether away, as was the habit of mysterious things when well examined.

He might see a reason for his friend's strange preference or bondage (call it which you please) and even for the startling clause of the will. At least it would be a face worth seeing: the face of a man who was without bowels of mercy: a face which had but to show itself to raise up, in the mind of the unimpressionable Enfield, a spirit of enduring hatred.

From that time forward, Mr. Utterson began to haunt the door in the by-street of shops. In the morning before office hours, at noon when business was plenty, and time scarce, at night under the face of the fogged city moon, by all lights and at all hours of solitude or concourse, the lawyer was to be found on his chosen post.

"If he be Mr. Hyde," he had thought, "I shall be Mr. Seek.""

Analysis

Utterson's Attraction to Hyde and Jekyll (The Dream)

The clues to his denial are soon revealed in Utterson's Freudian dreams, which are deeply symbolic: **"but now his imagination also was engaged, or rather enslaved; and as he lay and tossed in the gross darkness of the night and the curtained room."** The word **"enslaved"** suggests that he is helpless and forced not to suppress his **"imagination"**. We get the sense that his real desire is being revealed.

He dreams of **"a room in a rich house"**, suggesting that this wealth is something he also desires. This will explain his concern at Jekyll's will. Next, he sees **"where his friend lay asleep, dreaming and smiling at his dreams"**, which reveals a fixation on Jekyll. We must infer why Utterson chooses to imagine Jekyll in bed, also **"dreaming"**. One possibility is that this reveals his sexual desire.

Next he describes Hyde in a dominant position, **"the curtains of the bed plucked apart"**. **"Plucked"** is a specific verb*, which we associate with undressing, suggesting Utterson's desire to undress **"his friend"**. This is also emphasised with the use of the passive, instead of seeing Hyde pluck apart the **"curtains"** of the four poster bed.

(I hope you have noticed that telling the examiner a word is a verb, noun, adverb or adjective is something I hardly ever do. This is because it is usually not relevant to the point you are making. Here, the fact that it is a verb is very relevant to making it passive – Utterson does not make Hyde pluck the curtain – instead it is as though the force of sexual desire has done so).

Now he marvels at Hyde's power over Jekyll, "**and lo! there would stand by his side a figure to whom power was given, and even at that dead hour, he must rise and do its bidding.**" Again, Stevenson asks us to infer what power Hyde would want that would take Jekyll so deliberately from his bed.

A further clue is the passive again: "**power is given**" to Hyde. This suggests Jekyll himself has given Hyde this power. It implies that Jekyll is not an unwilling victim, but also desires Hyde to have this power. Again we infer this is a sexual attraction.

Now we can see Utterson's dream might reveal his own desire for Jekyll, and his sexual jealousy that Jekyll appears to be attracted to Hyde.

Before we proceed with this interpretation, we must be clear that Stevenson does not reveal this homosexual theme explicitly. However, it does help explain a real mystery in the novel. When Jekyll confesses, he claims that Hyde was finally able to take control of Jekyll's body once he has returned to sin in his own body, rather than through Hyde: "**no, it was in my own person, that I was once more tempted to trifle with my conscience; and it was as an ordinary secret sinner, that I at last fell before the assaults of temptation...and this brief condescension to evil finally destroyed the balance of my soul.**"

Jekyll is happy to tell us of his delight in clubbing Sir Danvers Carew to death, and yet he refuses to name this sin that finally gave Hyde ultimate power over his "**soul**". Only homosexuality, in the 1880s, would have been considered a more horrifying sin than murder. Indeed Lord Alfred Douglas called his love for Oscar Wilde "**the love that dare not speak its name**". In 1895, Wilde was imprisoned for homosexuality.

This context gives us a reason why Stevenson is not explicit in naming how Utterson is "**enslaved**" by homosexual desire. It also explains why Utterson bases his personality around denying himself pleasures.

As his dream reaches a conclusion, Stevenson emphasises Utterson's jealousy: "**He might see a reason for his friend's strange preference or bondage (call it which you please)**". Again, Jekyll's "**bondage**" is used to remind us of how Utterson as "**enslaved**". This implies that the cause of Jekyll's bondage is the same as Utterson's.

This is hinted at by Enfield when he imagines that Jekyll is being blackmailed by Hyde, "**Black-mail, I suppose; an honest man paying through the nose for some of the capers of his youth**." Because Jekyll is unmarried, no affair with a woman would be worthy of blackmail. Again, Stevenson manoeuvres us to imagine his "**capers**" to be homosexual love.

This invites us to think of the tragedy of the novel in a different light. Jekyll's need to create Hyde would now be because he is not allowed to express his homosexual nature. Similarly, Utterson's tragedy is that he cannot give in to any pleasures of his own, and instead lives vicariously through the sins of "**downward going men**".

Viewed in this light, Stevenson is arguing that homosexuality should not be considered a sin. He suggests that the efforts men have to go to to deny themselves ultimately destroys their personality, like Jekyll, or to live a life addicted to suppression and secrecy, like Utterson.

This is why Stevenson makes us see the world through Utterson's eyes, without having Utterson narrate it. It would be impossible for Utterson's personality to reveal all the secrets of the novel by telling its story, because he cannot speak about homosexuality.

From Chapter 4 THE CAREW MURDER CASE

"It was two o'clock when she came to herself and called for the police. The murderer was gone long ago; but there lay his victim in the middle of the lane, incredibly mangled. The stick with which the deed had been done, although it was of some rare and very tough and heavy wood, had broken in the middle under the stress of this insensate cruelty; and one splintered half had rolled in the neighbouring gutter—the other, without doubt, had been carried away by the murderer. A purse and a gold watch were found upon the victim: but no cards or papers, except a sealed and stamped envelope, which he had been probably carrying to the post, and which bore the name and address of Mr. Utterson.

This was brought to the lawyer the next morning, before he was out of bed; and he had no sooner seen it, and been told the circumstances, than he shot out a solemn lip. "I shall say nothing till I have seen the body," said he; "this may be very serious. Have the kindness to wait while I dress." And with the same grave countenance he hurried through his breakfast and drove to the police station, whither the body had been carried. As soon as he came into the cell, he nodded.

"Yes," said he, "I recognise him. I am sorry to say that this is Sir Danvers Carew."

"Good God, sir," exclaimed the officer, "is it possible?" And the next moment his eye lighted up with professional ambition. "This will make a deal of noise," he said. "And perhaps you can help us to the man." And he briefly narrated what the maid had seen, and showed the broken stick.

Mr. Utterson had already quailed at the name of Hyde; but when the stick was laid before him, he could doubt no longer; broken and battered as it was, he recognised it for one that he had himself presented many years before to Henry Jekyll.

"Is this Mr. Hyde a person of small stature?" he inquired.

"Particularly small and particularly wicked-looking, is what the maid calls him," said the officer.

Mr. Utterson reflected; and then, raising his head, "If you will come with me in my cab," he said, "I think I can take you to his house.""

Analysis

Sir Danvers Carew sends him a letter and the contents are never revealed. He does not open it yet.

Stevenson attaches these puzzles to Utterson in order to make us puzzle him out. While Utterson pursues the mystery of Hyde, **""If he be Mr. Hyde," he had thought, "I shall be Mr. Seek""**, Stevenson invites us to solve the mystery of Utterson.

Stevenson gives us the astonishing coincidence that, at the time of his death, Sir Danvers Carew was carrying a letter to Utterson, **"except a sealed and stamped envelope, which he had been probably carrying to the post, and which bore the name and address of Mr. Utterson."** And then astonishingly Stevenson refuses to mention it again.

It invites us to imagine the connection between Utterson and Carew may be the cause of Hyde's sudden desire to murder. For example, in Jekyll's confession we find that he had other opportunities to kill; he specifically mentions a female match seller, who (in comparison to the violence of the murder) he merely punches once in the face. This structural parallel invites us to suppose that killing Carew was not a random act. This is also emphasised by ensuring that we know Utterson knows Sir Danvers Carew: he is asked to identify the body. Once again, with no apparent relatives, we are asked why Stevenson has populated the novel with so many middle aged and single men.

In his confession, Jekyll also refuses to mention any motive. One explanation is that the confession is not written for the police, but specifically for Utterson. The police imagine that Danvers may have stopped to ask for directions to post the letter to Utterson, in which case the sight of Utterson's name drove Hyde to kill him. Alternatively, as we shall see later, the description of the killing strongly hints at Sir Danvers propositioning Hyde sexually, and Hyde kills him for his homosexual desires.

Whatever explanation we bring to this mysterious letter has to explain why Stevenson is highlighting a connection between Utterson and Carew, and Hyde's motive for killing him.

At the level of social commentary these men are all united by power and influence in society, and all of them seem attracted to or tempted by Hyde. Whatever Hyde's sins are, they aren't carried out simply among a criminal under class. Stevenson is explicit about this in choosing to have the murder witnessed by a maid who recognises Hyde because of his connection to her "**master**". Hyde is therefore part of the establishment. Stevenson symbolically suggests that Hyde represents the evil hypocrisy of powerful men in the establishment.

But, if we see Utterson as representing Hyde's opposite, Stevenson is also suggesting that even what seems moral and good in society, is also corrupt. As we will see, Utterson appears in his public actions to be a deeply moral and Christian man, but in fact is self-interested and criminal. However, unlike Jekyll who is tortured by guilt, Utterson feels no remorse.

Stevenson tantalises us with another coincidence. The murder weapon, a cane, belonged to Jekyll, but it was actually given to him by Utterson, "**he recognised it for one that he had himself presented many years before to Henry Jekyll**." Again, Stevenson implies that it is the connection to Utterson which drives Hyde to murder. Symbolically, he is also partly responsible for the murder.

So, Stevenson asks you to decide why? I am happy for you to develop your own theory. Whatever it is, explaining these coincidences coherently will ensure you get grades 8 or 9.

For me, the explanation is that Utterson is a symbol of society's repression of natural desire. When we consider the context of the time, society sought to suppress homosexual love. The most damaging sexual behaviour in society at the time is arguably the exponential growth in prostitution and the damage sexually transmitted diseases had on the health and life expectancy of wives and children. In a Christian novel which wished to attack middle class male hypocrisy in sinning, this would be the obvious target. Jekyll would be blackmailed because of his affairs, use of prostitutes, and would no doubt have at least a mistress. But Stevenson refuses us to imagine this can be the case. He doesn't just decide that Jekyll must be single, but that every other male character in the novel is also unmarried.

It is also a novel in which every portrayal of women is negative, from the foreign women and gin drinkers who populate Soho, to Hyde's vindictive housekeeper, to the maid who witnesses an apparently horrifying murder but seems to want to keep retelling the events which she claimed so upset her, "**Never (she used to say, with streaming tears, when she narrated that experience), never had she felt more at peace with all**

men or thought more kindly of the world." The brackets emphasise the incongruity of this, as she summons up **"streaming tears"** each time she **"narrated that experience"**.

This treatment of women in the novel might have many causes, not least Stevenson's anger at his wife who burned the first manuscript of the novel while he lay ill in bed. But the structural reason appears to be to alert the reader to a society which has rejected all women. Again, for me, he invites us to imagine a whole homosexual society which is forced to exist in secrecy and in denial, living in a Christian society which views homosexuality as a sin, and a secular society which has criminalised it. You don't have to agree.

But you will get grades 8 and 9 if you have a convincing explanation for this exclusively male focus, and the negative portrayal of every female character.

From Chapter 5 INCIDENT OF THE LETTER

"Guest had often been on business to the doctor's; he knew Poole; he could scarce have failed to hear of Mr. Hyde's familiarity about the house; he might draw conclusions: was it not as well, then, that he should see a letter which put that mystery to rights? and above all since Guest, being a great student and critic of handwriting, would consider the step natural and obliging? The clerk, besides, was a man of counsel; he would scarce read so strange a document without dropping a remark; and by that remark Mr. Utterson might shape his future course.

"This is a sad business about Sir Danvers," he said.

"Yes, sir, indeed. It has elicited a great deal of public feeling," returned Guest. "The man, of course, was mad."

"I should like to hear your views on that," replied Utterson. "I have a document here in his handwriting; it is between ourselves, for I scarce know what to do about it; it is an ugly business at the best. But there it is; quite in your way a murderer's autograph."

Guest's eyes brightened, and he sat down at once and studied it with passion. "No, sir," he said: "not mad; but it is an odd hand."

"And by all accounts a very odd writer," added the lawyer.

Just then the servant entered with a note.

"Is that from Dr. Jekyll, sir?" inquired the clerk. "I thought I knew the writing. Anything private, Mr. Utterson?"

"Only an invitation to dinner. Why? Do you want to see it?"

"One moment. I thank you, sir"; and the clerk laid the two sheets of paper alongside and sedulously compared their contents. "Thank you, sir," he said at last, returning both; "it's a very interesting autograph."

There was a pause, during which Mr. Utterson struggled with himself. "Why did you compare them, Guest?" he inquired suddenly.

"Well, sir," returned the clerk, "there's a rather singular resemblance; the two hands are in many points identical: only differently sloped."

"Rather quaint," said Utterson.

"It is, as you say, rather quaint," returned Guest.

"I wouldn't speak of this note, you know," said the master.

"No, sir," said the clerk. "I understand."

But no sooner was Mr. Utterson alone that night than he locked the note into his safe, where it reposed from that time forward. "What!" he thought. "Henry Jekyll forge for a murderer!" And his blood ran cold in his veins."

Analysis

The letter is a forgery.

Stevenson also uses Utterson to attack the law. The law should be each citizen's protection. However, if Utterson as a lawyer is corrupt, then by implication, so is the law. For this reason he introduces the secrecy between Utterson and Guest, who also represents the law.

They are both addicted to secrecy and suppression. Guest immediately recognises the handwriting as belonging to Jekyll, because Hyde's only disguise is to slant it. This strongly implies Utterson also knows this, which is why he imagines Guest will make such a powerful observation when he too recognises it, "**by that remark Mr. Utterson might shape his future course."**

Instead of taking this observation to the police, who we remember are hunting a murderer, he swears Guest to secrecy, "**I wouldn't speak of this note, you know**". He decides to keep the facts as he sees them, that Stevenson is aiding a murderer to escape, from the police, "**he locked the note into his safe, where it reposed from that time forward. "What!" he thought. "Henry Jekyll forge for a murderer!""**

We understand from this, that even at the end once Jekyll and Hyde are both dead, he keeps this secret from the police. There are no relatives to protect. This can only be to protect himself and his inheritance.

From Chapter 8 THE LAST NIGHT

"He caught up the next paper; it was a brief note in the doctor's hand and dated at the top.

"O Poole!" the lawyer cried, "he was alive and here this day. He cannot have been disposed of in so short a space, he must be still alive, he must have fled! And then, why fled? and how? and in that case, can we venture to declare this suicide? Oh, we must be careful. I foresee that we may yet involve your master in some dire catastrophe."

"Why don't you read it, sir?" asked Poole.

"Because I fear," replied the lawyer solemnly. "God grant I have no cause for it!" And with that he brought the paper to his eyes and read as follows:

"MY DEAR UTTERSON,—When this shall fall into your hands, I shall have disappeared, under what circumstances I have not the penetration to foresee, but my instinct and all the circumstances of my nameless situation tell me that the end is sure and must be early. Go then, and first read the narrative which Lanyon warned me he was to place in your hands; and if you care to hear more, turn to the confession of

"Your unworthy and unhappy friend,
"HENRY JEKYLL."

"There was a third enclosure?" asked Utterson.

"Here, sir," said Poole, and gave into his hands a considerable packet sealed in several places.

The lawyer put it in his pocket. "I would say nothing of this paper. If your master has fled or is dead, we may at least save his credit. It is now ten; I must go home and read these documents in quiet; but I shall be back before midnight, when we shall send for the police."

They went out, locking the door of the theatre behind them; and Utterson, once more leaving the servants gathered about the fire in the hall, trudged back to his office to read the two narratives in which this mystery was now to be explained."

Analysis

He hides the will and the letters from the police

"My head goes round," he said. "He has been all these days in possession; he had no cause to like me; he must have raged to see himself displaced; and he has not destroyed this document."

Hyde also understands that Utterson is corrupt, and relies on this to take revenge on Jekyll. It is extraordinary that Hyde does not destroy the new will. He knows that Jekyll will soon disappear – there is no more "salt" for his transformation, and everything will pass to him. Why does he let Utterson inherit it? Stevenson signposts that he wants his readers to answer this question themselves, by describing Utterson's shock that Hyde kept the will, **"He has been all these days in possession; he had no cause to like me; he must have raged to see himself displaced; and he has not destroyed this document."**

This is Hyde's perfect revenge on Jekyll. If Utterson inherits, he will suppress all the details of Jekyll's scientific discovery. Not only will Jekyll die, but his achievements will also die. He doesn't have the power to destroy Jekyll's legacy, but Utterson can. Unwittingly, he acts as Hyde's agent.

From Chapter 7 INCIDENT AT THE WINDOW

""That is just what I was about to venture to propose," returned the doctor with a smile. But the words were hardly uttered, before the smile was struck out of his face and succeeded by an expression of such abject terror and despair, as froze the very blood of the two gentlemen below. They saw it but for a glimpse, for the window was instantly thrust down; but that glimpse had been sufficient, and they turned and left the court without a word. In silence, too, they traversed the by-street; and it was not until they had come into a neighbouring thoroughfare, where even upon a Sunday there were still some stirrings of life, that Mr. Utterson at last turned and looked at his companion. They were both pale; and there was an answering horror in their eyes.

"God forgive us, God forgive us," said Mr. Utterson.

But Mr. Enfield only nodded his head very seriously and walked on once more in silence."

Analysis

He sees Jekyll change but wipes this from his memory

Utterson witnesses Jekyll turn into Hyde. On one level, Stevenson has him suppress this knowledge even from himself, "**They saw it but for a glimpse, for the window was instantly thrust down; but that glimpse had been sufficient, and they turned and left the court without a word…They were both pale; and there was an answering horror in their eyes**."

Enfield shares in this "**horror**", so it is clear "**the glimpse had been sufficient**" to see the transformation. However, rather than go inside to help Jekyll, they turn away. This is coupled with their silence, not speaking a "**word**".

Only Utterson speaks, exclaiming "**God forgive us**". To a Christian audience, this might suggest that Utterson sees the transformation as proof that mankind has sinned – Jekyll's creation of Hyde is just a symbol of the sins of all men.

But, we can also see it as proof that Utterson blames himself more personally. By turning away he is choosing to keep Hyde's identity secret.

Both Lanyon and Jekyll leave him their letters. They trust he will understand them. Jekyll leaves him his will, which gives Utterson a motive for hiding Jekyll's letter, sins and crimes.

Next they turned to the business-table. On the desk among the neat array of papers, a large envelope was uppermost, and bore, in the doctor's hand, the name of Mr. Utterson. The lawyer unsealed it, and several enclosures fell to the floor. The first was a will, drawn in the same eccentric terms as the one which he had returned six months before, to serve as a testament in case of death and as a deed of gift in case of disappearance; but, in place of the name of Edward Hyde, the lawyer, with indescribable amazement, read the name of Gabriel John Utterson. He looked at Poole, and then back at the paper, and last of all at the dead malefactor stretched upon the carpet.

"My head goes round," he said. "He has been all these days in possession; he had no cause to like me; he must have raged to see himself displaced; and he has not destroyed this document."

Analysis

The crucial detail here is the puzzle Stevenson sets us at the end. Jekyll explains it to Utterson in his confession, "**but if some time shall have elapsed after I have laid it by, his wonderful selfishness and Circumscription to the moment will probably save it once again**". This claim that Hyde will be too distracted is nonsense, especially when we see how orderly Hyde has kept the room before Utterson's entry.

Both men are exploiting their knowledge of Utterson. Jekyll believes that, as a loyal friend, Utterson will preserve his reputation once he is dead. Hyde also knows that Utterson will keep Jekyll's scientific discoveries secret, in order to preserve his own reputation from scandal when he inherits Jekyll's wealth. This is Hyde's final revenge on Jekyll.

Grade 9 Essay on Utterson

Beginning with the extract, how is the character of Utterson presented and developed?

The Extract from Chapter 2

Six o'clock struck on the bells of the church that was so conveniently near to Mr. Utterson's dwelling, and still he was digging at the problem. Hitherto it had touched him on the intellectual side alone; but now his imagination also was engaged, or rather enslaved; and as he lay and tossed in the gross darkness of the night and the curtained room, Mr. Enfield's tale went by before his mind in a scroll of lighted pictures.

He would be aware of the great field of lamps of a nocturnal city; then of the figure of a man walking swiftly; then of a child running from the doctor's; and then these met, and that human Juggernaut trod the child down and passed on regardless of her screams.

Or else he would see a room in a rich house, where his friend lay asleep, dreaming and smiling at his dreams; and then the door of that room would be opened, the curtains of the bed plucked apart, the sleeper recalled, and lo! there would stand by his side a figure to whom power was given, and even at that dead hour, he must rise and do its bidding.

The figure in these two phases haunted the lawyer all night; and if at any time he dozed over, it was but to see it glide more stealthily through sleeping houses, or move the more swiftly and still the more swiftly, even to dizziness, through wider labyrinths of lamplighted city, and at every street-corner crush a child and leave her screaming.

And still the figure had no face by which he might know it; even in his dreams, it had no face, or one that baffled him and melted before his eyes; and thus it was that there sprang up and grew apace in the lawyer's mind a singularly strong, almost an inordinate, curiosity to behold the features of the real Mr. Hyde. If he could but once set eyes on him, he thought the mystery would lighten and perhaps roll altogether away, as was the habit of mysterious things when well examined.

He might see a reason for his friend's strange preference or bondage (call it which you please) and even for the startling clause of the will. At least it would be a face worth seeing: the face of a man who was without bowels of mercy: a face which had but to show itself to raise up, in the mind of the unimpressionable Enfield, a spirit of enduring hatred.

From that time forward, Mr. Utterson began to haunt the door in the by-street of shops. In the morning before office hours, at noon when business was plenty, and time scarce, at night under the face of the fogged city moon, by all lights and at all hours of solitude or concourse, the lawyer was to be found on his chosen post.

"If he be Mr. Hyde," he had thought, "I shall be Mr. Seek."

Essay

(Remember, because I know I write at grade 7 and above, I know it is best to start with the extract. If you are not confident in doing this, it is much better to start with the novel as a whole.)

Stevenson presents Utterson as both an upstanding Christian gentleman, and as a representative of a corrupt life which is not worth living. Stevenson questions Utterson's Christian role in the novella by placing the "**church … so conveniently near**." "Conveniently" is ambiguous, perhaps a sign of his devout proximity to God, or perhaps conveying how little effort he wishes to expend in attending church, because it is done only out of convention or duty. The emphasis of "so" suggests the latter interpretation.

Having questioned Utterson's faith, Stevenson presents him as a proxy for the reader, "**his imagination also was engaged, or rather enslaved**" by the "**tale**". This subtly suggests the contemporary reader has more in common than their "imagination" and being "enslaved" by this great story: they are also suffering from a weakness in Christian faith.

The description is now filled with suppressed sexual desire, as Utterson "**tossed in the gross darkness**". "Darkness" works as a motif in the novella, continually reminding us of Hyde's evil, which always symbolises the evil of these hypocritical gentlemen. Utterson appears trapped in this "darkness" which represents his ignorance of Hyde's identity, his fear of Hyde's lack of "mercy", but also that Utterson shares his evil nature. This is powerfully emphasised by the sibilance, suggesting a sinister tone.

The "darkness" is also described metaphorically as "gross", meaning huge and thick. This allusion to impenetrability is emphasised by the "**curtained room**" which represents the theme of concealment which also runs as a motif in the novella, and is dramatised through Jekyll's alter ego's name, "Hyde".

Next Stevenson points to the reason that Hyde is evil: he personifies the evil hypocrisy of Victorian society. Consequently, Utterson fantasises about "**the great field of lamps of a nocturnal city**". This metaphor reveals that London's true nature is "nocturnal", and he emphasises this link to nature calling it a "field".

This prepares the ground for a discussion of Jekyll's true nature, and also that of the other bachelor, Utterson. Contemporary readers would also have noticed that Enfield and Dr Lanyon, the other protagonists, are also bachelors. Stevenson is hinting at what Oscar Wilde's lover called only a decade later, "the love which dare not speak its name", homosexuality.

Consequently, Utterson imagines Jekyll in bed, "**dreaming and smiling at his dreams**" which he immediately implies are dreams of Hyde. He is the figure who Utterson now imagines entering the bedroom and the "**curtains of the bed plucked apart**" is a metaphor for uncovering what has been concealed: homosexual desire. The use of "plucked" is also far more suggestive than 'pulled', as it implies nakedness, just as a bird is "plucked" of its feathers to reveal naked flesh. What is revealed is desire itself, personified by "**a figure to whom power was given, and even at that dead hour, he must rise and do its bidding**." Although this figure, in Utterson's mind, is the mysterious "Hyde", Jekyll is enslaved by the desire for the man "**to whom power was given**." This is the same "enslavement" of the "imagination" which has affected Utterson's dreams. Stevenson therefore suggests that Utterson shares the same sexual desire.

It is odd that Hyde has already been named, but that Utterson does not name him as the "figure". Stevenson wants us to focus on that oddness, because it means the figure could be Utterson himself, fantasising about a sexual relationship with his great friend, Jekyll.

To allude to this more strongly, Utterson distorts the memory of Hyde as a "Juggernaut" who he now imagines moving at ever increasing speed in a parody of sexual climax, to "glide" and then "**move the more swiftly and still the more swiftly, even to dizziness**". There was nothing dizzy in Hyde's trampling of the girl; this effect is being produced on Utterson, as a result of his own desires. Stevenson reveals them only in dreams, because they are forbidden. A man who is homosexual is literally lost to society, and Stevenson illustrates this with the metaphor of the city being made up of "**wider labyrinths**", which Utterson fears getting lost in, just as he fears his own desires.

Stevenson next employs repetition to suggest that this figure, standing beside Jekyll's bed is not just Hyde, or even just Utterson, but a personification of homosexual desire. Consequently**, "the figure had no face … it had no face, or one that baffled him and melted before his eyes".** One reason that Utterson can't hold on to the face is that he dare not admit that it is his own. Another reason perhaps is jealousy or sexual curiosity. He wonders what face has drawn Jekyll so successfully that Hyde can now **"blackmail"** him**.**

The final reference to his face is cleverly ironic. Utterson feels "**curiosity to behold the features of the real Mr. Hyde**". The emphasis of "real" tells the reader that Hyde is not who he seems. This again is a theme of the novella, because the "real" face of Hyde is of course Dr Jekyll. Hyde is not separate from Jekyll, he is only the evil part of his nature made flesh. But another irony is that perhaps Hyde's evil is just a social construct. He may only be disgusting to a Victorian audience because he is homosexual.

Stevenson makes this as explicit as he dare when Utterson wonders about Jekyll's **"reason for his friend's strange preference or bondage (call it which you please)".** "Strange" is a deliberate echo of the title, suggesting that Jekyll's duality of man is not just the science which allows him to create a new being, but the revelation this duality is potentially present in all men. "Bondage" is not used here as a modern sexual reference. However, it still implied "enslavement" to desire, and therefore once more suggests Jekyll's sexual desire for Hyde.

Their society dictates that homosexual desire is evil, and for this reason Utterson reminds himself that Hyde's face encouraged Enfield to have "**a spirit of enduring hatred**." We remember that in chapter one, Enfield had to hold back a desire to murder Hyde. Here Stevenson suggests that the social evil is not homosexual desire, but the hypocritical need to suppress it, which leads finally to Hyde, **"the self-destroyer"**, taking his own life, and why his readers demand an ending in which Jekyll is also killed for bringing his desires to life in the shape of Hyde.

1062 words

What is the Role of Doctor Lanyon?

Read the following extract from Chapter 6 and then answer the question that follows.

In this extract….

There at least he was not denied admittance; but when he came in, he was shocked at the change which had taken place in the doctor's appearance. He had his death-warrant written legibly upon his face. The rosy man had grown pale; his flesh had fallen away; he was visibly balder and older; and yet it was not so much, these tokens of a swift physical decay that arrested the lawyer's notice, as a look in the eye and quality of manner that seemed to testify to some deep-seated terror of the mind.

It was unlikely that the doctor should fear death; and yet that was what Utterson was tempted to suspect. "Yes," he thought; "he is a doctor, he must know his own state and that his days are counted; and the knowledge is more than he can bear."

And yet when Utterson remarked on his ill-looks, it was with an air of greatness that Lanyon declared himself a doomed man.

"I have had a shock," he said, "and I shall never recover. It is a question of weeks. Well, life has been pleasant; I liked it; yes, sir, I used to like it. I sometimes think if we knew all, we should be more glad to get away."

"Jekyll is ill, too," observed Utterson. "Have you seen him?"

But Lanyon's face changed, and he held up a trembling hand. "I wish to see or hear no more of Dr. Jekyll," he said in a loud, unsteady voice. "I am quite done with that person; and I beg that you will spare me any allusion to one whom I regard as dead."

"Tut-tut," said Mr. Utterson; and then after a considerable pause, "Can't I do anything?" he inquired. "We are three very old friends, Lanyon; we shall not live to make others."

"Nothing can be done," returned Lanyon; "ask himself."

"He will not see me," said the lawyer.

"I am not surprised at that," was the reply. "Some day, Utterson, after I am dead, you may perhaps come to learn the right and wrong of this. I cannot tell you. And in the meantime, if you can sit and talk with me of

other things, for God's sake, stay and do so; but if you cannot keep clear of this accursed topic, then, in God's name, go, for I cannot bear it."

In this extract and the rest of the novel, how does Stevenson present the character of Dr Hastie Lanyon?

Although this would be an unlikely question, understanding Lanyon will help lots of different interpretations of the themes of Jekyll and Hyde.

Thesis

Lanyon represents the moral, Christian Victorian reader, who fears that science threatens the power of God. It is a clear warning against scientific advance, which brings greater evil into the world.

His first name is symbolic. Hastie suggests rashness and suddenness. In this way, Stevenson hints that Lanyon's reaction is unwise. He dies when he should choose life. Even the evil Hyde is addicted to life: "But his love of life is wonderful".

<u>**Other references to Lanyon:**</u>

Chapter 2: SEARCH FOR MR. HYDE

With that he blew out his candle, put on a great-coat, and set forth in the direction of Cavendish Square, that citadel of medicine, where his friend, the great Dr. Lanyon, had his house and received his crowding patients. "If any one knows, it will be Lanyon," he had thought.

The solemn butler knew and welcomed him; he was subjected to no stage of delay, but ushered direct from the door to the dining-room where Dr. Lanyon sat alone over his wine.

This was a hearty, healthy, dapper, red-faced gentleman, with a shock of hair prematurely white, and a boisterous and decided manner. At sight of Mr. Utterson, he sprang up from his chair and welcomed him with both hands. The geniality, as was the way of the man, was somewhat theatrical to the eye; but it reposed on genuine feeling.

For these two were old friends, old mates both at school and college, both thorough respecters of themselves and of each other, and, what does not always follow, men who thoroughly enjoyed each other's company.

After a little rambling talk, the lawyer led up to the subject which so disagreeably pre-occupied his mind.

"I suppose, Lanyon," said he "you and I must be the two oldest friends that Henry Jekyll has?"

<u>**Analysis**</u>

Here the metaphor of "**Cavendish Square, that citadel of medicine**" suggests that medicine is under attack, and needs to be fortified. Stevenson presents medicine as already under attack by the advances in science. It is interesting that Jekyll's house (John Hunter's house remember) is far removed from Cavendish Square. Indeed, you have to cross through Soho to get from Lanyon's to Jekyll's house. This implies, like John Hunter's historical story, that medicine needs to break with accepted moral conventions if it is to make scientific discoveries which will benefit mankind. The "citadel" is therefore out dated, like a castle, no longer suited to the modern world.

So our first introduction to Lanyon portrays him as defensive and out of touch. This is added to by the description of him as **"the great Dr. Lanyon"** which hints at an obsession with his reputation, rather than his skill as a doctor (though equally, his reputation might be due to his great skill).

With this question raised in the minds of the reader, we can see that Stevenson is again presenting us with duality – here opposite interpretations of character.

This duality is also present in his physical appearance:

"This was a hearty, healthy, dapper, red-faced gentleman, with a shock of hair prematurely white, and a boisterous and decided manner."

"hearty, healthy" set up the shock we will face when we next meet him, and he is close to death. Stevenson uses this device to make us wonder what he could have witnessed that was so shocking in connection with Jekyll.

However, in the same sentence we find he is "red-faced", an easy association with high blood pressure and ill health: his "shock of har prematurely white" also foreshadows the shock of seeing Hyde's transformation, while the prematurely white hair suggests a premature death. Because this is how he appears now, Stevenson hints that Lanyon is already heading towards a premature death. This is symbolic of course. He is not just writing about Lanyon as an individual. Instead Stevenson uses him as a symbol of the medical profession. His is a "citadel" which is being undermined by its own weakness.

Lanyon is also used to portray upper class society and the ruling classes, alongside Utterson. This is why he decides they didn't just go to the same **"college"** but also the same **"school"**. This portrays society as controlled by a narrow range of men, from a select number of a few thousand families, from public schools such as Eton and Harrow. It is very relevant to Stevenson, an outsider from Scotland, who would notice the corruption of the 'old boys' network' in London. It hints at the corruption of that society.

Chapter 2: SEARCH FOR MR. HYDE

""I suppose, Lanyon," said he "you and I must be the two oldest friends that Henry Jekyll has?"

"I wish the friends were younger," chuckled Dr. Lanyon. "But I suppose we are. And what of that? I see little of him now."

"Indeed?" said Utterson. "I thought you had a bond of common interest."

"We had," was the reply. "But it is more than ten years since Henry Jekyll became too fanciful for me. He began to go wrong, wrong in mind; and though of course I continue to take an interest in him for old sake's sake, as they say, I see and I have seen devilish little of the man. Such unscientific balderdash," added the doctor, flushing suddenly purple, "would have estranged Damon and Pythias."'

Analysis

Here, Stevenson portrays Lanyon as the direct opposite of Jekyll in terms of his science. The comment **"unscientific balderdash"** shows that Lanyon has no belief that it can possibly work. The semantic field of **"devilish"** suggests that Jekyll's science is also potentially evil. His reference to **"Damon and Pythias"** who represent friends with the strongest bonds, who would risk their lives for each other in Greek myth, also tells us how betrayed Lanyon feels about Jekyll's scientific experiments

This prompts an interesting ethical debate. On the surface, it is simply an easy code. The good Christian, Lanyon, rejects the evil experiments of Jekyll, whom he had once considered the very closest of friends: the Christian reader is similarly appalled at Jekyll's dabbling with creation, creating Hyde, with "**Satan's signature**" written on his face.

However, the Christian interpretation is questioned by the nature of the allusion to a pagan and pre-Christian culture. There are examples of male love, loyalty and sacrifice in the bible, notably between David and Jonathan who work together in the face of a treacherous King, just as "**Damon and Pythias**" do.

Stevenson therefore promotes the Greek myth above the biblical story. One reason could be that he is likening the bible to a collection of myths, and finding the earlier, Greek versions superior. Another is the underlying hint of homosexuality. This is a theme of Greek myth, and causes speculation at the love between the two friends.

But, look more deeply, and we come back to how wrong Lanyon is in fact. Jekyll's work is not "**unscientific**", just as John Hunter's wasn't. Far from being "**balderdash**" it actually succeeds spectacularly – a wholly new being is created.

Stevenson invites us to go back "**ten years**" when Jekyll must have approached Lanyon for help in his research. Symbolically, this represents how he has reached out to the scientific and medical community for help. Lanyon's reaction shows how he has had to proceed in secret and alone. Lanyon's decision is perhaps hasty, hence his name, "**Hastie**".

This also implies that Jekyll's first instinct was to advance scientific discovery. It is only after he is rejected that he starts to think about the personal advantage he might have in creating an alter ego who can participate in his sinful pleasures. Lanyon also represents that lost opportunity to use that science for good, to create the "**angel**" instead of the "**fiend**".

Even though this happened ten years ago, its effect on Jekyll is still profound and painful:

DR. JEKYLL WAS QUITE AT EASE

 "'I never saw a man so distressed as you were by my will; unless it were that hide-bound pedant, Lanyon, at what he called my scientific heresies. Oh, I know he's a good fellow—you needn't frown—an excellent fellow, and I always mean to see more of him; but a hide-bound pedant for all that; an ignorant, blatant pedant. I was never more disappointed in any man than Lanyon."'

Analysis

The use of "**heresies**" shows that Lanyon's objections are Christian – again serving a dual purpose. Christian readers are confirmed in their belief that Jekyll's discoveries will be unchristian. Readers who look deeper will realise the Jekyll must have depended on Lanyon for help in his initial experiments. That he has never been "**more disappointed in any man than Lanyon**" lets us see how far he feels betrayed by Lanyon's rejection of science. In this way, we might infer that Lanyon is partly responsible for the creation of Hyde, rather than a noble alter ego.

Our next encounter is **REMARKABLE INCIDENT OF DR. LANYON**

"There at least he was not denied admittance; but when he came in, he was shocked at the change which had taken place in the doctor's appearance. He had his death-warrant written legibly upon his face. The rosy man had grown pale; his flesh had fallen away; he was visibly balder and older; and yet it was not so much,

these tokens of a swift physical decay that arrested the lawyer's notice, as a look in the eye and quality of manner that seemed to testify to some deep-seated terror of the mind."

Analysis

Stevenson uses the rapid decline in Lanyon's health to hint at the horror of what has happened with Jekyll. It deepens the mystery of Jekyll's relationship with Hyde, and hints that Jekyll is involved with evil.

But again, we have duality. Lanyon is the subject of a "**death warrant**". A warrant is issued by a court in pursuit of justice, pursuing a criminal. Once more, thinking more deeply, Stevenson invites us to see Lanyon as a criminal in his treatment of Jekyll. Why? Because Lanyon is first and foremost a scientist. Yet, when he is presented with the truth of scientific discovery, he chooses to die rather than learn more.

A Christian readership will sympathise with his rejection of "**heresies**". But Stevenson refuses to take this view. Indeed, many scientific discoveries were branded heresies by the church – Galileo proved the earth was not the centre of the universe, and was confined to house arrest by the church, for the rest of his life.

"It was unlikely that the doctor should fear death; and yet that was what Utterson was tempted to suspect. "Yes," he thought; "he is a doctor, he must know his own state and that his days are counted; and the knowledge is more than he can bear."

And yet when Utterson remarked on his ill-looks, it was with an air of greatness that Lanyon declared himself a doomed man."

This sentence is deeply critical of Lanyon. His "**air of greatness**" suggests he is deeply vain, and choosing to die out of a sense of pride, rather than a Christian rejection of Jekyll's science. "**Yet**" tells us that it is not that he can't "**bear**" the thought of the evil which Jekyll has created, instead it is an attempt to salvage his ego and pride: the "**shock**" is produced by his being proved wrong.

"I have had a shock," he said, "and I shall never recover. It is a question of weeks. Well, life has been pleasant; I liked it; yes, sir, I used to like it. I sometimes think if we knew all, we should be more glad to get away."

His reaction to his own death is also disappointingly cheerful. Stevenson juxtaposes this with Hyde's lust for life. Again, he asks us to question social morality. How good can Christianity be if it can make a man happy to give up on life. Does the existence of evil mean we also have to reject all that is good?

Stevenson suggests that Lanyon's death is simple vanity, a waste of life, and a product of delusion. Lanyon chooses to run away from reality.

In this way, he also asks his Christian readers to question the morality of Lanyon's faith.

"So great and unprepared a change pointed to madness; but in view of Lanyon's manner and words, there must lie for it some deeper ground.

A week afterwards Dr. Lanyon took to his bed, and in something less than a fortnight he was dead."

The phrasing of this "**Lanyon took to his bed**" suggests a deliberate choice to die. Stevenson links this to "**madness**" as a way to discredit the decision. The "**deeper ground**", Christian morality, will prove to the Christian reader that what seems mad is in fact a natural reaction to the evil of Jekyll's experiments. But to other readers, Stevenson may well point out that it is still madness, and therefore, so is Christianity. We are reminded that he took the mad decision to greet Jekyll with a "**revolve**r" at the beginning of this encounter. Christianity is therefore not only mad, but dangerous. Symbolically, Christianity brings death. It brings death to Dr Lanyon.

However, he assumes that Jekyll is both mad and violently dangerous, "**The more I reflected the more convinced I grew that I was dealing with a case of cerebral disease: and though I dismissed my servants to bed, I loaded an old revolver, that I might be found in some posture of self-defence.**"

Once again, this points to Lanyon's overreaction in the face of evidence. It also emphasises the symbolism we met earlier with the idea of the "**citadel of medicine**" which feel sunder attack by science. After all, all the ingredients in the drawer are entirely to do with scientific experiment. It is not really a fear of Jekyll's violence which causes him to bring a gun, it is a fear of scientific discovery.

When Lanyon describes his encounter with Hyde, Stevenson uses him as a proxy for the Christian viewpoint, "**I have since had reason to believe the cause to lie much deeper in the nature of man, and to turn on some nobler hinge than the principle of hatred.**" This suggests again that Hyde is evil. However, it is also that Hyde represents "**the nature of man**". This again implies that his choice to die is foolish – Hyde does not make mankind more evil. He is simply evidence that we carry the capacity for evil within us.

To emphasise this point Stevenson makes sure that Hyde is incredibly polite and considerate to Lanyon:

"'I beg your pardon, Dr. Lanyon," he replied civilly enough. "What you say is very well founded; and my impatience has shown its heels to my politeness. I come here at the instance of your colleague, Dr. Henry Jekyll, on a piece of business of some moment; and I understood..." He paused and put his hand to his throat, and I could see, in spite of his collected manner, that he was wrestling against the approaches of the hysteria—"I understood, a drawer..."'

This is not the behaviour of an evil man who has the youth and power to simply beat Lanyon with violence until he provides the drawer of drugs. But he doesn't behave in this way at all. In other words, Lanyon does not see true evil in Hyde. And remember, he has no knowledge that this is indeed Hyde, a murderer.

We could see the decision to make Lanyon witness his transformation into Jekyll as an evil one, knowing it would expose Lanyon's self-belief, and belief in his own scientific understand as entirely wrong.

But he doesn't make Lanyon see this. Instead, desperate though he is to take the potion, he pauses in order to give Lanyon a choice not to see the truth. In other words, he allows Lanyon to choose ignorance.

"My visitor, who had watched these metamorphoses with a keen eye, smiled, set down the glass upon the table, and then turned and looked upon me with an air of scrutiny.

"And now," said he, "to settle what remains. Will you be wise? Will you be guided? Will you suffer me to take this glass in my hand and to go forth from your house without further parley? Or has the greed of curiosity too much command of you?

Think before you answer, for it shall be done as you decide. As you decide, you shall be left as you were before, and neither richer nor wiser, unless the sense of service rendered to a man in mortal distress may be counted as a kind of riches of the soul.

Or, if you shall so prefer to choose, a new province of knowledge and new avenues to fame and power shall be laid open to you, here, in this room, upon the instant; and your sight shall be blasted by a prodigy to stagger the unbelief of Satan."'

Hyde presents Lanyon's lack of belief in the potential of science as like Satan's "**unbelief**" in the power of God. This is a pivotal moment.

Hyde suggests that Lanyon's lack of belief in Jekyll's science is like Satan's rejection of the power of God. In this way, he associates the experiment with goodness, rather than evil. Effectively, he dramatises scientific ignorance as an evil act, just like Satan's rebellion against God.

Of course, to a Christian reader this is simply proof of Hyde's evil nature, and his warped view of morality, replacing God with science. But, when we look at his self-restraint, his politeness, and the generosity of giving Lanyon the chance not to see the transformation, we might infer that Stevenson intends us to side with Hyde here.

Lanyon's sin is that he has rejected scientific advance: he has stood in the way of discovery and truth. And once he finds that he is wrong about science, he can no longer face life.

This is how Stevenson plays out the contemporary fear of science, and points out that this is ludicrous. It isn't science which has created Hyde – it is Jekyll's personality at the time of first taking the drug.

Even to a Christian, Lanyon's horrified rejection of life might seem unreasonable:

"My life is shaken to its roots; sleep has left me; the deadliest terror sits by me at all hours of the day and night; I feel that my days are numbered, and that I must die; and yet I shall die incredulous."

But it also contains a wilful disbelief. When he tells us "**yet I shall die incredulous**" he may mean that he chooses to die before he is forced to believe the truth. It is an extraordinary idea that someone would rather die than admit they are wrong.

In this way Stevenson uses Lanyon to force his Christian readers to examine their own fears and beliefs, if they dare. Notice that this could form your thesis.

How Does Stevenson use Setting?

Read the following extract from Chapter 1 and then answer the question that follows.

In this extract...

It chanced on one of these rambles that their way led them down a by-street in a busy quarter of London. The street was small and what is called quiet, but it drove a thriving trade on the week-days. The inhabitants were all doing well, it seemed, and all emulously hoping to do better still, and laying out the surplus of their gains in coquetry; so that the shop fronts stood along that thoroughfare with an air of invitation, like rows of smiling saleswomen. Even on Sunday, when it veiled its more florid charms and lay comparatively empty of passage, the street shone out in contrast to its dingy neighbourhood, like a fire in a forest; and with its freshly painted shutters, well-polished brasses, and general cleanliness and gaiety of note, instantly caught and pleased the eye of the passenger.

Two doors from one corner, on the left hand going east, the line was broken by the entry of a court; and just at that point, a certain sinister block of building thrust forward its gable on the street. It was two stories high; showed no window, nothing but a door on the lower story and a blind forehead of discoloured wall on the upper; and bore in every feature, the marks of prolonged and sordid negligence. The door, which was equipped with neither bell nor knocker, was blistered and distained. Tramps slouched into the recess and struck matches on the panels; children kept shop upon the steps; the schoolboy had tried his knife on the mouldings; and for close on a generation, no one had appeared to drive away these random visitors or to repair their ravages.

Mr. Enfield and the lawyer were on the other side of the by-street; but when they came abreast of the entry, the former lifted up his cane and pointed.

"Did you ever remark that door?" he asked; and when his companion had replied in the affirmative, "It is connected in my mind," added he, "with a very odd story."

"Indeed?" said Mr. Utterson, with a slight change of voice, "and what was that?"

Exam Question

Starting with the extract, how does Stevenson use settings throughout the novel?

Significant Aspects of Setting

1. Leicester Square is next door to Soho, like Hyde is next door to Jekyll, to the extent that they are two sides of the same place.

2. Utterson visits Soho after the killing of Sir Danvers Carew, in search of Hyde: "**It was by this time about nine in the morning, and the first fog of the season. A great chocolate-coloured pall lowered over heaven.**"

3. "**there would be a glow of a rich, lurid brown, like the light of some strange conflagration**".

4. The city of Utterson's dreams and nightmares: "**through wider labyrinths of lamplighted city, and at every street-corner crush a child and leave her screaming**".

5. The first description of Jekyll's house: "**Round the corner from the by-street, there was a square of ancient, handsome houses, now for the most part decayed from their high estate and let in flats and chambers to all sorts and conditions of men: map-engravers, architects, shady lawyers, and the agents of obscure enterprises. One house, however, second from the corner, was still occupied entire; and at the door of this, which wore a great air of wealth and comfort**".

6. Hyde's part of Jekyll's house, which we meet before Jekyll's: "**It was two stories high; showed no window, nothing but a door on the lower story and a blind forehead of discoloured wall on the upper.**"

7. Hyde's house in Soho: "**Mr. Hyde had only used a couple of rooms; but these were furnished with luxury and good taste. A closet was filled with wine; the plate was of silver, the napery elegant; a good picture hung upon the walls, a gift (as Utterson supposed) from Henry Jekyll, who was much of a connoisseur; and the carpets were of many plies and agreeable in colour**".

8. Lanyon's house: "**With that he blew out his candle, put on a great-coat, and set forth in the direction of Cavendish Square, that citadel of medicine, where his friend, the great Dr. Lanyon, had his house**".

9. The setting for the murder of Sir Danvers Carew: "**Although a fog rolled over the city in the small hours, the early part of the night was cloudless, and the lane, which the maid's window overlooked, was brilliantly lit by the full moon. It seems she was romantically given, for she sat down upon her box, which stood immediately under the window, and fell into a dream of musing**".

10. The murder scene: "**And next moment, with ape-like fury, he was trampling his victim under foot and hailing down a storm of blows, under which the bones were audibly shattered and the body jumped upon the roadway. At the horror of these sights and sounds, the maid fainted.**"

11. "Man's dual nature" is presented as a landscape: "**It was thus rather the exacting nature of my aspirations than any particular degradation in my faults, that made me what I was and, with even a deeper trench than in the majority of men, severed in me those provinces of good and ill which divide and compound man's dual nature.**"

12. The language associated with landscape is used to describe our "dual nature". "**I learned to recognise the thorough and primitive duality of man; I saw that, of the two natures that contended in the field of my consciousness, even if I could rightly be said to be either, it was only because I was radically both; and from an early date, even before the course of my scientific discoveries had begun to suggest the most naked possibility of such a miracle, I had learned to dwell with pleasure, as a beloved day-dream, on the thought of the separation of these elements.**"

Use parts of as many of these as you can to write a really full answer to the question.

Beyond Grade 9 Essay on Setting

Fanny, Stevenson's wife, burned his first draft of the novella, and asked him to write something less sensational and more "**allegorical**". So, in order to please her, he made sure so much in it was symbolic of something else. He writes the settings as symbols for the "**duality of man**".

He sets this up with one of the central symbols of the novel, which is the house shared by Jekyll and Hyde. Jekyll's respectable front of the house is "**handsome**". This symbolically represents Jekyll's façade, so to point this out, Stevenson uses exactly the same word, "handsome" to describe Jekyll.

The back of the house, where Hyde enters and exits, is apparently it's opposite, and "**sinister**". Again, Stevenson makes sure we understand this is also symbolic of Hyde, so that it is personified with a "forehead".

On the one hand this symbolises how well middle class men are able to hide their true natures.

But on the other hand, it suggests that the opposite is true. Hyde is not hidden at all – he is in plain sight. Anyone with legs can clearly see that Hyde's door is directly opposite, at the back, of Jekyll's. When he describes Hyde's entrance as having a "**blind forehead**" this perhaps reflects Utterson's blindness. It suggests that Utterson will never understand the truth, which is that we are all like Jekyll, a combination of a respectable front, and secret desires. He continues to see Hyde as a blackmailer even though he lives in the same house as Jekyll – he is "**blind**" to the level of consent this implies in their living together.

This house still stands in Leicester Square. More importantly, it is a house Stevenson knows is famous, and therefore expects his London readership in particular to know. Further proof of this is that Stevenson is not even in London when he writes this, but convalescing, apparently bedridden, in Bournemouth. The house is notorious. It is where the infamous surgeon, John Hunter lived. Hunter revolutionised medicine (just as Jekyll is trying to do) but he resorted to evil experiments (just as Jekyll does). In the 1700's Hunter paid grave robbers to bring him dead bodies, so that he could dissect them in the medical theatre he had specifically built in the middle of the house. In other words, his acts of evil were carried out in plain sight, with a theatre of medical students and doctors, watching him at work. He would lecture while dissecting.

By Stevenson's time Hunter was celebrated for the advances in surgery his experiments brought about, rather than for his immorality. This underpins Stevenson's portrayal of Hyde, who does not commit any evil act until Jekyll imprisons him for two months.

Stevenson does this to point out that notions of morality and sin are social constructs. With Victorian hindsight, the immoral grave robbing of Hunter can look like a service to mankind. Jekyll believes his experiments in creating an alter ego as a separate being might also prove a benefit to mankind.

Although his Christian readers will reject this, Stevenson still provokes them with his symbolism. Consequently, he portrays Hyde's lodgings in Soho in surprising ways. It is clearly the house of a gentleman, "**furnished with luxury and good taste**". More than that, Hyde has very refined tastes, so he is a "**connoisseur**". Although Jekyll has chosen these furnishings, they exactly match Hyde's tastes. Stevenson is pointing out that Hyde, too, is a gentleman, with gentlemen's tastes.

Here the setting is used to challenge us. Is Hyde any different from the gentlemen of London? On the one hand, this is an attack on their hypocrisy. Look beneath the surface, this challenge says, and you will find that all middle class men are hypocrites.

However, autobiographically, Stevenson did not share a Christian view of morality. While at university, he happily frequented brothels. He longed for a different kind of life, free of the social rules he found in Britain.

After Bournemouth, he left Britain for ever, eventually choosing a much more "**primitive**" life in Samoa, where he built his home.

Viewed from this perspective, his portrayal of Hyde is very sympathetic. He isn't just describing a veneer of respectability, but the real Hyde. After all, this is Hyde's private set of rooms, symbolic of his true nature. He is a man of "**good taste**" because, perhaps, he is a good man. What Victorian society considers to by Hyde's vices and sins are, perhaps to Stevenson, merely pleasures between consenting adults.

Another way Stevenson uses the setting to pull back the "**mask**" of respectability is in the choice of address. "Soho" is instantly recognisable to his readers as a symbol of immoral behaviour. It is full of immigrants, theatres, pubs, brothels, opium dens, a place to visit to satisfy any vice.

But Stevenson deliberately places Jekyll next door. "**Leicester Square**", where he lives, is literally a stone's throw away from "**Soho**". Hyde's lodging cannot be more than a five minute walk away. Stevenson does this to symbolise how the middle class respectability portrayed by all the men in the novel is simply a façade. They live right next door to Soho, because it exists to service their vices. Soho is just as much a part of their true nature, as the good Christian "works" they practice, like Jekyll.

On another level, Stevenson questions society's disapproval of Soho and its vices. Drug taking was not illegal in Victorian London, and neither was prostitution. The Guardian even suggests that Stevenson wrote Jekyll and Hyde while taking a version of cocaine in "a six day cocaine binge" as pain relief for his lung disease.

We can also see this attraction of vice in his other descriptions of London. When Utterson goes in search of Hyde, "**A great chocolate-coloured pall lowered over heaven**." A "pall" is a cloth covering a coffin. Interestingly, it does not cover the city, but the sky. Choosing to call this "heaven" is symbolic. To a Christian reader it suggests that the city has become sinful, and that the evils committed by its citizens are so great, that God is effectively dead – heaven is His coffin, and the "pall" covers it.

But to a reader who knows Stevenson better, the oxymoronic description stands out. The pall is "A great chocolate-coloured pall". "Chocolate" is brown in colour, but delicious in substance. "Great" means large, but also wonderful. The implication is that the death of God should be celebrated. He hints that we would build a freer and better society without the interference of Christian teaching. This is another clue as to why he would find Samoa so much more preferable to England, although by this time Samoan's had incorporated Christian beliefs into its cultural traditions.

So the settings therefore reveal Stevenson's "dual purpose". On the one hand, he wants his Christian readers to read a tale full of sensation and gothic elements. This tale must be resolved with good, and Christian, values triumphing. The sinful Jekyll is punished for his transgression against God. The evil Hyde must die to atone for his murder of Sir Danvers Carew.

But on the other hand he makes fun of these readers. In fact, Stevenson hated this novel, claiming it was the worst book he had ever written. We can infer from this that he disliked having to fit the plot to please his Christian readership, who he may well have seen as hypocritical.

https://www.telegraph.co.uk/books/authors/10-facts-about-robert-louis-stevenson-jekyll-hyde-author/

Again, for the discerning, alert reader, he actually makes fun of his typical readership. He portrays this in the setting he gives to the murder of Sir Danvers Carew. He picks a typical reader to witness this murder, "**the lane, which the maid's window overlooked, was brilliantly lit by the full moon**". She would appreciate the gothic "**moon**", the near midnight setting, the temporary absence of "**fog**", and she appears "**romantically given**". However, closer inspection of her description of the murder indicates how much she has relished watching the horrific, brutal assault unfold.

To illustrate this, Stevenson gives us a hyperbolic description which is not credible, "**the bones were audibly shattered and the body jumped upon the roadway**." Less bloodthirsty readers will spot that the idea of the dead body jumping is even more ridiculous, because Hyde is standing on it at the time!

It is also interesting that Hyde doesn't commit this murder in Soho, but in a more respectable area near the houses of Parliament, "**not far from the river**". On the one hand this plays to the Victorian's fears that crime will threaten rich and respectable people. But on the other, Stevenson is attacking the establishment. If Hyde acts out Jekyll's evil desires, this suggests an attack on Parliament and the law. Could Stevenson be voicing his own dissatisfaction with society and Parliament?

Finally, the setting which he wants us to take from the novel is not the geography of the city, but the symbolic setting of our own nature. He deliberately describes our desires by examining Jekyll's passions. His descriptions turn these into a symbolic landscape, so that we carry inside us "**provinces** of good and ill". Jekyll imagines his evil is in a "deeper **trench**" than other men's, but also realises that his sense of good and evil are at war, describing them as "two natures that contended in **the field** of my consciousness." Jekyll tries to escape this landscape in creating Hyde, "**I had learned to dwell with pleasure, as a beloved day dream, on the thought and separation of these elements**."

Stevenson also tries to escape from this Christian landscape, where a war is fought between "**good**" and "**evil**". It is a war he doesn't believe in: he doesn't see clear distinctions between good and evil, as Jekyll does. But he does believe we should "dwell with pleasure", and he also, like Jekyll, loves to dream as an escape from the current setting.

In his letters he reported that the idea came to him asleep, at war with his own illness, when he "**was dreaming a fine bogey tale**." We can see that his internal landscape, where he can express desires which society prevented him indulging, is an escape, in his dreams, in his writing, and ultimately in his final choice of setting, the primitive idyll of Samoa, rather than the hypocritical Christian suppression of England.

1720 words.

Even I would struggle to write this much in the exam. But most students, uninterrupted, could write 700 – 800 words. Here it is as a shorter Grade 6 answer, 528 words long.

Grade 6 Version

Thesis

Stevenson's wife asked him to write an "allegorical" novel. Consequently Stevenson uses the setting to symbolise the "duality of man".

Consequently, Jekyll's house is described as "handsome". This is just like Stevenson describes Jekyll, as a "handsome" man. Stevenson is suggesting that the men in the novel are just like this on the surface. Beneath the surface, they have evil desires. Hyde represents Jekyll's evil desires hiding beneath the surface.

Utterson describes Hyde's entrance to the back of Jekyll's house as "sinister". To make sure that we understand that this house symbolises Hyde, he describes it with personification. It has a "blind forehead", because it has no window. This suggests that it symbolises how Hyde and his evil nature is hidden by Dr Jekyll.

Stevenson created Jekyll's house to be exactly like John Hunter's house. His Victorian readers would know that this was infamous, because John Hunter was a surgeon who paid grave robbers to bring him dead bodies so he could practice surgery on them. This shows us that Stevenson sees Dr Jekyll as a partly evil character, who has taken scientific experiments too far. His readers would use this setting to be critical of his creation of Hyde.

When Doctor Lanyon sees Hyde transform into Jekyll he is so shocked by this that he chooses to die. This shows the horror that a Christian audience would have at the time. This is also why Stevenson decides that he has to punish Hyde as a murderer, and also decides Jekyll has to die for creating Hyde.

Another setting which Stevenson uses to show the evil of man's "dual nature" is placing Hyde's lodgings in "Soho". Soho was well known as a symbol of vice and crime. This means that Stevenson is criticising the middle class men in London, who go to Soho to use its brothels and satisfy their evil desires.

Stevenson places Dr Jekyll in Leicester Square, because it is next door to Soho. This suggests that middle class men are hypocrites. Like Jekyll has a handsome front, they also have secret desires. Soho symbolises those desires. Stevenson is suggesting that London would be a much better city if middle class men were not hypocrites, and instead behaved morally.

This might also be why he has Hyde kill the highly respected Carew away from Soho, in a respectable part of London, near "the river" and the houses of Parliament. Even the law-making government are hypocrites.

We can see that he thinks the whole of London is full of sin through the way he describes the city when Utterson goes to look for Hyde. He describes London as a dark place, covered by a "chocolate-coloured pall". This sounds unnatural, and suggests that the people in London are also unnatural.

Finally, a "pall" is also used to cover a coffin. This implies that Stevenson thinks that London is like a coffin. The metaphor suggests that the people who live there are dead. This is a Christian view. We know Stevenson wants us to think of this because he says it is "over heaven". This suggests that God is shocked by the behaviour of the people in London.

528 words

Here it is as an 823 word Grade 9 essay

Pay attention to the differences, so you can see how to improve. I hope reading it in this order also causes the internal lightbulb moment – 'aha, I get many of these ideas, I can steal them and quickly move to grades 7 and 8, perhaps 9!'

Thesis

Stevenson's wife asked him to write an "allegorical" novel. So Stevenson uses the setting to symbolise the "duality of man". It allows his readers to read the novella as a warning against the dangers of temptation. However, it also allows Stevenson to subvert and question the Christian values of his readers.

Consequently, Jekyll's house is like him, "handsome", but we also find out that this is actually a "mask" for his true nature, which is also reflected in Hyde.

Hyde exits from the "sinister" rear of the house. Stevenson personifies it with a "blind forehead" to illustrate Utterson's blindness, because he knows this "door" is to Jekyll's own home, but hides this knowledge and of Jekyll's criminally harbouring the murderer, Hyde. This symbolises the blindness of middle class men to their own hypocrisy, showing only their respectable fronts. Stevenson will present them all as having similar desires and vices to Jekyll.

Stevenson has Jekyll live in John Hunter's house, infamous for the surgeon's paying for grave robbers. Although this panders to the sensational tastes of his readership, he uses the setting to make a wider point. Hunter significantly advanced medical science and surgery. Stevenson therefore suggests that ideas of morality are social constructs. Hunter's experiments, by Stevenson's day, had proved to be for the greater good. This setting asks us to consider if Jekyll's experiments might also in time prove to be for the good of mankind.

This invites us to ask if Jekyll's vices might also be viewed as sinful only because of the social attitudes of the time. These were shaped by a Christian interpretation of moral behaviour, which we know Stevenson rejected, taking drugs and visiting brothels.

However, Stevenson must hide his atheism from his predominantly Christian readers, so he gives his novel a "dual nature". For them, he has to make sure that evil is punished, and good triumphs. Therefore, both Jekyll and Hyde are killed off, as though meeting God's justice.

Yet, his settings reveal a strong sympathy for his anti-hero Jekyll and alter ego Hyde. Hyde's private lodgings reflect his real nature (there are no guests he wishes to impress). It is clearly the house of a gentleman, "furnished with luxury and good taste". More than that, Hyde has very refined tastes, so he is a "connoisseur". On one level, this suggests that all middle class men are the same as Hyde, and therefore equally prone to evil. On the other hand, it suggests that Hyde simply has desires - there is nothing "evil" about them. Yes, he does kill Sir Danvers Carew, but until then has committed no crime. Indeed, Jekyll has kept him in solitary confinement up to this point.

If Hyde acts out Jekyll's evil desires, then we must decide if he picks on Sir Danvers Carew as a symbol of society. He represents Parliament. This is linked to the geographical location, near "the river", respectably close to Parliament, and removed from the sinful Soho. While Christian readers will see this as proof that crime is out of control, so no one is safe, sophisticated readers realise Stevenson is attacking British society and its law makers.

Another way the setting questions the Christian view of morality is in placing Hyde's lodgings in Soho. Though contemporary readers will have seen this as symbolic of vice, populated by theatres, gin palaces, opium dens and brothels, Londoners would pick out another symbolism. Soho is next door to Leicester Square, where gentlemen like Jekyll live. They are literally a stone's throw apart. One reading is that this points to the hypocrisy of middle class men, where the square reflects their public face, but Soho reflects their true, sinful nature.

However, Stevenson's decision to leave Britain altogether, living in the "primitive" society of Samoa suggests that it is not the vices of the middle classes which he finds hypocritical. Instead, it is the treatment of their natures and natural desires as sinful by a repressed, Christian moral code.

His description of London attacks this Christian viewpoint cleverly. When Utterson goes in search of Hyde, "A great chocolate-coloured pall lowered over heaven." The "pall" does not cover the city, instead the sky is the metaphorical coffin. Choosing to call this "heaven" is symbolic. To a Christian reader it suggests that the city has become sinful, and that the evils committed by its citizens are so great, that God is effectively dead – heaven is His coffin, and the "pall" covers it.

But to a reader who knows Stevenson better, the oxymoronic description stands out. The pall is "A great chocolate-coloured pall". "Chocolate" is brown in colour, but delicious in substance. "Great" means large, but also wonderful. The implication is that the death of God should be celebrated. He hints that we would build a freer and better society without the interference of Christian teaching. This is another clue as to why he would find Samoa so much more preferable to England. **823 words**

(Every reference to the setting, and explanation of why it is there, is a discussion of 'structure' in AO2. The reference to 'form' is in seeing the whole novel as allegorical. Tactically, I would control the examiner better by being more explicit: 'Stevenson's wife asked him to write **in the form of** an "allegorical" novel.')

Stevenson's Attack on the Victorian Gentleman

Read the following extract from Chapter 3 and then answer the question that follows.

In this extract…

A fortnight later, by excellent good fortune, the doctor gave one of his pleasant dinners to some five or six old cronies, all intelligent, reputable men and all judges of good wine; and Mr. Utterson so contrived that he remained behind after the others had departed. This was no new arrangement, but a thing that had befallen many scores of times. Where Utterson was liked, he was liked well. Hosts loved to detain the dry lawyer, when the light-hearted and the loose-tongued had already their foot on the threshold; they liked to sit a while in his unobtrusive company, practising for solitude, sobering their minds in the man's rich silence after the expense and strain of gaiety. To this rule, Dr. Jekyll was no exception; and as he now sat on the opposite side of the fire — a large, well-made, smooth-faced man of fifty, with something of a slyish cast perhaps, but every mark of capacity and kindness — you could see by his looks that he cherished for Mr. Utterson a sincere and warm affection.

"I have been wanting to speak to you, Jekyll," began the latter. "You know that will of yours?"

A close observer might have gathered that the topic was distasteful; but the doctor carried it off gaily. "My poor Utterson," said he, "you are unfortunate in such a client. I never saw a man so distressed as you were by my will; unless it were that hide-bound pedant, Lanyon, at what he called my scientific heresies. Oh, I know he's a good fellow — you needn't frown — an excellent fellow, and I always mean to see more of him; but a hide-bound pedant for all that; an ignorant, blatant pedant. I was never more disappointed in any man than Lanyon."

"You know I never approved of it," pursued Utterson, ruthlessly disregarding the fresh topic.

"My will? Yes, certainly, I know that," said the doctor, a trifle sharply. "You have told me so."

"Well, I tell you so again," continued the lawyer. "I have been learning something of young Hyde."

The large handsome face of Dr. Jekyll grew pale to the very lips, and there came a blackness about his eyes. "I do not care to hear more," said he. "This is a matter I thought we had agreed to drop."

"What I heard was abominable," said Utterson.

"It can make no change. You do not understand my position," returned the doctor, with a certain incoherency of manner. "I am painfully situated, Utterson; my position is a very strange — a very strange one. It is one of those affairs that cannot be mended by talking."

"Jekyll," said Utterson, "you know me: I am a man to be trusted. Make a clean breast of this in confidence; and I make no doubt I can get you out of it."

"My good Utterson," said the doctor, "this is very good of you, this is downright good of you, and I cannot find words to thank you in. I believe you fully; I would trust you before any man alive, ay, before myself, if I

could make the choice; but indeed it isn't what you fancy; it is not so bad as that; and just to put your good heart at rest, I will tell you one thing: the moment I choose, I can be rid of Mr. Hyde. I give you my hand upon that; and I thank you again and again; and I will just add one little word, Utterson, that I'm sure you'll take in good part: this is a private matter, and I beg of you to let it sleep."

Using the extract as a starting point, explore how Stevenson presents the idea of the Victorian gentleman?

<u>Possible Essay Plan</u>

Thesis

State why Stevenson focuses on gentlemen:

1. To show their hypocrisy
2. To show that power is in the hands of too few men, who are all inter-connected or went to the same schools
3. To show how secrecy is a cover for self-interest
4. To show that gentlemen's lives are being oppressed by Christian fear of homosexuality
5. To show that the law and Parliament is corrupt

Events to cover:

1. Lanyon, Jekyll and Utterson all going to the same school
2. Utterson at the centre of every man's life, including the murder victim, Sir Danvers Carew
3. Sir Danvers as a symbol of Parliament and the 1885 'gross indecency' Act
4. Hyde is a gentleman – his civility to Utterson and Lanyon, his lodgings, his visit to the master of the maid who witnessed the murder
5. Jekyll's reluctance to name his sin
6. Utterson's dream about Hyde's apparently sexual power over Jekyll
7. Enfield's and Utterson's fear of blackmail and homosexuality
8. The proximity of Soho to Leicester Square
9. Hyde's love of life, contrasted to Lanyon's love of death, and Utterson's love of abstinence
10. Utterson's avoidance of scandal and inheritance of Jekyll's estate
11. Stevenson's moving to Samoa

The Role of Violence

Read the following extract from Chapter 4 and then answer the question that follows.

In this extract….

Extract

Nearly a year later, in the month of October, 18—, London was startled by a crime of singular ferocity and rendered all the more notable by the high position of the victim. The details were few and startling.

A maid servant living alone in a house not far from the river, had gone up-stairs to bed about eleven. Although a fog rolled over the city in the small hours, the early part of the night was cloudless, and the lane, which the maid's window overlooked, was brilliantly lit by the full moon.

It seems she was romantically given, for she sat down upon her box, which stood immediately under the window, and fell into a dream of musing. Never (she used to say, with streaming tears, when she narrated that experience), never had she felt more at peace with all men or thought more kindly of the world.

And as she so sat she became aware of an aged and beautiful gentleman with white hair, drawing near along the lane; and advancing to meet him, another and very small gentleman, to whom at first she paid less attention. When they had come within speech (which was just under the maid's eyes) the older man bowed and accosted the other with a very pretty manner of politeness. It did not seem as if the subject of his address were of great importance; indeed, from his pointing, it sometimes appeared as if he were only inquiring his way; but the moon shone on his face as he spoke, and the girl was pleased to watch it, it seemed to breathe such an innocent and old-world kindness of disposition, yet with something high too, as of a well-founded self-content.

Presently her eye wandered to the other, and she was surprised to recognise in him a certain Mr. Hyde, who had once visited her master and for whom she had conceived a dislike. He had in his hand a heavy cane, with which he was trifling; but he answered never a word, and seemed to listen with an ill-contained impatience.

And then all of a sudden he broke out in a great flame of anger, stamping with his foot, brandishing the cane, and carrying on (as the maid described it) like a madman. The old gentleman took a step back, with the air of one very much surprised and a trifle hurt; and at that Mr. Hyde broke out of all bounds and clubbed him to the earth.

And next moment, with ape-like fury, he was trampling his victim under foot and hailing down a storm of blows, under which the bones were audibly shattered and the body jumped upon the roadway. At the horror of these sights and sounds, the maid fainted.

Beginning with the extract, how does Stevenson present violence and brutality in the novel?

Essay on Violence

Read this essay written only about the extract above. Those of you already getting grade 7 or higher will see that this is easy to do once you trust your instinct to write your thesis, then, as you read the extract, leap on any quotation which fits that thesis.

Thesis

Stevenson wants to shock his readers with the description of violence, and then hold a mirror up to them as seekers of this thrill. He seems to be asking his readers if they are any different from Doctor Jekyll. So, he writes about violence in a detached tone, as though he is unemotional about the very emotive subject matter.

Consequently, he is not startled, but "**London was startled**". Personifying London in this way also suggests that the whole population is alarmed by this murder. Stevenson adds to this by focusing on the "**high position of the victim**", because it suggests that no one is protected or immune from violence.

Stevenson expects his female readership to be most affected by the violence in London, and consequently the events are partly reported through the eyes of "**a maid**". Her circumstances make this more alarming, as she is "**living alone**" and has no one to protect her. So, she is a proxy for the vulnerability of his female readership.

There is also the possibility here that he begins to mock the reader's appetite for violence, experienced vicariously. So Stevenson also gives the scene a Gothic setting, where a "**fog rolled over the city**" and the murder will take place under "**the full moon**".

He next introduces an element of doubt into her testimony, commenting that "**It seems she was romantically given**". The use of "**seems**" implies that her account might not be as factual as we might wish. That she is "**romantically given**" also implies some exaggeration in her testimony. This impression is further added to when Stevenson points out the contradiction between her apparently heart felt "**streaming tears**" and the next information that "**she used to say…when she narrated that experience.**" Why would she keep retelling a story which was so distressing? The implication is that she takes great satisfaction from the violence of the tale. Here violence is used to mock the reader of Stevenson's own Gothic tale, as though to interrupt his narrative to tell the reader that he is giving them what they want – "**startling**", random and motiveless violence.

The use of "**that experience**" rather than "**the experience**" strongly implies that this is not the only narrative of violence that she enjoys retelling: it is "**that experience**" rather than 'this one'. A similar choice is made in telling us she "**narrated**" rather than described it – we are encouraged to suppose she has crafted and perhaps embellished the tale through retelling. This suggests violence is enjoyed vicariously and is a welcome distraction from everyday life. In this way, there is a strong parallel between the reader and Jekyll, who both enjoy their violent experience through others' actions.

Stevenson makes the violence seem more wicked and threatening by alluding to the goodness and gentleness of the victim, who is therefore both "**aged and beautiful**". His "**white hair**" suggests both age and innocence. Just in case we miss this, his face "**seemed to breathe such an innocent and old-world kindness**".

However, we now begin to sense a duality of purpose in the description of violence which is coming. The use of "**breathe**" to describe the innocence of his face feels ironic, as Sir Danvers is just about to breathe his last breath.

Next, the contrast between Sir Danvers and Hyde is comic. On the one hand the purpose is to show that he is an innocent victim of Hyde's motiveless rage, "**like a madman**". But we can read this another way. Carew has kept on demanding something of Hyde, not reading his body language in any way, while even the maid points out that he "**seemed to listen with an ill-contained impatience.**" Despite making his impatient obvious, Carew ignores Hyde.

When Hyde does threaten violence, Carew's reaction of being "**very much surprised**" rather than shocked, or in fear of his life, is potentially comic. The sudden addition that he looked "**a trifle hurt**" is wonderful understatement, as he completely misreads the danger. The irony of "**trifle**" is similar to that of "**breathe**" earlier, because he is now going to be very hurt indeed.

In the next moment, the level of violence is not comic, but shocking. For the Christian reader, Stevenson describes Hyde's violence as an "**ape-like fury**" to suggest that Jekyll has released a primitive, godless kind of evil. This horror is added to with the sound of the attack, so that the "**bones were audibly shattered**", and visually the scene becomes more macabre when Hyde beats Carew's body with such force that "**the body jumped on the roadway.**" The final horror is suggested when the maid cannot endure what she has witness, and "**fainted**".

However, the dual purpose which makes it comic is apparent again. The "**body jumped**" while Hyde was "**trampling**" on it, a very contradictory statement. The maid could not hear any of their conversation, but she can hear bones being shattered. The maid frequently retells the story, but it is so shocking it makes her faint. There is a suggestion that Stevenson is toying with the reader, giving them a sensational description of horror he knows they want, but filling it with contradictions and apparent irony as though to mock them for their salacious and vicarious joy in reading about it.

875 words

Your job now is to find other parts of the text to write about. You can find plenty of these by re-reading the earlier parts of the guide.

Because the examiners don't mind how many that is, I recommend the following –

1. Always relate your extract to the beginning of the novel – here it will be the violence of Hyde as the "damned Juggernaut" "trampling" the girl, and the different ways of reading this encounter. Contrast it to the behaviour of Enfield and the others.

2. Always relate your extract to the end of the novel – here it will be the violence Hyde inflicts on himself, and what this reveals about his desire for control and independence.

3. Any other example which occurs to you – here you could write about your interpretation for why his attack on the match seller is so slight, or why you believe he doesn't murder anyone else.

Once you have written those paragraphs, decide where they will fit in the overall essay.

Finally, rewrite it to a length you could write in 45 minutes. It's the best revision there is.

Or, you cold cheat, and look at my grade 9 interpretations of all the other examples of violence and brutality in the novel which follow!

<u>Other Examples of Violence with Analysis</u>

From **Chapter 10 HENRY JEKYLL'S FULL STATEMENT OF THE CASE**

"My devil had been long caged, he came out roaring. I was conscious, even when I took the draught, of a more unbridled, a more furious propensity to ill. It must have been this, I suppose, that stirred in my soul that tempest of impatience with which I listened to the civilities of my unhappy victim; I declare, at least, before God, no man morally sane could have been guilty of that crime upon so pitiful a provocation; and that I struck in no more reasonable spirit than that in which a sick child may break a plaything.

We have already seen that Jekyll's lack of a motive for the killing does not make sense with the rest of the novel. You can relate this to your knowledge of the 1885 Act if you wish to explore the homosexual context.

Here, Stevenson again presents the violence in a way which makes all readers feel they are potential victims. Hyde's rage in killing becomes like "**a sick child may break a plaything**", at once suggesting his lack of control and his immense strength. This makes violence doubly dangerous, because it can come without warning or provocation.

But I had voluntarily stripped myself of all those balancing instincts by which even the worst of us continues to walk with some degree of steadiness among temptations; and in my case, to be tempted, however slightly, was to fall.

Instantly the spirit of hell awoke in me and raged. With a transport of glee, I mauled the unresisting body, tasting delight from every blow; and it was not till weariness had begun to succeed, that I was suddenly, in the top fit of my delirium, struck through the heart by a cold thrill of terror.

Hyde's "**glee**" in the murder is also described in animalistic terms, as he "**mauled**" the body. It suggests that city life has created an environment in which civilisation is breaking down and men are reverting to a more primitive, animalistic version of themselves.

A mist dispersed; I saw my life to be forfeit; and fled from the scene of these excesses, at once glorying and trembling, my lust of evil gratified and stimulated, my love of life screwed to the topmost peg. I ran to the house in Soho, and (to make assurance doubly sure) destroyed my papers; thence I set out through the lamplit streets, in the same divided ecstasy of mind, gloating on my crime, light-headedly devising others in the future, and yet still hastening and still hearkening in my wake for the steps of the avenger.

The murderer feels "**terror**" at being caught, but this fear is also described as a "**thrill**". He both trembles, but is "**gratified and stimulated.**" The act of killing has led to him feeling most alive, his "**love of life screwed to the topmost peg**". Stevenson presents violence as seductive and life affirming. He doesn't just present a murderer as having no conscience, willing to kill in order to get what he wants. Here, the murderer simply wants the thrill of killing, which means a victim will not recognise the danger they are in, and cannot protect themselves.

Hyde had a song upon his lips as he compounded the draught, and as he drank it, pledged the dead man. The pangs of transformation had not done tearing him, before Henry Jekyll, with streaming tears of gratitude and remorse, had fallen upon his knees and lifted his clasped hands to God."

Jekyll presents Hyde as showing no remorse. However, remember that we do not have to trust Jekyll's description, because Hyde has ample opportunity to kill again, but refuses to do so.

....

From Chapter 1 STORY OF THE DOOR

 "All at once, I saw two figures: one a little man who was stumping along eastward at a good walk, and the other a girl of maybe eight or ten who was running as hard as she was able down a cross street. Well, sir, the two ran into one another naturally enough at the corner; and then came the horrible part of the thing; for the man trampled calmly over the child's body and left her screaming on the ground.

It sounds nothing to hear, but it was hellish to see. It wasn't like a man; it was like some damned Juggernaut. I gave a view-halloa, took to my heels, collared my gentleman, and brought him back to where there was already quite a group about the screaming child. He was perfectly cool and made no resistance, but gave me one look, so ugly that it brought out the sweat on me like running.

The people who had turned out were the girl's own family; and pretty soon, the doctor, for whom she had been sent, put in his appearance. Well, the child was not much the worse, more frightened, according to the Sawbones; and there you might have supposed would be an end to it.

But there was one curious circumstance. I had taken a loathing to my gentleman at first sight. So had the child's family, which was only natural. But the doctor's case was what struck me. He was the usual cut-and-dry apothecary, of no particular age and colour, with a strong Edinburgh accent, and about as emotional as a bagpipe. Well, sir, he was like the rest of us; every time he looked at my prisoner, I saw that Sawbones turn sick and white with the desire to kill him. I knew what was in his mind, just as he knew what was in mine; and killing being out of the question, we did the next best.

Hyde's first act of violence is not what it seems. Although Enfield describes it as "**hellish to see**", we are asked to question his judgement, just as Stevenson asks us to question the judgement of the maid. Hyde "**trampled calmly over the girl**", but we can see from the description that he has not seen her as she ran into him, that she has fallen while he has walked "**calmly**" on. Given her age and size, this would involve one foot standing on her as he continues striding. Even the doctor admits that she is unharmed by this. When Enfield chases him, he makes no resistance. We see that Hyde has not been violent at all.

We told the man we could and would make such a scandal out of this, as should make his name stink from one end of London to the other. If he had any friends or any credit, we undertook that he should lose them. And all the time, as we were pitching it in red hot, we were keeping the women off him as best we could, for they were as wild as harpies. I never saw a circle of such hateful faces; and there was the man in the middle, with a kind of black, sneering coolness—frightened too, I could see that—but carrying it off, sir, really like Satan.

'If you choose to make capital out of this accident,' said he, 'I am naturally helpless. No gentleman but wishes to avoid a scene,' says he. 'Name your figure.'

Well, we screwed him up to a hundred pounds for the child's family; he would have clearly liked to stick out; but there was something about the lot of us that meant mischief, and at last he struck.

Yet the apparently civilised onlookers all want to kill him. This is so urgent an instinct that Enfield watches the doctor "**turn sick and white with the desire to kill him**". He confesses that this was also his desire. Even the women want to tear him apart, being "**wild as harpies**". Stevenson presents us with the paradox of Enfield's description, that Hyde was "**really like Satan**". This doesn't match the events in any way. Any objective assessment would see that he, the doctor, and the women, are far more wicked than Hyde. They prove this by blackmailing him for a hundred pounds, the equivalent of a year's wages for an average man.

A Christian reader might not see this, but latch on to the Satanic reference, the idea that Hyde was "**damned**", the size and youth of the victim at now more than ten, her terrible "**screaming**" all point to his incredible evil. But an astute reader will notice the incredible contradiction, that the accuser, Enfield, behaves in a much more evil way.

This strongly suggests that civilisation is just a veneer, and all men will threaten violence when they feel they can get away with it. It also suggests that the desire to kill is universal and very close to the surface. It wouldn't take much for social order to break down, and murder to be much more common.

....

From **Chapter 10 HENRY JEKYLL'S FULL STATEMENT OF THE CASE**

"He walked fast, hunted by his fears, chattering to himself, skulking through the less-frequented thoroughfares, counting the minutes that still divided him from midnight. Once a woman spoke to him, offering, I think, a box of lights. He smote her in the face, and she fled.

Although a murderer, Hyde is now presented as a victim of violence. He is "**chattering to himself**" as though becoming yet more primitive and ape-like, and is being "**hunted by his fears**". The moral message might be that violence turns on the aggressor, so that he is suffers because of what he has done. His moral decline is also suggested in the way he "**smote**" a woman "**in the face**". Jekyll also suggests Hyde's mental decline here, because he can't remember what the woman had offered or said to Hyde, only adding "**I think**".

But, on another level, the violence also serves to shock us in how weak Hyde appears to be, as though this is a half-hearted attempt at evil. He doesn't try to rob or rape her, which thousands of other Londoners might well have tried seeing an opportunity in the **"less-frequented"** streets. He is hardly the embodiment of evil. And of course, Hyde can only be executed once – there is nothing to stop him murdering this woman except his apparent desire not to murder her. This strongly suggests that Jekyll's evil nature is not that great. It also asks us to wonder again at the murder of Sir Danvers Carew, which clearly was very violent. What was so different in that circumstance to this?

When I came to myself at Lanyon's, the horror of my old friend perhaps affected me somewhat: I do not know; it was at least but a drop in the sea to the abhorrence with which I looked back upon these hours. A change had come over me. It was no longer the fear of the gallows, it was the horror of being Hyde that racked me. I received Lanyon's condemnation partly in a dream; it was partly in a dream that I came home to my own house and got into bed."

....

From Chapter 8 THE LAST NIGHT

""Jekyll," cried Utterson, with a loud voice, "I demand to see you." He paused a moment, but there came no reply. "I give you fair warning, our suspicions are aroused, and I must and shall see you," he resumed; "if not by fair means, then by foul! if not of your consent, then by brute force!"

"Utterson," said the voice, "for God's sake, have mercy!"

"Ah, that's not Jekyll's voice—it's Hyde's!" cried Utterson. "Down with the door, Poole!"

Poole swung the axe over his shoulder; the blow shook the building, and the red baize door leaped against the lock and hinges. A dismal screech, as of mere animal terror, rang from the cabinet. Up went the axe again, and again the panels crashed and the frame bounded; four times the blow fell; but the wood was tough and the fittings were of excellent workmanship; and it was not until the fifth, that the lock burst in sunder and the wreck of the door fell inwards on the carpet.

This is another moment in the novel where we question Hyde's presentation by others. The axe has merely come from outside the theatre. Hyde could easily have kept this for himself, yet he has made no effort to defend himself. Utterson and Poole do not notice this: Stevenson makes us work for the knowledge.

Inside the cabinet, all the evidence is of a calm man. He has **"a good fire going"**, papers are **"neatly laid out"** and he is about to have **"tea"**. Hyde is a middle class gentleman at leisure. This is totally at odds with his response to the break in, with **"a dismal screech, as if of mere animal terror"**.

As usual, Utterson has misinterpreted the scene. Hyde has been calm, waiting for this moment which he knows is coming. We know he has chosen cyanide from Stevenson's description of it having **"a strong smell of kernels"** – cyanide is well known for its smell of bitter almond.

His scream is not of terror, it is of pain. He has clearly planned to have cyanide at his side, and now drinks it in such a high dose that it appears to kill him in the time it takes for Poole to swing the axe 5 times. This would be an extraordinarily large and painful overdose, which burns the body from the inside. In reality, liquid cyanide would take up to 11 minutes to kill, which is also what we see with Hyde's still **"twitching"** body, and a face which still has **"semblance of life"**.

Being a gentleman, Utterson will not allow himself to wield the axe, and lower himself to use violence. However, he orders Poole to use it. In other words, he is control of that violence. It makes us look at Hyde's violence and ask how far it is controlled by the Jekyll.

This also makes us ask questions about Jekyll's control of Hyde's violence. If we accept that Hyde only exists in order to commit acts, and experience pleasures, which Jekyll wanted to experience, then the ultimate act of violence, killing Sir Danvers Carew must have satisfied Jekyll on some level. Because it appears to be motiveless, it asks us to consider what motive Jekyll could be blind to. What has he suppressed, and hidden from his own thoughts? Or perhaps he is not blind to his own motive, but wishes to keep it secret from Utterson? It is up to the reader to guess at this, from few clues.

Any detective would ask, who gains from the murder of Sir Danvers Carew? Not Hyde. He has to remain hidden, because to appear is to risk being caught and executed. Who gains from that? Jekyll. Hyde does not have the power to appear while Jekyll is awake, and killing Sir Danvers Carew has not given Hyde more strength or power to do so. Jekyll has not woken up as Hyde since the killing. This is a strong clue that killing Carew was done to satisfy Jekyll more than Hyde. The next strong clue is the final event which tips the power relationship into Hyde's favour. Hyde has been unable to appear without the drug until Jekyll decides to commit a sin in his own person, as Jekyll:

"Not that I dreamed of resuscitating Hyde; the bare idea of that would startle me to frenzy: no, it was in my own person, that I was once more tempted to trifle with my conscience; and it was as an ordinary secret sinner, that I at last fell before the assaults of temptation."

We can see here that Jekyll's plan is to keep Hyde not just locked away, but experiencing his own death, as "**resuscitating**" implies. His motive in killing Carew is therefore his desire to kill Hyde, without also killing Jekyll.

To a Christian audience, Jekyll deserves his punishment because he ultimately gives Hyde power by returning as a "**secret sinner**" as Jekyll. To Stevenson, the moment is more interesting because it tells us that Jekyll is in control of Hyde until this moment. It suggests that Hyde had been created for just this purpose. He needed Hyde to kill Sir Danvers Carew. He didn't need Hyde to enjoy his life as a "**secret sinner**", as he is able to go back to that life once Hyde is repressed.

Stevenson suggests, then, that Hyde only gains power once Jekyll can no longer tell himself that Hyde is responsible for his sin. The idea that Hyde is "**pure evil**" is a fiction dreamed up by Jekyll to blame Hyde, and hide his own control of Hyde's actions. The logic of Jekyll's argument would have to be that Hyde only gains control once he commits the most evil act, murdering the "**innocent**" Carew. But this pointedly doesn't happen. Hyde gains control only once Jekyll has no more excuses, and embraces his own sin.

Stevenson therefore points out that Jekyll was always Hyde. When we return to the will, we know this to be true. He always planned for Hyde to survive and Jekyll to disappear. The tragedy happens when Jekyll goes back on this plan and tries to stop Hyde and his "**love of life**" from appearing.

Is Stevenson suggesting that Hyde would have been a preferable state than Jekyll? If Hyde had not been "**caged**", he would not have come "out roaring". The sins he commits before this seem minor. They certainly haven't attracted any attention. There are no scandals.

What is wrong with society is that it has created men whose main method of engaging with the world is suppressing their own desires. Utterson is the embodiment of repression, and kills his own desires. Lanyon kills himself in order to suppress the truth of Jekyll's scientific discoveries and the proof that God alone is not the creator of life. Jekyll kills himself because he tries to kill his own desires, and tries to repress Hyde. It isn't really Hyde who lashes out at society and its rule makers in killing Carew. Why would he? Hyde is at home in society. It is Jekyll who has reason to want revenge on what society has done to him.

In a better society, Utterson would still drink wine and visit the theatre instead of reading "**dry divinity**". Lanyon and Jekyll would have collaborated on the science, and made a better, public use of it. Jekyll would have indulged his pleasures without fear of scandal, or social disapproval.

This also brings us back to the John Hunter house. Hunter's sinful use of dead bodies, without the families' consent, is morally wrong. But his experiments on the bodies were not carried out in secret, for personal gain. Instead they were on display, in the "**theatre**" he had especially built in his house. His fame, rather than social disapproval, is caused by sharing his discoveries with the medical community, for the medical benefit of mankind.

How very personal this might have felt to Stevenson, who has suffered from infancy with undiagnosed conditions with his lungs. How he must have longed for a specific treatment, rather than bed rest, drugs, and the pursuit of a warm climate. Stevenson ultimately gives Jekyll the John Hunter house not to point out the similarities between them as "**secret sinner**"s. It is to point to the terrible crime of secrecy. Jekyll's secrecy ultimately destroys his science, so that we can never test whether it can create an "**angel**" rather than a "**fiend**". Lanyon's secrecy is the same: he refused to participate in the science when they were younger, and he refuses to leave any clues as to the science in his posthumous letter.

In the end, Lanyon and Jekyll both choose death. Stevenson probably finds this unforgiveable. Hyde does not choose death, he is going to be executed anyway. He only chooses the manner of his death.

Finally, who would Stevenson blame for these deaths? Is it the giving in to "**temptation**", the natural punishment for those who commit sins against Christian teaching? Or is it Christian society itself, forcing secrecy, criminalising natural desires and pleasures and creating a society which represses us?

The besiegers, appalled by their own riot and the stillness that had succeeded, stood back a little and peered in. There lay the cabinet before their eyes in the quiet lamplight, a good fire glowing and chattering on the hearth, the kettle singing its thin strain, a drawer or two open, papers neatly set forth on the business-table, and nearer the fire, the things laid out for tea: the quietest room, you would have said, and, but for the glazed presses full of chemicals, the most commonplace that night in London.

Right in the midst there lay the body of a man sorely contorted and still twitching. They drew near on tiptoe, turned it on its back and beheld the face of Edward Hyde. He was dressed in clothes far too large for him, clothes of the doctor's bigness; the cords of his face still moved with a semblance of life, but life was quite gone; and by the crushed phial in the hand and the strong smell of kernels that hung upon the air, Utterson knew that he was looking on the body of a self-destroyer."

The Role of Secrecy

Read the following extract from Chapter 5 and then answer the question that follows.

Extract

"And now," said Mr. Utterson, as soon as Poole had left them, "you have heard the news?"

The doctor shuddered. "They were crying it in the square," he said. "I heard them in my dining-room."

"One word," said the lawyer. "Carew was my client, but so are you, and I want to know what I am doing. You have not been mad enough to hide this fellow?"

"Utterson, I swear to God," cried the doctor, "I swear to God I will never set eyes on him again. I bind my honour to you that I am done with him in this world. It is all at an end. And indeed he does not want my help; you do not know him as I do; he is safe, he is quite safe; mark my words, he will never more be heard of."

The lawyer listened gloomily; he did not like his friend's feverish manner. "You seem pretty sure of him," said he; "and for your sake, I hope you may be right. If it came to a trial, your name might appear."

"I am quite sure of him," replied Jekyll ; "I have grounds for certainty that I cannot share with any one. But there is one thing on which you may advise me. I have — I have received a letter; and I am at a loss whether I should show it to the police. I should like to leave it in your hands, Utterson; you would judge wisely, I am sure; I have so great a trust in you."

"You fear, I suppose, that it might lead to his detection?" asked the lawyer.

"No," said the other. "I cannot say that I care what becomes of Hyde; I am quite done with him. I was thinking of my own character, which this hateful business has rather exposed."

Utterson ruminated a while; he was surprised at his friend's selfishness, and yet relieved by it. "Well," said he, at last, "let me see the letter."

The letter was written in an odd, upright hand and signed "Edward Hyde": and it signified, briefly enough, that the writer's benefactor, Dr. Jekyll, whom he had long so unworthily repaid for a thousand generosities, need labour under no alarm for his safety, as he had means of escape on which he placed a sure dependence. The lawyer liked this letter well enough; it put a better colour on the intimacy than he had looked for; and he blamed himself for some of his past suspicions.

Beginning with this extract, how does Stevenson present the theme of secrecy in the novel?

- This is pretty much the essay on Utterson. You'll notice that there are only so many questions the examiners can ask – they will play around with the wording, but the content is always the same.
- The only other character we need to consider is Enfield.

This comes from the opening of the novel and so sets the theme of secrecy for the whole novel:

*"I see you feel as I do," said Mr. Enfield. "Yes, it's a bad story. For my man was a fellow that nobody could have to do with, a really damnable man; and the person that drew the cheque **is the very pink of the proprieties, celebrated too, and (what makes it worse) one of your fellows who do what they call good**. Black-mail, I suppose; an honest man paying through the nose for some of the capers of his youth. Black-Mail House is what I call that place with the door, in consequence. Though even that, you know, is far from explaining all," he added, and with the words fell into a vein of musing.*

From this he was recalled by Mr. Utterson asking rather suddenly:

"And you don't know if the drawer of the cheque lives there?"

"A likely place, isn't it?" returned Mr. Enfield. "But I happen to have noticed his address; he lives in some square or other."

"And you never asked about the—place with the door?" said Mr. Utterson.

"No, sir: I had a delicacy," was the reply. "I feel very strongly about putting questions; it partakes too much of the style of the day of judgment. You start a question, and it's like starting a stone. You sit quietly on the top of a hill; and away the stone goes, starting others; and presently some bland old bird (the last you would have thought of) is knocked on the head in his own back-garden and the family have to change their name. No, sir, I make it a rule of mine: the more it looks like Queer Street, the less I ask."

"A very good rule, too," said the lawyer."

This extended metaphor and simile invite us to decide on the moral purpose of secrecy in the book. Is the rejection of "the day of judgement" (which is a biblical reference) therefore a rejection of Christianity? Or does it suggest people should be tolerant of each other's sins, allowing God to decide how we should be judged in death?

Does exposing the sins of "some bland old bird" suggest the victim of society's disapproval is harmless, and undeserving of this scorn, or does his blandness and age suggest that everyone, no matter how insignificant in appearance, is full of secret sins, pretending to be good as a mask for their evil natures.

Similarly, is "the family have to change their name" comedic hyperbole, intended to be humorous, or is it an actual description of the severity of the sin the man must have committed?

Stevenson sets the novel up this way in order to test our view of morality, and whether we see secrecy as allowing hypocrisy and sin to continue, or whether we see it as a kindness, given that no one is without sin. The reference to the "stone" is a deliberate allusion to Jesus's instruction, "let he who is without sin cast the first stone" (John 8:7), which places us firmly on Enfield's side, forgiving the sinner because they are similar to ourselves.

However, by the end of the novel, Utterson has kept all of Jekyll's secrets. The only other person who knows the truth, Doctor Lanyon, has effectively committed suicide rather than live with the secret. Utterson, taking Enfield's description of the need to change name, would not be able to live with Jekyll's social disgrace. He would need to distance himself from Jekyll's name, and his inheritance.

So we can see there is a clear self interest in Utterson's desire to keep Jekyll's discovery secret.

Stevenson also invites us to see the suppression of scientific advancement as a moral issue. In Jekyll's own words, the drug could have created angelic forms, much better versions of ourselves:

HENRY JEKYLL'S FULL STATEMENT OF THE CASE

"That night I had come to the fatal cross-roads. Had I approached my discovery in a more noble spirit, had I risked the experiment while under the empire of generous or pious aspirations, all must have been otherwise, and from these agonies of death and birth, I had come forth an angel instead of a fiend. The drug had no discriminating action; it was neither diabolical nor divine".

Imagine a society in which such "angel"s were commonplace? Is it right to deny the chance of repeating this scientific discovery?

The Battle Between Good and Evil

Read the following extract from Chapter 6 and then answer the question that follows.

Extract

Time ran on; thousands of pounds were offered in reward, for the death of Sir Danvers was resented as a public injury; but Mr. Hyde had disappeared out of the ken of the police as though he had never existed.

Much of his past was unearthed, indeed, and all disreputable: tales came out of the man's cruelty, at once so callous and violent; of his vile life, of his strange associates, of the hatred that seemed to have surrounded his career; but of his present whereabouts, not a whisper.

From the time he had left the house in Soho on the morning of the murder, he was simply blotted out; and gradually, as time drew on, Mr. Utterson began to recover from the hotness of his alarm, and to grow more at quiet with himself.

The death of Sir Danvers was, to his way of thinking, more than paid for by the disappearance of Mr. Hyde. Now that that evil influence had been withdrawn, a new life began for Dr. Jekyll. He came out of his seclusion, renewed relations with his friends, became once more their familiar guest and entertainer; and whilst he had always been known for charities, he was now no less distinguished for religion. He was busy, he was much in the open air, he did good; his face seemed to open and brighten, as if with an inward consciousness of service; and for more than two months, the doctor was at peace.

Starting with the extract, how does Stevenson present ideas about good and evil in the novel?

Use my grade 9 notes to write an essay. Your essay doesn't have to be grade 9, of course, but it can be.

You might begin by simply ordering the points I make into a logical sequence, to build the argument you want to put forward.

Then you can try to write it in fewer words – which points will you keep, and which will you get rid of?

Grade 9 Notes

Thesis

We can argue that the novel convinces us that Stevenson sees no such thing as good. We are all, to varying degrees, evil. We can certainly look at all the characters in the novel and argue that this is so.

Next, we must consider if this is because Stevenson wants us to identify with them, because they represent mankind. Or, whether he is attacking a particularly male society of wealthy, privileged gentlemen, who represent London society and the corrupt ruling classes, and not necessarily mankind.

Points to Consider:

Here is a quick run through of the potential corruption of each character. Utterson we have already covered fully.

Enfield has been coming from "the ends of the earth" when he first meets Hyde. Stevenson therefore implies that he is similar to Hyde in his sinful habits. Moreover, though Hyde has trodden with one foot on the unharmed young girl, Enfield has immediately longed to murder him, and then extorted him with threats of violence and blackmail, out of £100, a small fortune.

Guest has willingly gone along with Utterson's desire to keep Jekyll's identity as the killer of Sir Danvers Carew a secret from the police.

Poole has agreed to keep the documents, left by Jekyll and Hyde to Utterson, a secret, without going to the police.

Even Doctor Lanyon gives up on life once he realises Jekyll's secret. On the one hand, this might be seen as noble self-sacrifice, escaping a world which is too full of sin. But on the other hand it is the ultimate act of vanity to give up God's most precious gift, life, because Jekyll has proved Lanyon's view of science to be too narrow and therefore wrong.

Lanyon too has left nothing for the police, even though he dramatically reveals both that Jekyll is Hyde, and Hyde is a murderer.

Stevenson asks us to be detectives after the events of the novel are over. These are the secrets kept from the reader:

1. Why does Jekyll not give a reason for killing Sir Danvers Carew?

Because it is the secret of homosexuality, which is at the centre of the novel – Carew has probably propositioned him.

"It must have been this, I suppose, that stirred in my soul that tempest of impatience with which I listened to the civilities of my unhappy victim; I declare, at least, before God, no man morally sane could have been guilty of that crime upon so pitiful a provocation"

Look at the phrase, "it must have been this, I suppose". The must sounds like someone desperate to believe something they want to believe. "I suppose" shows how he doesn't succeed – he realises this is just wishful thinking. This is followed by "I declare, at least" that he is certain only of what comes next, not what went before.

The idea that Hyde was not "morally insane" is not the same as saying he was mad. Jekyll implies that Hyde was acting in a "sane" way, in other words, a logical way. In other words, that is was reasoned. But because Hyde is amoral, he has no moral reason for behaving as he did.

Again, this is Stevenson's way of forcing us to ask, 'what was his reason?' This is a secret he forces us to answer for ourselves. This would possibly be too much to bear for Jekyll if he is homosexual, faced with the hypocrisy of the 1885 Act.

2. Why is he the only murder victim? Why does he only punch the match seller once, and move on?

Because Stevenson does not quite believe in the evil nature of his creation – he has too much sympathy for Hyde and his love of life.

Because it shows us that Carew has done something to invite this reaction – it is not just a random act. It suggests this is Jekyll's revenge.

3. Why was Sir Danvers Carew out walking the streets close to midnight?

Because he is looking to meet other homosexual men, looking for sex. This also suggests why the maid has seen Hyde with her master before.

4. Why was he sending a letter to Utterson?

Everyone is linked to Utterson. Utterson therefore represents the social force which binds them all – repressive, secretive, corrupt.

5. Why did Utterson stop going to the theatre?

Because he is afraid of his own pleasures. He represents how a repressive society forces people even to repress their own desires.

6. Why don't Enfield and Utterson discuss the change they saw in Jekyll at the window?

Because they believe in repression. Because it is a denial of God – if man can create another human being, through science, it is an attack on God's power.

7. Why don't we hear of anything Hyde does when he is indulging in sin, apart from the killing of Sir Danvers Carew?

Because Stevenson is hinting that these sins are more socially unacceptable than discussing murder! This means homosexuality.

Again, Stevenson is also suggesting that he does not really believe in this idea of pleasure seeking as a sin.

Perhaps we see this through Jekyll, "I concealed my pleasures; and that when I reached years of reflection, and began to look round me and take stock of my progress and position in the world, I stood already committed to a profound duplicity of life. Many a man would have even blazoned such irregularities as I was guilty of; but from the high views that I had set before me, I regarded and hid them with an almost morbid sense of shame."

So, society makes him hide his pleasures – notice he cannot bring himself to call them sins, or evil, and he points out that "many a man" would have indulged in these pleasures and even let everyone know about them – they would be "blazoned". The problem, then, is social repression.

8. What sin did Jekyll give in to before Hyde was able to first take control of his body? Why doesn't Stevenson mention this?

Again, this suggests homosexuality. Prostitution, gambling, drug taking would not be so shocking that they could not be mentioned.

"The pleasures which I made haste to seek in my disguise were, as I have said, undignified; I would scarce use a harder term. But in the hands of Edward Hyde, they soon began to turn toward the monstrous. When I would come back from these excursions, I was often plunged into a kind of wonder at my vicarious depravity. This familiar that I called out of my own soul, and sent forth alone to do his good pleasure, was a being inherently malign and villainous; his every act and thought centred on self; drinking pleasure with bestial avidity from any degree of torture to another; relentless like a man of stone."

Notice that he calls his own pleasures only "undignified" – as though in his own form as Jekyll, he can't do what he really wants. As Hyde, he can. So what are they? Well, he calls them ironically "his good pleasure". But it also suggests a truth, that he is delighted he can now enjoy them. Not that he can now enjoy them in secret, without being detected, but that these pleasures are new to Jekyll.

9. It is also interesting that Hyde takes pleasure in control – the degree of torture.

Ultimately, his greatest pleasure is perhaps his control of Jekyll, which he achieves at the end.

10. Why does Hyde not destroy the new will which leaves everything to Utterson, and why doesn't he destroy Lanyon's letter and Jekyll's confession?

(Because he can rely on Utterson to keep Jekyll's scientific success a secret). It is the perfect revenge.

11. Why does Hyde commit suicide?

(To keep Jekyll's success a secret, so he will never achieve scientific fame: he will be the opposite of John Hunter).

"With every day, and from both sides of my intelligence, the moral and the intellectual, I thus drew steadily nearer to that truth, by whose partial discovery I have been doomed to such a dreadful shipwreck: that man is not truly one, but truly two. I say two, because the state of my own knowledge does not pass beyond that point. Others will follow, others will outstrip me on the same lines; and I hazard the guess that man will be ultimately known for a mere polity of multifarious, incongruous, and independent denizens.

I, for my part, from the nature of my life, advanced infallibly in one direction and in one direction only. It was on the moral side, and in my own person, that I learned to recognise the thorough and primitive duality of man; I saw that, of the two natures that contended in the field of my consciousness, even if I could rightly be said to be either, it was only because I was radically both; and from an early date, even before the course of my scientific discoveries had begun to suggest the most naked possibility of such a miracle, I had learned to dwell with pleasure, as a beloved day-dream, on the thought of the separation of these elements."

So we can see that Jekyll is convinced he will leave a legacy which will lead to huge developments in science that will change "man", and therefore mankind, forever. His use of "miracle" to describe this also shows how incredibly important he feels his discovery has been, even though it has destroyed him.

12. Why doesn't Jekyll try to create others like him, but angelic and good?

"That night I had come to the fatal cross-roads. Had I approached my discovery in a more noble spirit, had I risked the experiment while under the empire of generous or pious aspirations, all must have been otherwise, and from these agonies of death and birth, I had come forth an angel instead of a fiend."

13. Why doesn't he tell us what Jekyll's final sin was, committed as Jekyll?

This is the sin that tipped the balance, giving Hyde full control:

"it was in my own person, that I was once more tempted to trifle with my conscience; and it was as an ordinary secret sinner, that I at last fell before the assaults of temptation."

This panders to his Christian readers. It is the accumulation of sins that finally gives Hyde control. It is a warning that we must always be vigilant against our own evil desires. In other words, it is a call for society to repress desire.

However, another way to look at this to doubt the severity of Hyde's other crimes. He has apparently been "monstrous" before killing Sir Danvers. Then even adding that murder to his previous sin does not give power to his evil self. This makes it highly unlikely that an ordinary sin would do it.

In this way, Stevenson questions the idea of an evil person. We are all "comingled" out of good and evil in the sense that good people can commit evil acts. This does not make people irredeemably evil. The trivial nature of Jekyll's sin calls attention to this. Are the acts of evil society judges as a sin really sinful? The juxtaposition of the murder with this forces us to question society's view of sin., because we can't imagine that whatever Jekyll has done is worse than murder.

We can contrast the murder of Carew with his self-restraint later, once he has changed into Hyde while awake for the first time.

"Hyde in danger of his life was a creature new to me; shaken with inordinate anger, strung to the pitch of murder, lusting to inflict pain. Yet the creature was astute; mastered his fury with a great effort of the will."

This contradicts his description of Hyde's overwhelming desire to kill Carew. Both descriptions of Hyde can't be true. Therefore, Stevenson is challenging us to look deeper into Jekyll's motives and desires.

Hyde's lack of motive for killing Sir Danvers is even more unconvincing when Jekyll describes how he felt when waiting for Lanyon to get the salts for him.

"He, I say—I cannot say, I. That child of Hell had nothing human; nothing lived in him but fear and hatred… into the midst of the nocturnal passengers, these two base passions raged within him like a tempest…

Once a woman spoke to him, offering, I think, a box of lights. He smote her in the face, and she fled."

Despite the strongest description of Hyde's emotional state, he hits her only once, and with such little force that she is able to turn and run away from him. We are left with the distinct impression that killing Carew is totally out of character for Hyde. This again hints at Jekyll's own motive for killing him.

Now write your essay and email it to me at sallesdominic@gmail.com if you would like me to take a look at it.

Mystery and Suspense

Starting with the extract from Chapter 7, how does Stevenson present ideas about good and evil in the novel?

Extract

The court was very cool and a little damp, and full of premature twilight, although the sky, high up overhead, was still bright with sunset. The middle one of the three windows was half-way open; and sitting close beside it, taking the air with an infinite sadness of mien, like some disconsolate prisoner, Utterson saw Dr. Jekyll.

"What! Jekyll!" he cried. "I trust you are better."

"I am very low, Utterson," replied the doctor, drearily, "very low. It will not last long, thank God."

"You stay too much indoors," said the lawyer. "You should be out, whipping up the circulation like Mr. Enfield and me. (This is my cousin — Mr. Enfield — Dr. Jekyll.) Come, now; get your hat and take a quick turn with us."

"You are very good," sighed the other. "I should like to very much; but no, no, no, it is quite impossible; I dare not. But indeed, Utterson, I am very glad to see you; this is really a great pleasure; I would ask you and Mr. Enfield up, but the place is really not fit."

"Why then," said the lawyer, good-naturedly, "the best thing we can do is to stay down here and speak with you from where we are."

"That is just what I was about to venture to propose," returned the doctor with a smile. But the words were hardly uttered, before the smile was struck out of his face and succeeded by an expression of such abject terror and despair, as froze the very blood of the two gentlemen below.

They saw it but for a glimpse, for the window was instantly thrust down; but that glimpse had been sufficient, and they turned and left the court without a word. In silence, too, they traversed the by-street; and it was not until they had come into a neighbouring thoroughfare, where even upon a Sunday there were still some stirrings of life, that Mr. Utterson at last turned and looked at his companion. They were both pale; and there was an answering horror in their eyes.

"God forgive us, God forgive us," said Mr. Utterson.

But Mr. Enfield only nodded his head very seriously and walked on once more in silence.

In this extract, how does Stevenson create a sense of mystery in the text?

We've looked at this question before in several guises. You could simply go through the points you learned in the section on the structure of the novel. Or you could look at the previous section, and simply use the 13 points you have just read.

The Extract

What is most interesting here is that Enfield and Utterson have both clearly seen the transformation. It is a mystery they refuse to acknowledge. They refuse to discuss it, and in effect pretend it never happened.

They both echo the same language that Lanyon used, turning repeatedly to "God".

Like Utterson, they turn away from the truth. Utterson began by trying to solve the mystery of Mr Hyde, but when the truth presents itself to him, he would rather not know. This is why Stevenson gives him Lanyon's letter and Jekyll's confession. This is the only way that Utterson, and the society he represents, can accept the truth of Jekyll's scientific discovery.

But instead, he buries this truth in his safe.

The Role of Fear and Tension

Read the following extract from Chapter 8 and then answer the question that follows.

It was a wild, cold, seasonable night of March, with a pale moon, lying on her back as though the wind had tilted her, and a flying wrack of the most diaphanous and lawny texture. The wind made talking difficult, and flecked the blood into the face.

It seemed to have swept the streets unusually bare of passengers, besides; for Mr. Utterson thought he had never seen that part of London so deserted. He could have wished it otherwise; never in his life had he been conscious of so sharp a wish to see and touch his fellow-creatures; for struggle as he might, there was borne in upon his mind a crushing anticipation of calamity.

The square, when they got there, was all full of wind and dust, and the thin trees in the garden were lashing themselves along the railing. Poole, who had kept all the way a pace or two ahead, now pulled up in the middle of the pavement, and in spite of the biting weather, took off his hat and mopped his brow with a red pocket-handkerchief.

But for all the hurry of his coming, these were not the dews of exertion that he wiped away, but the moisture of some strangling anguish; for his face was white and his voice, when he spoke, harsh and broken.

"Well, sir," he said, "here we are, and God grant there be nothing wrong."

"Amen, Poole," said the lawyer.

Thereupon the servant knocked in a very guarded manner; the door was opened on the chain; and a voice asked from within, "Is that you, Poole?"

"It's all right," said Poole. "Open the door."

The hall, when they entered it, was brightly lighted up; the fire was built high; and about the hearth the whole of the servants, men and women, stood huddled together like a flock of sheep.

At the sight of Mr. Utterson, the housemaid broke into hysterical whimpering; and the cook, crying out, "Bless God! it's Mr. Utterson," ran forward as if to take him in her arms.

"What, what? Are you all here?" said the lawyer peevishly. "Very irregular, very unseemly; your master would be far from pleased."

"They're all afraid," said Poole.

Blank silence followed, no one protesting; only the maid lifted up her voice and now wept loudly.

Starting with this extract, how does Stevenson present fear in the text?

Thesis

The greatest fear Stevenson addresses is the Victorian's fear of pleasures which they have characterised as sin. As an atheist, Stevenson wants his readers to break free from fear of being "human" and reject the oppressive, fearful society they live in.

Points for your essay plan:

In this extract fear is presented as a weakness, appropriate only for the lower classes, and even here it is criticised by Utterson.

The bravest character is clearly Jekyll, who risks death in the pursuit of his experiment.

Amongst the middle class men in this novel there appears to be only a fear of life. They all doubt their pleasures in life and try to curb them. This denial reduces the experience of life, which we can see in the mortification of Utterson, and Jekyll's refusal to enjoy pleasures himself because of scandal, sending out Hyde to experience them for him.

The only character who does not embrace death is Hyde, who longs for life and freedom.

The fears are therefore social. They are fears shared by the readers:

- The fear of immigration – which we see in Soho
- Science – which we see from Lanyon
- Evolution – which we see in the descriptions of the ape-like Hyde
- Lack of faith in Christianity – when we see in the satanic descriptions of Hyde
- Drugs – visible in Hyde's desperation for the drug to return him to Jekyll
- Homosexuality – which we see in Utterson's dreams and the killing of Carew, and the fear of blackmail.
- The vicarious fear of reading a Gothic novel – which we see in the description of the maid.

Using the guide so far, can you find quotations for each of these?

Feel free to write your essay and email it to me – I may give you some feedback or make a video.

Tension

Read the following extract from Chapter 8 and then answer the question that follows.

Extract

"But now the ten minutes drew to an end. Poole disinterred the axe from under a stack of packing straw; the candle was set upon the nearest table to light them to the attack; and they drew near with bated breath to where that patient foot was still going up and down, up and down, in the quiet of the night.

"Jekyll," cried Utterson, with a loud voice, "I demand to see you."

He paused a moment, but there came no reply. "I give you fair warning, our suspicions are aroused, and I must and shall see you," he resumed; "if not by fair means, then by foul! if not of your consent, then by brute force!"

"Utterson," said the voice, "for God's sake, have mercy!"

"Ah, that's not Jekyll's voice — it's Hyde's!" cried Utterson. "Down with the door, Poole!"

Poole swung the axe over his shoulder; the blow shook the building, and the red baize door leaped against the lock and hinges. A dismal screech, as of mere animal terror, rang from the cabinet. Up went the axe again, and again the panels crashed and the frame bounded; four times the blow fell; but the wood was tough and the fittings were of excellent workmanship; and it was not until the fifth, that the lock burst in sunder and the wreck of the door fell inwards on the carpet.

The besiegers, appalled by their own riot and the stillness that had succeeded, stood back a little and peered in. There lay the cabinet before their eyes in the quiet lamplight, a good fire glowing and chattering on the hearth, the kettle singing its thin strain, a drawer or two open, papers neatly set forth on the business-table, and nearer the fire, the things laid out for tea: the quietest room, you would have said, and, but for the glazed presses full of chemicals, the most commonplace that night in London.

Right in the midst there lay the body of a man sorely contorted and still twitching. They drew near on tiptoe, turned it on its back and beheld the face of Edward Hyde. He was dressed in clothes far too large for him,

153

clothes of the doctor's bigness; the cords of his face still moved with a semblance of life, but life was quite gone; and by the crushed phial in the hand and the strong smell of kernels that hung upon the air, Utterson knew that he was looking on the body of a self-destroyer."

Beginning with this extract, how does Stevenson create tension?

Essay Plan

This is really a question about structure. Stevenson asks us to solve a set of mysteries. The obvious one is the relationship between Hyde and Jekyll.

You can answer the question using the points in the Structure section of the guide.

The more troubling tensions are those caused by the gaps in the narrative, or what is not said. Ultimately, the absences are far more tense than what we do discover.

Causes of Tension

1. Enfield refuses to tell us who signed Hyde's cheque, though we know he is in the "pink of proprieties".
2. Utterson wants to know, as we do, why Jekyll's will includes the clause about him disappearing.
3. We wonder what the cause of blackmail might be between Jekyll and Hyde.
4. We wonder why Enfield and the doctor are so repulsed by Hyde that they want to kill him, even though he has caused no injury to the girl who ran into him, and why they "screw him" for one hundred pounds.
5. Why does Lanyon die so suddenly?
6. What is the cause of his attack on Jekyll's "scientific balderdash"?
7. We wonder why Hyde kills Sir Danvers Carew, but not anyone else, and why in a fit of rage he punches the match seller only once, so that she is easily able to run away. Jekyll's explanation does not satisfy us.
8. Why doesn't Utterson tell the police that he has evidence Jekyll forged a letter from Hyde, and not tell the police about their relationship? Why does he break the law in this way?
9. Why do Utterson and Enfield refuse to talk to each other about the transformation they witness at Jekyll's window, when he transforms into Hyde. And, when it happens, Stevenson only refers to it as 'it', so we wonder what 'it' is.
10. Why does Utterson keep hold of the confession, Lanyon's letter, and the new will, and not give them to the police?
11. We only find out the truth of the scientific experiments in the final two chapters.
12. Why does Hyde not destroy Jekyll's papers, but allow the new will and Jekyll's confession to pass to Utterson?
13. Does Hyde achieve a revenge over Jekyll in preventing his scientific discovery being known?
14. Why does Stevenson concentrate only on a male society?
15. Why does Utterson dream of Jekyll in his bed?
16. Why does Hyde stay in London and not try to escape abroad?

17. Why doesn't Stevenson tell us what Hyde does for his pleasures?

18. Why does he choose Sir Danvers to be Hyde's chosen victim?

19. Why was Sir Danvers out walking close to midnight, and why is he sending a letter to Utterson?

What is the Purpose of Tension?

Then you can look at the deeper questions, which make us wonder about Stevenson's wider themes and ideas.

To suggest that:

1. Society is corrupt

2. Middle class men are hypocrites, and self-interested and full of sinful desires

3. The problems in society are caused by social pressures which forces men to repress their natural desires, especially homosexuality

4. We all have evil desires and need to learn to manage them rather than repress them, as symbolised by Hyde

5. British society is broken, and the only solution is to escape it – symbolised by the deaths of Jekyll and Hyde

6. Drug taking is dangerous and will rob you of your identity and sanity

7. Christianity is a cause of social repression which make it impossible for Christians to love live, but instead glorify death.

8. Christianity trades on myth, and the scientific discoveries of the 19th century, particularly evolution, prove that it has no basis in truth.

Write this essay and email it to me if you would like me to look at it – I may have time, and would be delighted to make a video if it is any good!

Conflict Between Science and Christianity

Read the following extract from Chapter 9 and then answer the question that follows.

Extract

And now," said he, "to settle what remains. Will you be wise? will you be guided? will you suffer me to take this glass in my hand and to go forth from your house without further parley? or has the greed of curiosity too much command of you? Think before you answer, for it shall be done as you decide. As you decide, you shall be left as you were before, and neither richer nor wiser, unless the sense of service rendered to a man in mortal distress may be counted as a kind of riches of the soul. Or, if you shall so prefer to choose, a new province of knowledge and new avenues to fame and power shall be laid open to you, here, in this room, upon the instant; and your sight shall be blasted by a prodigy to stagger the unbelief of Satan."

"Sir," said I, affecting a coolness that I was far from truly possessing," you speak enigmas, and you will perhaps not wonder that I hear you with no very strong impression of belief. But I have gone too far in the way of inexplicable services to pause before I see the end."

"It is well," replied my visitor. "Lanyon, you remember your vows: what follows is under the seal of our profession. And now, you who have so long been bound to the most narrow and material views, you who have denied the virtue of transcendental medicine, you who have derided your superiors — behold!"

He put the glass to his lips and drank at one gulp. A cry followed; he reeled, staggered, clutched at the table and held on, staring with injected eyes, gasping with open mouth; and as I looked there came, I thought, a change — he seemed to swell — his face became suddenly black and the features seemed to melt and alter — and the next moment, I had sprung to my feet and leaped back against the wall, my arm raised to shield me from that prodigy, my mind submerged in terror.

"O God!" I screamed, and "O God!" again and again; for there before my eyes — pale and shaken, and half-fainting, and groping before him with his hands, like a man restored from death — there stood Henry Jekyll!

What he told me in the next hour, I cannot bring my mind to set on paper. I saw what I saw, I heard what I heard, and my soul sickened at it; and yet now when that sight has faded from my eyes, I ask myself if I believe it, and I cannot answer. My life is shaken to its roots; sleep has left me; the deadliest terror sits by me at all hours of the day and night; I feel that my days are numbered, and that I must die; and yet I shall die incredulous. As for the moral turpitude that man unveiled to me, even with tears of penitence, I cannot, even in memory, dwell on it without a start of horror.

Beginning with this extract, how does Stevenson show the struggles between science and religion?

Essay Plan

Thesis

Stevenson views Christianity and science with a "dual" purpose. To a Christian reader, Stevenson writes an allegorical novel, warning of the dangers of science which is being developed without ethics. To the more astute reader, Stevenson presents Christianity as a fiction, and the fear of science as a social problem.

The John Hunter house explores the ethics of science, and the later acceptance of scientific discovery which benefits mankind.

The Christian reader is likely to be troubled by science. This is represented in Lanyon's reaction, and choice to die, which horrifies Stevenson, the invalid who fights for life.

It is also why Hyde eventually commits murder, and chooses as a victim one of the most important men in London. To a Christian audience, this symbolises the dangers of science to wider society.

On the other hand, Christian morality has forced society to persecute homosexuality, which is the real motive for Jekyll's use of Hyde as a "bravo" to kill Carew for his hypocritical support of the 1885 Act banning "gross indecency".

To the Christian reader, science is linked to recklessness in the way that Jekyll experiments on himself and becomes addicted to drugs – science is allied to poor judgement and immorality.

On the other hand, Stevenson might well be excited about scientific development. He creates a Hyde because this will satisfy the salacious interests of his readers who want tales of crime and sinful behaviour which they can experience vicariously while still leading moral lives. In this way, he likens his readers to Jekyll!

He points out that Hyde might have been created as an angel – in other words, scientific discovery is neutral, it is how people use it that can be characterised as good or evil.

He might also criticise Christian morality. The Christian characters in the novel are obsessed with denial – they mortify themselves and deny themselves pleasures. He presents this as diminishing life. Ultimately, Jekyll doesn't envy Hyde's ability to act sinfully. He envies his sheer joy in living.

When he creates the "divinity" reading Utterson, he asks us if the Christian life is worth living. Utterson derives no pleasure from it, and even he seeks out the lives of downward going men in order to make his existence more bearable. Ironically, this simply leads to an accumulation of wealth, but no increase in happiness.

Stevenson had himself rejected Christianity and left England forever shortly after publication. We might infer he gives the novel its Christian plot in order to satisfy a Christian readership, but his subtle depiction of Utterson rejects the benefits of Christianity as a worthless goal, and one that leads to a diminished life.

Doctor Jekyll and the Duality of Man

Read the following extract from Chapter 10 and then answer the question that follows.

Extract

Instantly the spirit of hell awoke in me and raged. With a transport of glee, I mauled the unresisting body, tasting delight from every blow; and it was not till weariness had begun to succeed, that I was suddenly, in the top fit of my delirium, struck through the heart by a cold thrill of terror.

A mist dispersed; I saw my life to be forfeit; and fled from the scene of these excesses, at once glorying and trembling, my lust of evil gratified and stimulated, my love of life screwed to the topmost peg. I ran to the house in Soho, and (to make assurance doubly sure) destroyed my papers; thence I set out through the lamplit streets, in the same divided ecstasy of mind, gloating on my crime, light-headedly devising others in the future, and yet still hastening and still hearkening in my wake for the steps of the avenger.

Hyde had a song upon his lips as he compounded the draught, and as he drank it, pledged the dead man. The pangs of transformation had not done tearing him, before Henry Jekyll, with streaming tears of gratitude and remorse, had fallen upon his knees and lifted his clasped hands to God.

The veil of self-indulgence was rent from head to foot, I saw my life as a whole: I followed it up from the days of childhood, when I had walked with my father's hand, and through the self-denying toils of my professional life, to arrive again and again, with the same sense of unreality, at the damned horrors of the evening.

I could have screamed aloud; I sought with tears and prayers to smother down the crowd of hideous images and sounds with which my memory swarmed against me; and still, between the petitions, the ugly face of my iniquity stared into my soul.

As the acuteness of this remorse began to die away, it was succeeded by a sense of joy. The problem of my conduct was solved. Hyde was thenceforth impossible; whether I would or not, I was now confined to the better part of my existence; and oh, how I rejoiced to think it! with what willing humility, I embraced anew the restrictions of natural life! with what sincere renunciation, I locked the door by which I had so often gone and come, and ground the key under my heel!

Beginning with this extract, how does Stevenson present duality in the text?

Look at the use of the personal pronoun here. This is where Jekyll admits that he killed Carew as Jekyll, not just Hyde. Other references to Hyde are in the third person. Here he writes in the first person, because Hyde represents Jekyll at this moment, in this act, in this murder.

This is really a question about Jekyll.

Grade 9 Analysis of Doctor Henry Jekyll

Thesis

Stevenson uses Jekyll to represent the hypocrisy of London gentlemen, who show society a respectable façade, while secretly enjoying private vices. He also represents the advances in scientific discovery which challenge Christianity. Yet Stevenson writes for a Christian audience, and portrays Jekyll's downfall in biblical terms, a man giving in to temptation as a sinner. Science is discredited as part of that sin.

However, as an atheist, Stevenson subtly uses Jekyll to expose Christian morality as oppressive and damaging to society, and damaging scientific advances.

As a gentleman, Jekyll is born with "**a large fortune**" but society encourages him to suppress his "**gaiety of disposition**". To maintain high social status, he keeps this joyous side of his nature secret, which leads to "**a profound duplicity of life**". This duplicity is not just his, but represents all gentlemen who Stevenson believes are forced into hypocrisy.

His pleasures leave him "**plunged in shame**" but he refuses to tell us what these are. He appears to be critical of "**religion**", saying it is the "**root**" of "**one of the most plentiful springs of distress**". This juxtaposition of the kind of imagery we find in praise of nature, coupled with "**distress**" suggests that religion takes what is natural and pure, like a spring, and makes us view it as corrupt and evil.

He describes this state as "**man's dual nature**" and for himself "**a dreadful shipwreck**". This realisation comes to him *before* he creates Edward Hyde. In other words, Stevenson portrays society's views of pleasure and sin as the "root" of Jekyll's tragedy. Society creates "**man's dual nature**". Without Christian rules, he would be able to live freely, simply expressing his nature without fear of being judged as evil.

Jekyll, as a part of that society, does not blame Christianity, and accepts his vices as evil – so much so that he can't bring himself to tell Utterson what they are.

However, he does not count his scientific experiments in creating an alter ego as a sin. His readers are likely to share Lanyon's horror at his heretical challenge to God in creating a new being. Yet Jekyll himself imagines that other scientists will follow and "**outstrip me on the same lines**". We can see that his confession is also written for posterity: he wants his scientific discoveries to be developed, even though he does not leave behind a precise record of how to do so. He tells us that he doesn't want to leave a proper scientific record of his experiments in case future scientists recreate another Edward Hyde, rather than a more angelic version of themselves.

A Christian readership might approve of Utterson silencing Jekyll's legacy, but Stevenson himself might argue that Jekyll's science might well create an "**angel**" rather than a "**fiend**". He suggests the science itself is neutral. It is for this reason that he gives Jekyll John Hunter's house, specifically to remind his readers that what was once considered sinful (grave robbing) has led to significant scientific advance which has benefited mankind in improving surgery. This subtly questions Lanyon's horror, and by extension he asks his readers to think more deeply about their own Christian faith.

Stevenson also makes us sympathetic toward Jekyll who creates Hyde so that Jekyll is no longer "**exposed to disgrace and penitence**". It isn't just that he does not want people to know what pleasures he seeks out, he particularly doesn't want to feel guilty about them. It is society's repression which makes him feel this guilt and "**shame**". The evil creation of Hyde is therefore directly linked to society's repression. Symbolically, science creates the alter ego, but society's repression creates its evil nature.

Stevenson also questions which is the more real version of Jekyll. When he first becomes Hyde, he observes: "**I came to myself as if out of the great sickness**". The symbolism suggests that Hyde, the pleasure seeker, is his more natural state, while Dr Jekyll, the product of society, is a kind of sickness. This is another attack on society's moral values.

He describes the sensation of being Hyde in very sensual language, as "**not an innocent freedom of the soul**". The reader might well ask what the soul needs freedom from? Perhaps it suggests the soul needs freedom from Christianity, and the moral codes of 19th-century British society. By linking this freedom to the "soul", he also suggests that Christianity, with its moral code, is repressing something fundamentally human but also holy.

Jekyll points out that his new identity is "**natural and human**". Instead of God looking down on him, he imagines being judged by "**the constellations**" who would observe him "**with wonder**". These are the pagan constellations of the Greeks, whose Gods did not have the same moral views as Christian theology. Just as all men are "commingled out of good and evil" so were the Greek Gods. In other words, standards of morality were very different then. Homosexuality was celebrated, as every male middle and upper class reader would know – they would have studied such stories in the original Greek while at school.

The Christian reader will see this as proof of Jekyll's vanity and hubris, celebrating his own evil nature. However, Jekyll does not reject Christianity. He keeps judging Hyde in terms of Christian morality. It is Stevenson who undermines this with Jekyll's references.

Consequently, he points out that the idea of "**pure evil**" embodied by Edward Hyde is a Christian construct. While Jekyll appears to agree with this view of Edward Hyde, his actions, and choice of imagery suggests that he doesn't accept this Christian definition.

Stevenson needs Jekyll to conform to a Christian perspective in order to satisfy his Christian readers. However, his more astute readership will read a different story behind Dr Jekyll's words.

Dr Jekyll can only describe one truly evil act, the killing of Sir Danvers Carew. This is hardly "**pure evil**", or the act of somebody "**alone in the ranks of mankind**". If this were the case, Sir Danvers Carew's murder would be only the first murder in history, never mind the only murder Hyde commits.

Stevenson describes the secret pleasures of his life as "**undignified**" as though he struggles to find them horrifying, while society describes them as evil. He also suggests that they were more difficult to enjoy because he was "**growing towards the elderly man**". This is another hint that the pleasures might be physically strenuous, needing a young man's energy.

Alternatively, they may require the cooperation of other young people, who would not be attracted to "the elderly" Dr Jekyll. This is another prompt that the secret pleasures are sexual, but also consensual. Hyde doesn't have to pay for them. If he did, his age would not matter.

He describes the "**undignified**" pleasures as turning "**towards the monstrous**". However, his language contradicts this kind of morality, referring to Hyde's doing "**his good pleasure**". Although he speaks of "**any degree of torture to another**" he is unable to give us any examples. Added to this, he gets tremendous vicarious pleasure from Hyde's actions. Again we wonder if these are simply pleasures society rejects, but which at the level of the individual are entirely acceptable.

Stevenson strongly hints that Jekyll's shameful vice is homosexuality. This would explain the need to create Hyde as a younger man, a man whose face Jekyll finds so attractive that he places a mirror in the cabinet where he transforms!

Parliament's Act of 1885, criminalising homosexuality, also provides a homosexual Jekyll with the unspoken motive to murder Sir Danvers Carew. Stevenson implies Carew himself is homosexual in the way he appears to proposition Hyde in a "**pretty**" way, and in the suspicious time he is cruising his own neighbourhood, and the even more unlikely need to ask Hyde the way. Carew's sin, in Stevenson's eyes, will be that he has voted for an Act which criminalises his own nature. For this betrayal, Hyde kills him.

Jekyll is unable to give Utterson any explanation for Hyde's murder. He says there was "**so pitiful a provocation**" and compares it to a child breaking "**a plaything**". This lack of a motive makes no sense. Sir Danvers Carew cannot have been the first person Hyde met on his walk. Nor is Hyde lying in wait, hoping to murder the first person who comes along.

This strongly suggests a motive. Stevenson challenges us to fill in the blanks. A further clue is in Jekyll's name, a compound of the French 'je' and the homophone 'kill'. This strongly implies that Hyde is not the real murderer, he is acting as Jekyll's "**bravo**".

Jekyll's description of the murder does not tally with the maid's. Instead of clubbing him to death with a cane and stamping on his body, he describes it much more intimately as "**with a transport of glee, I mauled the unresisting body, tasting delight from every blow**". Animals maul with teeth and claws, and the use of "tasting" to describe his delight similarly suggests different actions. In Victorian times mauling also held these sexual connotations, so Stevenson nudges us toward a sexual motive for the murder.

Jekyll explains that two months before the murder of Sir Danvers Carew he woke up for the first time as Edward Hyde after having taken the potion to go to sleep as Dr Jekyll. He claims that from this moment he realised that Edward Hyde would become stronger than Dr Jekyll. Hyde's wholly evil personality overcomes Jekyll's which was "**commingled**" out of good and evil.

However, we remember that he drew up the will over a year before this: becoming Edward Hyde was always part of the plan. Jekyll has always imagined that being Hyde would be a more satisfying existence than being Jekyll.

When he views himself as the doctor it is as **"elderly and discontented"**, while as Edward Hyde he felt **"liberty, the comparative youth, the light step, leaping impulses and secret pleasures."** This is the full list in his comparison. Astute readers will notice the absence of **"evil"**. This is another clue that Jekyll's life as Edward Hyde is not in fact full of evil deeds, but simply the freedom to pursue pleasures which are rejected by Christian society.

Jekyll tries to portray Hyde as the evil creature who murders out of animalistic desire. He describes Hyde toasting the dead victim, gloating about his crime, and planning to carry out other murders in the future. Again, the astute reader will notice that he doesn't commit any future crimes. He barely injures a woman selling matches, and only **"gnashed"** his teeth at a hansom cab driver. Consequently, he does not appear in his actions to be motivated by evil, but by pleasure.

A very strong clue that he is actually providing Jekyll pleasure is his treatment of Dr Lanyon. He would be an easy victim of murder. Instead, he gives Jekyll his revenge – Lanyon is forced to see that Jekyll's **"unscientific balderdash"** was actually scientific genius. Forcing Lanyon to see that he was always wrong is Jekyll's best revenge. This again powerfully suggests killing Carew was also for Jekyll's pleasure.

We might also infer that, when this leads to Lanyon's death, Jekyll has orchestrated the killing of Stevenson's enemies: Lanyon as representative of Christian morality, and Carew as representative of the social repression of homosexuality. We know of at least two homosexuals that Stevenson counted as friends: Lang the critic for whom he wrote a poem, and Sergent the artist who painted him.

However, for the Christian reader, Jekyll expresses apparent regret. Although he describes feeling guilty at this murder, once he realises that he cannot be caught, he describes only feeling **"joy"**. He is struck not just that the murder was **"a crime, it had been a tragic folly"**. The emphasis of placing "folly" last suggests that this mistake was a bigger regret (because Hyde was "overlooked" by the maid), rather than the sin of murder.

Edward Hyde is finally able to overcome Jekyll's resistance, without requiring the potion, after Dr Jekyll indulges in one of his secret pleasures **"in my own person"**, rather than in the form of Hyde. The symbolism here is that once he accepts himself for who he is, and owns these pleasures, Hyde takes over.

To the Christian reader this is clear evidence that Jekyll has abandoned Christian morality, with the consequence that his soul has been lost forever, he has forever become the evil Edward Hyde, and his soul will now go to hell.

To the astute reader Dr Jekyll's fate is more complicated. The killing of Sir Danvers Carew, a member of Parliament, is now symbolic of an attack on the laws in society. This suggests that Edward Hyde is driven to crime through society's criminalisation and condemnation of his more innocent pleasures. This suggests that true evil is created by society: it is the constant repression which has led to this violent outburst, rather than a growing evil.

Although Jekyll uses the language of Christian morality to portray Hyde as **"hellish"** and **"inorganic"** he notes that Hyde is disgusted by Dr Jekyll's **"despondency"** and lack of **"life"**. He attacks Jekyll by scrawling **"blasphemies"** in his books, attacking Jekyll's Christian faith. This implies that he blames Christian morality for the **"dislike"** others feel for him

Dr Jekyll contrasts himself with Hyde's **"love of life"** which **"is wonderful"**. Even before he is about to cease to be Dr Jekyll forever, he realises the great joy in being Edward Hyde. The tragedy now seems that Dr Jekyll has not been allowed to be himself by society, and has not been allowed to enjoy his pleasures openly. The tragedy is that society has forced him to create Edward Hyde and then, symbolically, destroyed his own and

Hyde's "**love of life**". This appears to be a much more real description of Hyde, addicted to the pleasures of living, than the description of him as the ultimate evil in mankind.

His final comment on Edward Hyde is that he suggests suicide would be an act of "**courage**". This courage would be to "**release himself**". This strongly suggests that Jekyll does not believe in the notion of hell, because that could not be a "release". Dr Jekyll can only use this language if he ultimately rejects Christianity, and the concept of hell.

It suggests that the Christian language, the duality between good and evil, the despair at his own sin, the claim that Hyde is the most evil of men, has all been a posture, a pose, a façade. It is the message he believes Christian society wants to hear, presented in terms which Utterson will understand. But Jekyll doesn't really believe it.

This is why death can be a "release", and why the description of Hyde's ultimate evil is so unconvincing. It is why his last words about Hyde contain a note of admiration.

And what is he releasing himself from? Not from death, obviously. Instead the release is from public condemnation, a public death on "**the scaffold**". He is being released from society's moral condemnation of his pursuit of pleasure. Dr Jekyll clearly sees Edward Hyde's crime in killing Sir Danvers Carew as a result of social repression, not the result of Edward Hyde's innate evil.

The Christian reader will not spot this, instead seeing Jekyll's story as an allegory, warning faithful readers not to be tempted by their evil impulses, not to seek out hedonistic pleasures, not to embrace scientific discoveries as though they offer hope for a better future.

But to Stevenson it presents Christian society as hypocritical and repressive. Perhaps Stevenson could not make his true feelings any clearer than by abandoning Britain for ever, and choosing the much more primitive Samoa where, like Hyde, he might experience "not an innocent freedom of the soul" without fear of social condemnation.

2637 words

Grade 9 Essay on Doctor Jekyll

Thesis

Stevenson creates Jekyll with a dual purpose: firstly, to expose the hypocrisy of the male ruling classes, and the dangers of sinning against Christian morality. But secondly, he subverts this. Stevenson is an atheist, challenging his readers to reimagine sin as simply natural pleasure seeking, to reject Christian belief and create a more liberal society.

Consequently Jekyll's sins are first portrayed as a love of life, a "**gaiety of disposition**". He feels forced to hide his true nature, and lead "**a profound duplicity of life**". Christian morality leaves him "**plunged in shame**" after enjoying these pleasures.

However, he observes that "**at the root of religion**" is "**one of the most plentiful springs of distress**". This juxtaposition of "**natural springs**" with "**distress**" suggests that religion takes what is natural and pure, like a spring, and makes us view it as corrupt and evil, inviting his readers to question their Christian morality.

Before he creates Hyde, Jekyll describes this state as "**man's dual nature**" and for himself "**a dreadful shipwreck**". In other words, he has been wrecked by society's standards even before enjoying Hyde's sins. To a Christian reader this suggests he is irredeemably a sinner, but to Stevenson it suggests that Christianity simply brands everyone as sinful as its moral standards are too negative.

Although Christian readers will see his creation of Hyde as a heretical challenge to God, Jekyll believes other scientists will "**outstrip me on the same lines**" and he wants his scientific discoveries to be developed so that an "**angel**" might be created instead of a "**fiend**"

Stevenson suggests science is neutral. Consequently, he gives Jekyll John Hunter's house, reminding his readers that what was once considered sinful (grave robbing) has led to significant scientific advance which has benefited mankind in improving surgery. This subtly questions Lanyon's Christian horror, and by extension he asks his readers to think more deeply.

Stevenson also makes us sympathetic toward Jekyll who creates Hyde so that Jekyll is no longer "**exposed to disgrace and penitence**". "**Penitence**" reveals he particularly doesn't want to feel guilty. Society's repression makes Jekyll feel this "**shame**", and so society is responsible for Hyde's creation.

When Jekyll first becomes Hyde, he observes, "**I came to myself as if out of the great sickness**". The symbolism suggests that Hyde, the pleasure seeker, is his more natural state, while Dr Jekyll, the product of society, is a kind of "**sickness**". This is another attack on society's moral values.

He describes being Hyde as "**not an innocent freedom of the soul**". This horrifies a Christian reader, as his "**soul**" is free from fear of sin. To Stevenson it is wonderful, as Jekyll's soul is free to enjoy pleasures which society represses and forbids.

Consequently, Jekyll points out that his new identity is "**natural and human**". Instead of God, he imagines being judged by "**the constellations**", who would observe him "**with wonder**". This reference to the Greeks reminds us of their Gods who were "**commingled out of good and evil**", like mankind. They celebrated homosexuality, as middle class readers would know, having studied such stories in the original Greek at school.

He hints that he requires youthfulness to enjoy his "**undignified**" pleasures, which is difficult as Jekyll is "**growing towards the elderly man**". This suggests these pleasures are sexual, but also consensual. Hyde doesn't have to pay for them. If he did, his age would not matter. Thus Stevenson strongly hints that Jekyll's shameful vice is homosexuality.

This explains why Hyde is created as a younger man, whose face Jekyll finds so attractive that he acquires a mirror to see the transformation. Parliament's Act of 1885, criminalising homosexuality, also provides a homosexual Jekyll with the unspoken motive to murder Sir Danvers Carew. Stevenson implies Carew himself is homosexual in the way he appears to proposition Hyde in a "**pretty**" way. Carew's sin, in Stevenson's eyes, will be that he has voted for an Act which criminalises his own nature. For this betrayal, Hyde kills him to satisfy Jekyll's desire.

This undermines Jekyll's Christian rhetoric about Hyde's evil. He only describes one truly evil act, the killing of Sir Danvers Carew. This is hardly "**pure evil**", or the act of somebody "**alone in the ranks of mankind**". Jekyll uses these words to cover up his own desire to kill Carew.

This is why he says the murder was committed with "**so pitiful a provocation**". This lack of motive makes no sense. But Jekyll's name is a clue, compounding 'I' and 'kill', implying that Hyde kills Carew acting as Jekyll's "**bravo**".

This also explains the will, giving everything to Hyde, written over a year before Hyde could appear without the potion. Consequently, permanently becoming Hyde was always Jekyll's plan; being Hyde would be a more satisfying existence than being Jekyll.

Consequently, Jekyll describes himself as "**elderly and discontented**", while as Hyde he felt "**liberty, the comparative youth, the light step, leaping impulses and secret pleasures.**" Astute readers will notice the absence of "**evil**" in this list. It also explains why Hyde commits no other murders.

This also explains why Jekyll doesn't mention Hyde's temptation of Lanyon, to watch the transformation. Hyde is acting on Jekyll's motive for revenge on the "**pedant**" who called Jekyll's experiments "**unscientific balderdash**".

Jekyll's enemies are Stevenson's enemies: Lanyon as representative of Christian morality, and Carew as representative of the social repression of homosexuality. We know of at least two homosexuals whom Stevenson counted as friends, Lang the critic for whom he wrote a poem, and Sergent the artist who painted him.

Jekyll contrasts himself with Hyde's "**love of life**" which "**is wonderful**". The tragedy now seems that Jekyll has not been allowed to be himself by society, and is forbidden to enjoy his pleasures openly. Society has forced him to create Hyde and then, symbolically, destroyed his own and Hyde's "**love of life**".

Jekyll finally suggests Hyde's suicide would be an act of "**courage**" to "**release himself**". Hell could not be a "**release**", so Jekyll ultimately rejects Christianity. He rejects Christian repression, just as Stevenson does, when choosing the more primitive Samoa where, like Hyde, he might experience "**not an innocent freedom of the soul**" without fear of social condemnation.

1031 words

Printed in Great Britain
by Amazon

79400872R00095